POETRY, GEO(

Gender Studies in Wales
Astudiaethau Rhywedd yng Nghymru

The aim of this series is to fill a current gap in knowledge. As a number of historians, sociologists and literary critics have for some time been pointing out, there is a dearth of published research on the characteristics and effects of gender difference in Wales, both as it affected lives in the past and as it continues to shape present-day experience. Socially constructed concepts of masculine and feminine difference influence every aspect of individuals' lives; experiences in employment, in education, in culture and politics, as well as in personal relationships, are all shaped by them. Ethnic identities are also gendered; a country's history affects its concepts of gender difference so that what is seen as appropriately 'masculine' or 'feminine' varies within different cultures. What is needed in the Welsh context is more detailed research on the ways in which gender difference has operated and continues to operate within Welsh societies. Accordingly, this interdisciplinary and bilingual series of volumes on Gender Studies in Wales, authored by academics who are leaders in their particular fields of study, is designed to explore the diverse aspects of male and female identities in Wales, past and present. The series is bilingual, in the sense that some of its intended volumes will be in Welsh and some in English.

POETRY, GEOGRAPHY, GENDER

Women Rewriting Contemporary Wales

Alice Entwistle

UNIVERSITY OF WALES PRESS
CARDIFF
2013

www.uwp.co.uk

British Library Cataloguing-in-Publication Data
A catalogue record for this book is available from the British Library.

ISBN 978-0-7083-2669-5
e-ISBN 978-0-7083-2670-1

Typeset by Mark Heslington Ltd, Scarborough, North Yorkshire
Printed by CPI Antony Rowe, Chippenham, Wiltshire

For Claire Coghlin and Gareth Reeves
who showed me how,
and for Tom, with love

Contents

	Acknowledgements	ix
	Abbreviations	xi
	Preface	xv
	Introduction	1
1	On the Border(s): The Interstitial Poetries of the Contact Zone	16
2	'Not without strangeness': Ruth Bidgood's Unhomely Mid Wales	47
3	Frontier Country: Christine Evans	69
4	'A kind of authentic lie': Gwyneth Lewis's English-Language Sequences	92
5	Traverses: Gillian Clarke, Christine Evans, Catherine Fisher and Ireland/Wales	112
6	Wales and/or Thereabouts: Sheenagh Pugh, Wendy Mulford and Zoë Skoulding	135
	Afterword	159
	Notes	167
	Bibliography	196
	Index of Names	215
	General Index	223

Acknowledgements

Thanks are due first to the publishers, especially Sarah Lewis, Dafydd Jones, Siân Chapman and Teleri Williams† at the University of Wales Press, and my editor and colleague Professor Jane Aaron. I am also indebted to the original commissioners, Cary Archard and Mick Felton at Seren, for their forbearance and generosity in recent months. I am likewise very grateful to colleagues past and present at the University of Glamorgan, now the University of South Wales, for all kinds of support including a crucial sabbatical: Tony Curtis, Gavin Edwards, Philip Gross, Jeremy Hooker, Ruth McElroy, Chris Meredith, Bryony Randall, Fiona Reid, Andy Smith, Diana Wallace, Jeff Wallace and Martin Willis. I owe a particular debt to Katie Gramich, and especially to that most assiduous of readers, Kevin Mills, for his unstinting practical and scholarly help in the project's crucial later stages. Other kinds of thanks go to Neil Astley at Bloodaxe Books, William Ayot of Poetry on the Border, Claire Connolly, Jarlath Costello, Jo Gill, John Goodby, Matthew Jarvis, Jane Moore, Francesca Rhydderch, Pete Vokes and the tireless staff at the National Library for Wales, and the Poetry Library, especially Miriam.

I am grateful to the following authors and publishers for granting me permission to publish extracts from: Tiffany Atkinson: *Kink and Particle* (Seren Publishing, 2006) and *Catulla et Al* (Bloodaxe Books, 2011); Ruth Bidgood, *Selected Poems* (Seren Publishing, 1995), *New and Selected Poems* (Seren Publishing, 2004), *Hearing Voices* (Cinnamon Press, 2008) and *Time Being* (Seren Publishing, 2009); Gillian Clarke: *Letting in the Rumour* (Carcanet Press, 1989), *Collected Poems* (Carcanet Press, 1997); Anne Cluysenaar, *Timeslips: New and Selected Poems* (Carcanet Press, 1997) and *Migrations* (Cinnamon Press, 2011); Sarah Corbett, *The Red Wardrobe* (Seren Publishing, 1998); Menna Elfyn, *Perffaith Nam: Dau Ddetholiad a Cherddi Newydd / Perfect Blemish: New and Selected Poems 1995–2007* (Gomer/Bloodaxe Books, 2007); Christine Evans, *Looking Inland* (Poetry Wales Press, 1983), *Cometary Phases* (Seren Publishing, 1989),

Island of Dark Horses (Seren Publishing, 1995) and *Burning the Candle* (Gomer, 2006); Catherine Fisher, *Immrama* (Seren Publishing, 1988), *The Unexplored Ocean* (Seren Publishing, 1994), *Altered States* (Seren Publishing, 1999); Gwyneth Lewis, *Parables and Faxes* (Bloodaxe, 1998), *Chaotic Angels: Poems in English* (Bloodaxe, 2005), *A Hospital Odyssey* (Bloodaxe, 2010) and *Sparrow Tree* (Bloodaxe, 2011); Hilary Llewellyn-Williams, *Animaculture* (Seren Publishing, 1997); Wendy Mulford, *And Suddenly, Supposing: Selected Poems* (Etruscan Books, 2002), 'Alltud' (Scintilla, 2009) and *The Land Between* (Reality Street, 2009); Pascale Petit, *The Zoo Father* (Seren Publishing, 2001); Sheenagh Pugh, *Sing for the Taxman* (Seren Publishing, 1993), *Id's Hospit* (Seren Publishing, 1997), *Stonelight* (Seren Publishing, 1999), *The Beautiful Lie* (Seren Publishing, 2002) and *Long Haul Travellers* (Seren Publishing, 2008); Deryn Rees-Jones, *The Memory Tray* (Seren Publishing, 1994), *Signs Round a Dead Body* (Seren Publishing, 1998) and *Quiver* (Seren Publishing, 2004); Jo Shapcott, *Tender Taxes: Versions of Rilke's French Poems* (Faber and Faber 2001); Zoë Skoulding, *Remains of a Future City* (Seren Publishing, 2008); Anne Stevenson, 'Binoculars in Ardudwy' (Bloodaxe, 2005); Samantha Wynne-Rhydderch, *Banjo* (Picador/ PanMacmillan, 2012).

This book could not have happened without the cooperation of the poets themselves, especially those I have been able to interview. Thanks are due to Tiffany Atkinson, Ruth Bidgood, Anne Cluysenaar, Menna Elfyn, Christine Evans, Catherine Fisher, Wendy Mulford, Hilary Llewellyn-Williams, Pascale Petit, Sheenagh Pugh, Deryn Rees-Jones, Samantha Wynne Rhydderch, Zoë Skoulding and Anne Stevenson. I am especially grateful to Gwyneth Lewis for – among many kindnesses – an epigraph which was for so long my title, and to the artist Sarah Jane Brown, for allowing me to reproduce *Chimerical Coast* on the front cover.

Finally I want to offer heartfelt thanks to the people who, as friends and family, have had to endure the writing of this book at close quarters, and have done so with unfailing understanding, interest and support: my mother and siblings; Lisa Beaumont, a source of continuing inspiration and respect, Nikki, Shelley, Ann, Helen and Hilary; and above all Tom, Alf and Clem, who between them have made so much possible.

Abbreviations

Ruth Bidgood

HV	*Hearing Voices*
NSP	*New and Selected Poems*
RBSP	*Selected Poems*

Gillian Clarke

GCCP	*Collected Poems*

Sarah Corbett

RW	*The Red Wardrobe*
TWB	*The Witch Bag*

Menna Elfyn

PN	*Perfect Blemish / Perffaith Nam*

Christine Evans

BtC	*Burning the Candle*
CP	*Cometary Phases*
IDH	*Island of Dark Horses*
LI	*Looking Inland*

Catherine Fisher

AS	*Altered States*
TUO	*The Unexplored Ocean*

Gwyneth Lewis

AHO	*A Hospital Odyssey*
CA	*Chaotic Angels*
SR	*Sunbathing in the Rain*
ST	*Sparrow Tree*

Wendy Mulford

ASS	*And Suddenly Supposing*
TLB	*The Land Between*

Pascale Petit

TZF	*The Zoo Father*

Sheenagh Pugh

IH	*Id's Hospit*
LHT	*Long-Haul Travellers*
SFTT	*Sing for the Taxman*
TBL	*The Beautiful Lie*

Creu Gwir fel gwydr o ffwrnais awen / In these stones horizons sing

Gwyneth Lewis

Look at any word long enough and you will see it open into a series of faults, into a terrain of particles each containing its own void.

Robert Smithson

Preface

Creu Gwir fel gwydr o ffwrnais awen / In these stones horizons sing

Standing some 6 feet tall, the physically enormous words slicing through the burnished sides of the Wales Millennium Centre, rearing beside the new Senedd at the heart of Cardiff's regenerating bay, signify in diverse ways. Mediating between the bustle of Roald Dahl Plas and the soaring interior of Wales's largest performance space which they help to illumine, materially speaking they comprise a giant poem-window, operating simultaneously as both installation artwork and architectural feature. In this functionality, the poem is a threshold: it stands, liminally, between the domains it spans, linking and separating seen and unseen, art and dailiness, cultural and socio-economic and, perhaps most obviously, its two languages. At the same time, from its elevated vantage point (as from the numerous publicity materials on which it appears) it beams out, across the artificial lake now marking the congested historic space of Cardiff Bay, towards the commercial traffic of the Bristol Channel and the vaster cultural-economic domains on which the seaway gives. In its own complex referentiality, and the dialoguing which it conducts with its partnering Welsh-language text (translated as 'Creating truth like glass from the furnace of inspiration', and similarly yoking functionality with aesthetic expression), this work succinctly utters both the actual and imagined creative resonances of the edifice which houses it and the actual and imaginable cultural and creative possibilities of post-millennial Wales as a whole. Its few words frame (as window space) and enshrine (as poem/song) the imaginative scope – the 'horizons' – on which they open.

In Welsh the word for 'poem' (*cerdd*) takes the feminine gender; meanwhile, as Welsh-language poet Menna Elfyn points out, 'in Welsh, stone can be female'.[1] It is perhaps less than coincidental, then, that the self-consciously millennial poem I have just been reading was commissioned from bilingual poet Gwyneth Lewis, and written in the wake of her appointment as Wales's very first national poet. I borrow it as much for that special history as for the resonances I have just described. Vicki Bertram identifies poetry by women as 'a valuable index of cultural change; yielding insights into the placing and construction of women in culture and society, and [recording their] changes and challenges to the status quo'.[2] Part cultural criticism, part poetic ethnography, in the wake of Bertram and others, this book explores how the female poet is shaped by, imagines and helps shape the geo-cultural politics of a partly devolved, newly self-conscious and outward-looking twenty-first-century Wales.

In Jahan Ramazani's words, 'By sound, structure, and self-reflexivity, poems enunciate and play on the construction of, and movement through, multiple worlds'.[3] I find the processes and effects of any poetic text's formal and linguistic 'play' as diverting as any of the worlds on which it might open. As Angela Leighton's virtuosic study shows, the word 'form' comes to seem chimerical in the endless paradoxes which it enshrines:

> [It] can signify both the finished object, the art form in its completion, or the parts that make up its technical apparatus. It can signify a visionary apparition in the mind, or the real, physical properties of a work. In addition, it can suggest the force that drives to completion: a resource, a goad, a ghost, an intention, a struggle, a desire.[4]

It is in such complexities that, for me, poetry compels. The formal decisions in which the poem's voice is made are invariably what help to propel it beyond any merely lexical/textual existence. As Maggie Humm rightly warns, 'How something is spoken about reveals a great deal about the operation of power relations'.[5]

For me as for both Humm and Bertram, any text's signifying possibilities are sharpened by knowledge of the differences that gender can make both to the processes which bring it into being, and to the literary traditions by which it is judged and valued. However, this study takes less interest in feminist and nationalist ideological positions per se than in the ways that any ideology might be uttered, critiqued and/or contested in and through a poem's form, as well as its language and/or theme. For Gwyneth Lewis, the material and prosodic choices which admit any poem's fullest expressive possibilities lend it ethical agency; she constructs in its specialised spatio-textual domain, crucially, 'a form of discernment'.[6] In other words, the poem gives shape to the hermeneutic processes (of 'discernment') which it produces in as well as for its reader, as 'a form of energy which links . . . your truth to the world around you'.[7] The conviction – that the aesthetic can utter truth on its own 'discern[ing]' terms – openly obtains in the closing pages of Lewis's boldly political epic *A Hospital Odyssey* (2010):

> Matter never sees fit to die
> and if life is the transfer of energy
>
> from one state to another – this poem from me
> to you – then this continual exchange
> must be our purpose
> . . .
> Some say that energy
> vibrates, that stuff's made up of superstrings,
> that physicists study harmony
> and that particles aren't billiard balls, things,
> but notes, all matter a coherent song
>
> for many voices . . . (*AHO*, pp. 146–7)

The energy-flow between text, author and reader which Lewis prizes is politicised by both the gender of its author and its form. Angela Leighton affirms that 'What is formed may be transformed, deformed, reformed; it may contain a formative or forming purpose; it may be formal, informed or multiform'.[8] In such plasticities, many poems ask to be read against and back into the cultural milieux from which they emerge. Lewis's own writing practice tirelessly confirms the socio-cultural and political valency of the aesthetic: 'It seems to me that the trick of writing out of your own language or idiom without being parochial is to use the material you find at your feet but using the highest aesthetic standards.'[9] Filtering the materials which come thus to hand (the 'truth like glass' to be found, as it were, 'in these stones') through the visual and aural economies of genre, stanza, lineation, metre and rhyme, Lewis's poems search the cultural-political complexities of her historical moment. In their often disruptive formalities her poems can be construed – along with those of a perhaps surprisingly broad range of other poets – as 'producing' a subtly expressive topos, a kind of verbal-textual analogue of Henri Lefebvre's 'social space'.[10]

Lewis's success might serve to remind us that, poetically speaking, women in Wales have never had it so good. Of three national poets to have held the appointment so far, two have been women; the current incumbent is Gillian Clarke. At the time of writing, Wales's foremost and oldest poetry publisher Seren could count thirty-one women on its books, Parthian six and Cinnamon a triumphant thirty-four; Welsh-language publishers Gomer include nine. Arguably perhaps nowhere else in the UK can women writing poetry enjoy the sense of critical mass which Wales and Wales-based publishers today make available. Like Lewis's giant poem-window, many of their works are choreographed in ways which are self-consciously self-troubling: the uncertain aesthetic topoi they produce hint at the restive imaginary of a post-millennial and increasingly transcultural Wales. In their prodigality, of literary and/or aesthetic mode, cultural-political stance and in some cases language, these poems seem to me above all to insist on what Homi K. Bhabha calls 'the impossible unity of nation as symbolic force'. Conversely, they also prove the prodigiousness of the creative and cultural possibilities to be found at or within 'the ambivalent margin of the nation-space'.[11]

I propose that the aesthetically, culturally, geopolitically and/or ethnographically complex spaces such poems produce invariably approximate to – even if they do not explicitly figure – Bhabha's 'ambivalent space of enunciation'. Partly because they have themselves been produced by *women*, they recall his accommodating vision of the 'beyond'; that . . . *in-between* space – that carries the burden of the meaning of culture'.[12] Again and again the poets I read 'envisage a different cultural horizon for writing and for women [and for Wales]' in the relatively confined geopolitical territory, but proliferative imaginary, of the national space in and out of which they choose to write. To be fair, none could be said self-consciously to align herself with the shifting inter- and/or trans-cultural horizons of Bhabha's 'beyond'.[13] It is, rather, my readings which swing the critical lens in the direction of that 'contingent, in-between space'.[14] Indeed, this book's gender emphases surely affirm how far, as a woman writing in and out of, constructed and conditioned by, the same geopolitical and linguistic complexities as my subjects, my map of their poetic topoi is itself a production, as implicated as I am in the sociocultural architectonics I trace. As Christian Jacob notes, any 'map results from a double construction, that of its author and that of its readers – a symmetrical process, a twofold construction . . . of encoding and decoding'.[15]

My writing of this book has always been charged by a sense of critical and cultural relationship with the writers and works I read. This makes the cartographer's provisional relation to the map, its 'contingent' signifying system as uncertain as any text's, worth reiterating.[16]

No wonder Ned Thomas urges makers of the critical map in Wales to stay alert to 'the forces that shape our drawing of it', and writer/editor Francesca Rhydderch calls for more attention to be paid to 'the difficulties of placing and voicing oneself as a critic'.[17]

Those difficulties leave me thinking of this study as less map than critical travelogue, the textual-aesthetic spaces it simultaneously produces and tours emerging in conversation with the writers I cite. For Rhydderch, the 'linguistic and cultural schizophrenia' of our shared geopolitical context marks 'a point beyond which Welsh critics could and perhaps should struggle to pass'.[18] I hope that the reflexive critical space I have produced here can, like the texts, admit without overdetermining the aesthetic horizons in and through which a vibrant group of poets 'sing' (to quote Lewis's huge poem) into being the reoriented topology of a post-millennial Wales they are themselves helping to shape.

Introduction

> It is only by remaining dynamic, by evolving, that a culture or a literary tradition continues to live.[1]

Writing just ahead of the referendum which initiated political devolution in Wales, Stephen Knight wonders: 'Do people shape a culture or does culture shape people? The answer, no doubt, lies somewhere between the two.'[2] He is treading a terrain theorised by Henri Lefebvre, for whom space is produced in and through social interaction engendered by and assimilating 'Everything: living beings, things, objects, works, signs, symbols . . . Social space per se is at once work and product – a materialization of social being'.[3]

Doreen Massey's influential description of space, inflected by Lefebvre's, characterises it as multiplicitous, multidimensional and 'always in the process of being made. It is never finished; never closed. Perhaps we could imagine space as a simultaneity of stories-so-far.'[4] A formula that works in two directions (the 'stories' producing space are surely also produced in and by that space) overlooks how *place* influences the matrix it describes, if (as Edward Relph argues) 'Space is claimed for place by naming it'.[5] The 'simultaneity of stories-so-far' telling and told by post-millennial Wales combines in a manifestly equivocal socio-historical space. The poems which help produce and are produced by that ambivalence can likewise rarely reduce the places which contextualise them. The texts which I tour here seem, separately and together, to inscribe a mobile and proliferative aesthetic and cultural geography of selfhood and political affiliation.

Historically, Wales's poets have been influential in the self-fashioning social processes Lefebvre theorises. Their special history contextualises my interest in the contemporary poet's unsettling of sanctified constructions of Wales as secure and securing 'place', in and through the spatio-textual domain of the poem. The destabilising urge echoes Massey, arguing that 'the identities of place are always unfixed, contested, multiple . . . Places viewed in this way are porous and open.'[6]

Nudging us towards a permeable domain she calls 'that beyond', Massey suggests and illumines the overlap between these poets' destabilising of their shared domain, and the 'in-between', equivocal simultaneities of Homi K. Bhabha's hybridic, theoretically unrepresentable, 'Third Space'.

I want to reconfigure Knight's question: do authors and places, like the communities they treat, produce texts and their readings, or vice versa? Three guiding emphases shape my construction of the Wales producing and produced by/in the readings which follow. First, there is the extent to which we can, or might want to, construct Wales as national context. The American poet Charles Bernstein warns that 'for writing, or reading, to assume . . . a national identity is as problematic as for writing to assume a self or group identity'.[7] His words reflect justifiable scepticism about the links which many understand to exist between identity and place. Secondly, in our cyber/networked contemporary moment, this study inscribes my conviction that the people Gwyn Alf Williams could in 1970 call 'Welsh' (leaving aside the incipient political problems of defining the term) can no longer be held solely responsible for producing the artefact of 'Wales', cultural or otherwise. Given the slippage-ridden intersections between national and cultural identity, the question of *Welshness* has long seemed to me to be more tangential to this enquiry than, to echo Jeremy Hooker treading a similar path some twenty years ago, 'the different ways certain writers form ideas or shape *visions* of Wales in their work'.[8]

For one reason or another, most of the writers I discuss are less accurately defined as Welsh than Wales-affiliated, or more precisely still perhaps, in one neat locution, 'elective' Welsh.[9] They are, however, all women. The cultural-political discourse of the later twentieth century leaves no doubt that the story of a nation's changing sense of cultural identity can be re-understood in and through the herstories its history must frame. Women are always as firmly, if less visibly, embedded in the political as the psychic dramas of the nation:

> Men are incorporated into the nation metonymically[:] the nation is embodied within each man, and each man comes to embody the nation . . . Women are scripted into the national imaginary in a different manner. Women are not equal to the nation but symbolic of it.[10]

For me – as for many – gender issues trouble and complicate the links, however contingent and uncertain, which Bernstein and others make between writing (specifically 'poetry and songs') and nationhood.[11] I explore women's mediation of Wales as a locus of cultural-political activity and experience, in and through the female-centred poetry which *helps produce* as much as it is produced by that locus. In Wales, the work of scholars like Deirdre Beddoe, Ursula Masson, Angela John, Jane Aaron and Katie Gramich has helped to loosen some of the gendered/ing effects of those constraints.[12] Collectively such writers show how, in Wales as elsewhere in western culture, women's literary productions, 'rooted . . . in the materiality of women's existence in real life [have been] denied validity and legitimation in a culture still very much dominated by men'.[13]

This study seeks to build on the foundations which these and other critics of poetry by Anglo-American/'British' women offer. By comparison with their English, Scottish and Irish peers, women have been writing poetry in Wales for an unusually long time.[14] Insofar as this, the first major critical study of its kind, seeks to offer its female subjects the contemporaneous literary-critical legitimation their foremothers lacked, it must be considered feminist. In writing this book I have wanted to widen the kinds of literary critical horizon against which a diverse array of poets and texts might be silhouetted. If my motives have been ideological, they have been so in the name of a literary-critical rather than any more instrumentally political agenda. Whatever this study lacks in political edge, I hope it makes up for in its foregrounding of poetry written by women 'as primary and as constitutive of a different [Wales]'.[15]

Writing identity and place

In this book, what Gillian Rose calls 'a geopolitics of location' is both brought into focus and unsettled in the textual terrain of the (female-authored) poem.[16] I find the poem 'geopolitical' both in its capacity at once *to be* a location, in its particular spatialised/aesthetic existence as text, and, simultaneously, *to represent* the cultural contexts and locations, the socioculturally produced spaces and places out of which it emerged. The paradigm is complicated by the ways in which any poetic construct is conditioned by its ethnographic origins and contexts.

First, given 'the variegated transnational poetries' of our time, there seems little point in trying to overplay the lyric poem's sense of cultural affiliation, still less in the context of Wales's arguably postcolonial literary imaginary and aesthetic.[17] Rather, for me, poetry acutely registers the contingent sociocultural agendas of 'decentered subjects . . . who are plural, differentiated, and conflicted because they are constituted as subject-citizens in and by a world that is not – no more than they themselves are – rationally and singly authored'.[18] Secondly, there is the gendering effect on that aesthetic of what Hélène Cixous calls the 'spacious singing Flesh: . . . that bursts partitions, classes, and rhetorics, orders and codes, must inundate, run through, go *beyond* the discourse with its last reserves'.[19] Time and again, the texts I read seem to write themselves out of their geopolitical contexts in reaching beyond conventional aesthetic (formal and/or generic) expectations towards freshly imagined cultural, political and poetic horizons.

Place(s) enshrine as well as help make sense of the space(s) in and of which they are constituted.[20] It is chiefly in the capacity to locate, or fix, that the idea of place becomes entangled with questions of identity. Hence Hooker's assumption that any writer 're-creates the place he lives in, at the same time as he is re-created by it'.[21] Take Gillian Clarke, in a reflective moment which Hooker points out elsewhere:

> From where I write I see a landscape open like a book, a landscape of valleys and hills typical of the view from the . . . writing desk of many a Welsh writer from any of the seven counties of Wales . . . I can name the fields on my side of the valley, and a few on the other side. Valleys, and a land that is tilted to face its neighbour, makes for tight communities and open lives.[22]

Spoken from that much-loved Ceredigion landscape which has long embedded her in its demonstrably 'tight communities', Clarke's words manifest the powerful nature of the relationship 'between community and place' which Matthew Jarvis senses in the Welsh *cynefin*, meaning 'a landscape with everything in it . . . rendering the physicality of the Welsh environment a vitally *human* space'.[23] For me, it is partly in their introversion that the notionally 'open' horizons which Clarke projects seem so exclusive: the 'gratitude' Hooker himself hears in them hints that he shares my sense of their self-involved nature.[24]

The mutually confirming consonances between place and selfhood are not easily reduced: 'when the question "'Who am I?" . . . becomes "Where am I?" . . . place takes the place of essence'.[25] Clarke's words hint that an essentialising tendency can still tell in a landscape where, as Kirsti Bohata shows, places have long been ideologically constructed.[26] So confessedly, in the passage I have quoted, a (belated) product of the landscape she constructs from her desk, the Cardiff-born Clarke's remarks seem to me to be haunted by various kinds of 'uncomfortable questions about essentialism, about "authentic" or legitimate culture, about rights, about ethnicity, language and experience embedded in landscape', all of which, Jasmine Donahaye rightly suspects, stem from cultural constructions of place 'as a fixture'.[27] Unsettling just such constraining fixities of location and subjectivity, with women in mind, Susan Stanford Friedman constructs identity in spatio-territorial terms as 'a terrain, an intersection, a network, a crossroads of multiply situated knowledges'.[28]

The complexities of self-positioning in what was once called the 'British Isles' find Robert Crawford concluding that 'Identity . . . always lives through and is determined by a "debatable land", a shifting, dynamic border territory'.[29] His argument might seem to resist the historic grain of Wales's culture, where poets 'as keepers of the word' are often, determiningly, tied into local and historic traditions.[30] This is why the ancient links between poet and a 'poetry-loving society' are often recovered in the form of *y bardd gwlad*, the 'country' or 'folk' poet linked with an originary *gwerin* or 'common people'.[31] Elsewhere amid the political realities of a newly post-millennial Wales, Jane Aaron and M. Wynn Thomas refresh an 'identifying attachment to *bro* (locality) rather than nation' in the place-bound terms of 'local patriotism'.[32] In both cases, however, the use of *Cymraeg* silently queries 'the ability of the English language to mediate Welshness'.[33] Amid the linguistic chauvinism still haunting all kinds of anglophone writing in Wales, my privileging of English-language texts perhaps needs defending. Regrettably, I am monolingual. I should dearly love to speak Welsh well enough to savour the full complexities of its use in contemporary poetics. Until then I can only speculate with Crawford that, as in Scotland and Ireland and many other bilingual cultures, Wales may speak itself more eloquently in the dialogues between its two languages than either can separately.

According to Francesca Rhydderch, for French novelist Andre Gide a country's unifying sense of identity derives from the extent to which its constituents 'mix, intersect and merge with each other.'[34] Gide seems to anticipate the inter-cultural melange to which new communication technologies give rise. In a Wales which must increasingly view itself as the product of the temporal and topological confusions of our age, cultural affiliations of all kinds surely begin to seem chimerical: 'Who on earth knows who they themselves are in all this mess of movement, migration, tacit segregation and attempted acculturation?'[35]

Amid the roiling cross-currents – local, national, inter- and/or trans-national, and technologically mediated – of their complex historical, arguably 'intercultural' moment, the poets I read can hardly but unsettle the 'unitary and homogeneous Welsh identity' cherished by their predecessors.[36] In the different materials each brings to Gwyn's 'mess', Gwyneth Lewis and her peers propose various forms of 'cultural and historical relationship' that reach beyond the ethnic, geopolitical and aesthetic horizons marking and marked by 'the tired old Welsh-English binary'.[37] It is perhaps as a result of the same linguistically self-conscious 'mess' that Jarvis sketches a twenty-first-century Wales more frequently constructed by its poets as 'a place to begin thinking about something else' than as 'a subject of outright concern'.[38]

My own gendered readings confirm Leigh Gilmore, noticing how often, for

> women writers, the community into which one is born is not, ultimately, the community to which one belongs. Women . . . who cross classes and regions [and/or] who politicise female identity . . . locate themselves in complex relation to their communities or homes of origin and to the communities they join.[39]

The poet Frances Williams is frank: 'I simply don't belong to Wales in that unquestioning, uncomplicated way.'[40] Few of Williams's peers disagree with her, not least Wales-identifying Israeli-Palestinian in-migrant Donahaye, who insists that 'identification . . . is not the same as belonging; identification *with* is not the same as identity as'.[41] Donahaye's greater point is equally germane: being 'Welsh', insofar as the claim is any longer possible, should neither legitimate nor preclude any creative artist's contribution to the collective, ongoing and always provisional cultural production of Wales. Different groupings, like different individuals, produce their own versions of their cultural home or hinterland. In the words of Ned Thomas, 'There is every reason, in Wales as elsewhere, to prefer a view of culture which allows for plurality, fluidity, dialogue, interaction and even conflict, over a definition which is totalizing and static and essentialist'.[42]

The writers I treat – whether of identifiably 'Welsh' extraction (Clarke, Ruth Bidgood and Catherine Fisher, Menna Elfyn and Gwyneth Lewis, Alison Bielski, Samantha Wynne-Rhydderch and Nerys Williams, say), less certainly affiliated writers (like Christine Evans, Pascale Petit, Wendy Mulford and Deryn Rees-Jones), self-consciously 'elective Welsh' in-migrants (like Hilary Llewellyn-Williams, Sarah

Corbett and Donahaye) or those who (like Anne Stevenson, Anne Cluysenaar, Sheenagh Pugh, Tiffany Atkinson and Zoë Skoulding) have lived, or (Jo Shapcott) habitually write, in Wales – centralise the problematic of identity, and the processes of identification, in its numerous contexts. Their poems inscribe in Wales (or *Cymru*) a heterogeneous and permissive place, in which such powerful issues can 'be productively entered into, without the risk of shattering the national into meaningless fragments'.[43]

The variously equivocal textual spaces/places in and out of which these writers write chime with Lewis's gigantically indeterminate millennial text, not least its wide-angled admission of what Massey calls 'the global as part of what constitutes the local, the outside as part of the inside'.[44] Energetically implicated in the 'creation of a vital cultural identity [dependent] less on a looking in than on a looking out', their collective imaginary typically asks us, in Bhabha's terms,

> To think beyond narratives of originary and initial subjectivities [in focusing] on those moments or processes that are produced in the articulation of cultural differences [and read in their texts a] terrain for elaborating strategies of self-hood – singular or communal – that initiate new signs of identity . . .[45]

Writing out of the 'far country'

Clarke's long poem 'Letter from a Far Country' did much to encourage women writing poetry to turn to their gender-community for the 'instrument of expression' best suited to the circumstances of their common ground. Published in 1981, Clarke's letter crucially authorised the value of the woman-centred history and experiences it imaged and which, alongside peers like Sally Roberts-Jones, Alison Bielski, Gladys Mary Coles, Sandra Anstey and Penny Windsor, she would import into the literary and poetic traditions of her time. As Linden Peach comments, in their visibility such writers provided the female role models to counter the masculinity of Wales's national imaginary.[46] The acclaim which 'Letter' earned also did much to strengthen critical interest in the work of women poets in and beyond Wales in the later twentieth century. The very role in which Gwyneth Lewis's gigantic millennial poem was commissioned from her, as first national poet for Wales, confirms the success of the shift which Clarke helped engineer. Lewis is herself quite clear: 'What Gillian did was to make a massive claim for that domesticity, as being equal in high seriousness to anything that male poets were writing about . . . which has meant that we are free *not* to consider that realm. I've been freed up by Gillian's work to look at other things.'[47]

For Massey, space 'is a product of . . . relations which are necessarily embedded material practices which have to be carried out'.[48] The creative arts are implicit in those 'material practices', as Lewis's text again suggests, hinging the territorial, socio-historical and linguistic riches of Wales's 'stones' with the country's traditionally vigorous creative life. They might recall Clarke's 'The Wind Chimes', written 'after a slate sculpture by Howard Bowcott', in which one set of (material) significations gives, synaesthetically, onto a different if equally traditional aesthetic and expressive mode:

> From sunrise to afternoon
> the wind harp drinks the sun,
> notes slowly giving to mellowness
> . . . the warm stones singing. (*GCCP*, p. 169)

Clarke often uses the at once immutable and malleable properties of rock and its cognates to trope the sociocultural history staged in Wales's perhaps too easily romanticised landscapes. 'Slate Mine' genuflects at the metonymic threshold of an industrial imaginary ('We stoop through its porch') which 'Roofing' re-centres in the 'domestic geometry' of a craft ('Neat as a darn they lap and overlap') it honours in four equally neat para-rhymed tercets resolving in a rhyming couplet (*GCCP*, pp. 112, 113). In 'Slate' a palimpsestic new hearthstone opens up and anchors the home in its prehistoric materiality:

> Milky planets
> trapped in its sheets
> when the book was printed,
> float in the slate,
>
> water-marked pages
> under a stove's feet. (*Letting In The Rumour*, p. 54)

Poems like this seem to anticipate the 'horizons' of Lewis's millennial text in several ways. Formally and thematically Clarke's best work uncovers new horizons – a 'far country' – in the most mundane-seeming materials ('stones'). The regulating effort which 'Letter' describes, with a mixture of satisfaction and resentment ('The chests and cupboards are full, / the house sweet as a honeycomb. / I move in and out of the hive / all day, harvesting, ordering. / You will find all in its proper place, when I have gone') is replayed in the ordering of the poem's semi-sequential architecture (*GCCP*, 45–6). Part dramatic, part lyric, poised between narrative and epistolary modes, like the other landmark texts of Clarke's productive middle career (including 'Cofiant' and the looser-limbed 'The King of Britain's Daughter' [1993], both of which I touch on later), 'Letter' embeds Clarke in the cultural processes I describe. Among the first women to achieve recognition in the patriarchal Wales of the later 1960s, she remains a crucial progenitor for the poets who followed her, mediating between the contemporaries named a moment ago, together with figures like Sheenagh Pugh, Anne Stevenson and Jean Earle (whose death in 2002 places her just outside my scope); the successors on whom I focus in the main body of this account, and the writers who arguably acted as path breakers for them all: Tony Conran's 'heroic' generation, comprising Lynette Roberts (1909–95), Margiad Evans (1909–58) and Brenda Chamberlain (1912–71), with the addition suggested by Kenneth Rexroth in 1949 – he omits Evans – of Denise Levertov (1923–97).[49]

If they are rarely acknowledged as exemplars by today's poets, this group can nevertheless be said both to have 'produced' and been produced by the Wales they knew in ways which seem pertinent to their twenty-first-century successors. Yet none could be called 'authentically' Welsh. For Conran, the collectively 'problematic relation to Wales' of his three models, all 'expatriate and exotic in their chosen culture', defines them as 'heroic', their work the expression of poetic courage rather than coincidence or expedience.[50] The daring of Evans, Roberts, Chamberlain and Levertov confirms the 'formal pleasure' they afford Conran: the different ways each finds (the first three were all, like their still neglected neo-modernist successor Bielski, talented visual artists) to make *aesthetic* sense of their cultural-political position. Signally, their commonly problematic sense(s) of relationship with the places in and out of which each writes sharpens not so much *what* they write about as *how* they choose to say it: the shaping of an idea, in the spatial constraints of the text (and its immediate material contexts), in and through the linguistic and formal energies which poetic expression uniquely affords.

The two collections of poetry published by Margiad Evans, shortest-lived but most intensely Wales-identifying of the four (perhaps with least reason), have yet to be properly read.[51] Evans's searching miniaturism – often earthed by an instant of epiphanic communion with the natural world – emerges from a sensibility reminiscent of Dickinson,

Hardy and Edward Thomas, although for me her tiny, tense lyrics more powerfully invoke the differently interiorised poetics of John Clare and Charlotte Mew respectively. Evans's formal economy masks her impatience with metric and stanzaic convention; her psychic sense of cultural dislocation echoes as much in self-rupturing lineation and syntax as in a shadowy imagery. Evans's innovations are less ostentatious than the verbal pyrotechnics for which her Argentian-born contemporary Lynette Roberts, another in-migrant, is now honoured. Roberts wrote more rapidly out of the Welsh/London literary networks in which marriage to Keidrych Rhys in 1939 immersed her, although her small poetic oeuvre reflects another foreshortened career: after moving away from Wales following her marriage breakdown she ceased publishing, despite returning to Carmarthenshire where she lived for the rest of her life.

In Margiad Evans's work topography and place rarely obtrude; Roberts's work is by contrast 'grounded in a variety of places: West Wales, Latin America, metropolitan London'; hence the 'prodigal and worldflung' idiom admired by her friend Alun Lewis in 1941.[52] For Conran, however, Roberts's is an imaginary in which Wales always prevails: 'There is no question that she was aware of what she was doing when she allowed Welsh influence to mould her work . . . her constant sense of experiment, her interest in the Welsh tradition as an excitement and challenge.'[53] Bangor-born Brenda Chamberlain, like Evans and Roberts a trained painter who travelled in and out of her native Welsh context, enjoyed a much longer career. The highly wrought intensity of Chamberlain's fine prose work *Tide Race*, about her years on Bardsey Island, has tended to draw attention from the muscular poems of *The Green Heart* (1958). Deriving (too closely for some) from the passionate correspondence between the poet and her erstwhile German lover, the collection merits recuperation as the adept found or even progressively collaborative work it asks to be read as today. The youngest but in transatlantic terms best known of the four, British-born 'Black Mountain' poet Denise Levertov, one of the constellation of writers influenced by Charles Olson's 'open field' poetics, identified with her adored mother's native Wales throughout her lengthy career, as poems like 'The Instant', 'The Quarry Pool' and 'An Arrival (North Wales 1897)' confirm.[54]

That these sketchy links still await concerted critical study testifies to the 'inbuilt sexism' which Conran rebukes in 'centuries of male dominance and self-esteem'. Any of them might have forestalled Randal

Jenkins, who in 1972, reproving Clarke's predecessors for a 'scarcity of technical innovation', takes to bespeak 'the scarcity of a radically different outlook in search of a different means of expressing it'.[55] Even without Roberts, whose idiosyncratic voice had fallen silent by 1950, Chamberlain and Levertov inarguably provide such an outlook; innovative Welsh-language poet Menna Elfyn recently revealed the importance of Levertov's example to her own work.[56]

Randal Jenkins's now myopic-seeming complaint is interesting if only for investing 'technical innovation' with some cultural or political purpose ('outlook'), in and beyond its aesthetic qualities. For Irigaray, 'change[s] in discourse' likewise occur only when writers 'go beyond the utterance into the creation of new forms'.[57] Lee M. Jenkins echoes the view of these strange bedfellows in charting a poetics in which, for reasons of gender, 'displacement, relocation, cultural translation and untranslatability are registered in formal and stylistic as well as in thematic terms'.[58] I hope what follows bears her out; giving directly and metonymically onto the bewitchingly mobile interpretative terrain of the aesthetic, the signifying notion of poetic form seems worth pausing on.

Angela Leighton persuades us that the complex semantic associations of the word 'form' link it with space – absence – as much as substance:

> it holds off from objects, being nothing but form, pure and singular; at the same time, its whole bent is towards materialization, towards being the shape or body of something. Form which seems self-sufficient and self-defining, is restless, tendentious, a noun lying in wait for its object.[59]

The poets I discuss share a seemingly collective will to use poetic form/ality for precisely the possibilities which Leighton uncovers, appropriating for poetry what Bhabha calls 'those spaces that are continually, contingently, "opening out", remaking boundaries, exposing [how] difference is neither one or the other, but *something else besides*, in-between . . .'[60]

Evoking the political and cultural 'horizons' promised in Lewis's reflexively fenestral millennial text, the 'beyond' which Irigaray identifies seems to me to echo the prodigal, self-displacing 'Beyond' which, for Bhabha, 'signifies spatial distance, marks progress, promises the future . . .'[61] Like Clarke and her modernist predecessors, Lewis and her female peers use the poetic construct literally and metaphorically, to script aesthetic but also cultural-political change: to go *beyond* the generic and formal horizons of their creative and geopolitical situation.[62] To open up Wales's cultural imaginary to their 'stories-so-far', such writers produce in the material/textual and often generically undecideable poetic construct an aesthetic *and* political space in which to test the complexities of their cultural moment. Their 'heroic' foremothers figure the decades of back-story, the historical, critical and creative continuities inflecting the ethnographically nuanced cultural/aesthetic processes which I appraise.

Women writing Wales 'now'

If literary and poetic genre can be read as a synecdoche for other forms of cultural (and political) taxonomy, critical labels (like borders) constrain.[63] This irony returns me to Neil Smith and Cindi Katz: 'multiple identities, borders and borderlands, margins, and escape from place are all in different ways a response to the political inviability of absolute location'.[64] It also explains Ramazani's noticing how writers seek 'imaginative forms to articulate the dualities, ironies, and ambiguities of this cultural in-betweenness': 'Poetry – a genre rich in paradox and multivalent symbols, irony and metaphor – is well-suited to mediating and registering the contradictions of split cultural experience.'[65] I hope this book makes clear my conviction that poetry in its spatio-prosodic wizardry engages in imaginative and critical dialogue with its cultural-political moment in ways which frequently take it, and us, 'beyond identitarian boundaries'.[66]

Prosodically speaking, the range of poetries in Wales is perhaps uniquely broad, thanks partly to the spectrum of 'strict metres', many deriving from medieval models, on which today's Welsh-language poets are still taught to draw.[67] Their English-language counterparts prize formal innovation no less highly. Pushing poetic utterance past the norms of formal and generic convention, the women I read inscribe their variously uncertain senses of relation, and/or identification, with the cultural complex which is Wales today. In their hands, both public and private narrative and lyric modes are subverted, often in the fractured linearity of the lyric sequence. In the same way, subgenres like pastoral, confessional and travel/quest poetries become as self-consciously equivocal and discreetly political as the anti-referential textual – sometimes eloquently intertextual – spaces of the found, macaronic and/or translated poem. In all these ways, the generically indexed architecture of the poetic text comes to seem to 'open out' the kinds of cultural spaces which for Bhabha insistently mark in difference 'neither one or the other, but *something else besides*, in-between. . .'[68]

I begin by surveying the attraction of the interstitial for more than one generation of Wales-identifying poet. Some of the writers I survey in chapter 1 search the contours, both actual and historical, of Wales's famously compelling, conflict-laden landscapes. Others parallel that still-contested terrain with the multiply marked, text-like (not always female, human nor even necessarily animate) body; one registers it in the linguistically undecideable quasi-collaborative space of the parallel (translated) text. Chapters 2, 3 and 4 elicit the cultural-textual and to some extent regional geographies of the Wales variously producing and produced by three very different poets. Chapter 2 finds local historian Bidgood too alive to the effects of socio-historical change on her much-loved Mid Wales to assume too much of the often ruinous traces left by the ebb and flow of human habitation on its enigmatic topology. For me, the dialogue between natural and manmade produced by the complex relationship between the indigenous and incoming inhabitants of rural Powys, and their un/homely environs reaches its apotheosis in the weirdly dis/embodied possibilities of the found poems which this prize-winning nonagenarian has only belatedly collected.

Chapter 3 investigates the effects on the Welsh-speaking but Yorkshire-born Evans of a domestic life driven as remorselessly by the socio-linguistic norms of the far north-west coast of Wales – where the Llŷn peninsula reaches south towards the mound of Bardsey Island – as by the seasons and weather. For Evans, life has long revolved, both reassuringly and disruptively, around her farming family's annual migration between isthmus and island, in a rhythm which marks the degree of cultural dis/connection inscribed in the imaginary, linguistic and sociocultural frontiers of her home(s). Uncertainty charges and enriches a self-questioning poetics which deflects, as much as it reflects on, the tensions it probes. Chapter 4 meanwhile reads in Lewis's provocative manipulation of language and form a kind of eloquent cultural topography, as it discerns in her playful poetics the strategic effort to frustrate political, linguistic and generic over-determination. In the flexible hybrid forms she favours, the distinctions between truth and fiction, real and fabricated, self and other are strenuously troubled, until the term 'confession' comes to signify only mocking awareness of its own provisionality.

The two remaining chapters each deal with a small group of poets. Chapter 5 probes Wales's deeply rooted sense of historic, socio-political, imaginative and at some level linguistic sense of cultural kinship with neighbouring Ireland, as channelled through the poetic story-telling of Gillian Clarke, Christine Evans and Catherine Fisher. The final chapter explores the contrasts to be found among the works, and especially the attitude to form and mode, of three very different in-migrant and emigrant writers, Sheenagh Pugh, Wendy Mulford and Zoë Skoulding. As it demonstrates, each finds her own innovative way of traversing in order to dislocate – or unfix – the Wales in and out of which she writes.

Gillian Rose's performative critique notes that no distinction between any variety of 'real' space, and 'absolute' (or 'symbolic') space, is tenable; each version can always be proved as solid/unfixed as the other. For me, Wales (as both real and symbolic space) and its poets/poems interrelate and thus produce each other, mutually and simultaneously, materially and symbolically, all the time, in and through the spaces of representation and representational spaces which Lefebvre identifies. Wales's poets can always be said to have helped produce the cultural-political space(s) they write in and out of, and are themselves produced by, as they renew the textual and formal models which their cultural situation (imagined or actual, elective or not) offers. As for the poetic, so for the *critical* imaginary: my project, to describe, review, *map*, reflexively embeds both me and this book in a process of cultural production which mirrors the aesthetic manoeuvring I explore. Thus, the interviews and biographical materials I produce to illumine the poets' shifting orientations towards Wales simultaneously lay bare the dialogical character of my own scholarly practice. I am not minded to apologise for the effort to give poets vocal space in those broader critical conversations which so often silence as well as position them; to enable them to speak to and within as well as about that discourse, without ever wanting to appear to reduce the always complex relationship between any author and the creative materials (the places, experiences and personae) on which a text might draw.

In much the same spirit, I am happy to admit that the readings I offer here construct me as inevitably as my own and others' interviews play their part in constructing the poets I have talked to. This book is no different from any other scholarly work in its making of the map it tours. And, as Kathleen Kirby warns, 'Cartography [is] a site of interface, mediating the relationship between space and the subject and constructing each in its own particularly ossified way'.[69] That entangling implicates me, and this book, in a freighted 'critical' space which is itself always under construction. As reader and writer, I have tried to remember throughout that I am myself always navigating the same socio-political contingencies and dilemmas of cultural affiliation, language use and representation as the poets. For J. Hillis Miller, any community is 'an artificial, deconstructible construct fabricated out of words or other signs'.[70] Since it is as true of critical as it is of any socio-cultural community, that recognition leaves me for professional as well as personal reasons endorsing the decision of Menna Elfyn, once imprisoned for her political beliefs, to define her birthplace – that is, Wales itself – as 'desire'.

Elfyn's word reiterates the troping power of the horizon, the Bhabhaesque 'beyond', in the poetry which she and her female peers are writing, in and out of a Wales in which none feels (or seems to want to feel) entirely at ease. In their desiring relationship with Wales, such writers often render it seductively 'impossible'. Likewise, Bhabha's assertion that 'identification, as it is spoken in the desire of the other, is always a question of interpretation' points the way to geographer Nigel Thrift's account of place as 'permanently in a state of enunciation, between addresses, always deferred'.[71] As if in agreement, the poets' deployment of literary forms and genres which are distractingly compound, always work to draw their readers beyond their own textual topography, towards an elusive hermeneutic horizon – an ethnographic Third Space – we none of us can fully delineate or inhabit.

1

On the Border(s): The Interstitial Poetries of the Contact Zone

> The contact zone where differences meet is as real and as significant a part of cultural formations, including the formations of identity, as the spaces of difference.[1]

To the Edwardian mind of the writer H. V. Morton, the inherently secret (rather than secret*ive*) nature of Wales is its most compelling quality. Morton's courteous and percipient travelogue of 1930s Wales, *In Search of Wales*, seems at least partly driven by the expectation of its own failure. Making his leisurely approach from Ludlow, Morton rehearses Wales's painful history of cultural border making with circumspect sympathy; implicitly he urges us to understand Wales as having been taught to construct itself, like its embattled community, in defensively bounded terms. His arrival in Llangollen is accordingly marked, with respectful curiosity, by 'the feeling that I had crossed a frontier. I was in a foreign country.'[2]

The American writer Anne Stevenson, who spends some of each year in a remote Gwynedd cottage owned by her husband's family, is sanguine about the sense of cultural alienation she shares with Morton: 'In Wales I cannot be more than a passionate observer, a student of its geology and Neolithic past, an admirer of its mountains as I learn stumblingly to name them.'[3] Appearing at the close of the 1990 essay ('Poetry and place') in which these remarks appear, Stevenson's poem 'Binoculars in Ardudwy' echoes her sense of separateness from the landscape it captures, expressively, 'in the . . . noose' of the watcher's binoculars,

> hauling hill, yard, barn, man, house
> and a line of blown washing across
> . . .
> a mile of diluvian marsh.

However, in an irony compounded – as this intensely self-aware text knows – by the metonymically obscuring weather, the 'noose' confines the speaker as well as the scene:

> . . ., just as I frame it, the farm
>
> wraps its windows in lichenous weather
> and buries itself in its tongue.
> Not my eyes but my language is wrong.
> And the cloud is between us forever.
>
> Under cover of mist and myth
> the pieced fields whisper together,
> 'Find invisible *Maesygarnedd* . . .,
>
> Y Llethr . . . Foel Ddu . . . Foel Wen.' ('Binoculars in Ardudwy', in Lothar Fietz et al. (eds), *Regionalität*, p. 211; *Poems 1955–2005*, p. 185)

Both dividing and eliding the different elements of the scene they 'haul' into view, the binoculars honour the cultural separatism enshrined in, and shrouding, the farm and its spell-like field names. They also testify to the stranger's imaginatively double perception of the continuities yoking Ardudwy's figuratively misty patchworked ('pieced') landscape.

The recondite air which at once attracts and alienates Stevenson and Morton might derive partly from the relationship between demography and topography in Wales: its much-mythologised tracts of sparsely inhabited uplands can today still make its chief centres of population seem peripheral, Derridean supplements located with self-doubling ambivalence on the very margins of the marginal. The strangeness to which Morton and Stevenson both respond seems at once reified and troubled by the trope for which each reaches: the border. Like the boundary, which I have touched on already, borders are definitively liminal, permeable, polysemous spaces in which division and conjunction meet and interpenetrate. Susan Stanford Friedman puts it more elegantly:

> Borders between individuals, genders, groups and nations erect categorical and material walls between identities . . . But borders also specify the liminal space in between, the interstitial site of interaction, interconnection, and exchange. Borders enforce silence, miscommunication, misrecognition. They also invite transgression, dissolution, reconciliation, and mixing.[4]

For a range of strategic reasons, later twentieth-century feminist literary criticism laid energetic claim to the cultural power of the liminal. On behalf of readers and writers alike, as my epigraph suggests, critics like Friedman came to prize the border above all as 'contact zone', a site 'of constant movement and change, the locus of syncretist intermingling and hybrid interfusions of self and other', in which conventional discriminations driven by hierarchies of sameness and difference are interrogated and refused.[5] The gender emphases of Friedman's argument are of course germane to this account. I also want to keep Homi Bhabha in mind, for his confident reaching beyond the constraints of gender into what we might call the inter-cultural: 'the overlap and displacement of domains of difference [in which] the intersubjective and collective experiences of nationness, community interest, or cultural values are negotiated'.[6]

This chapter situates a number of poetries amid the productive uncertainties of the interstitial. As I show, the term can be applied as readily to textual as to territorial space(s), to material as to metaphoric forms of expression, as writers track the dynamic processes of cultural individuation in and through the complex contact zones of Wales's ethnographic and sometimes psycho-social terrain. For political and aesthetic reasons, the poems I read below explore these interstices in the variegated languages of two central tropes: the human, pre-human and mythopoeic histories and topographies of Wales's landscape; and the relational morphologies of the body, human and not. Again and again their authors exploit, with a poetic intelligence as likely to be playful as protective, both the aesthetic and the cultural-political opportunities of this eloquent, embodied, liminality.[7] To adapt a point made by Clair Wills, they use genre to register the ethnographic uncertainties of their situation, by reconfiguring 'the relationship between text and [culturally identifying] body'.[8]

Writing the March

The equivocal space of the 'contact zone' is writ large in Wales if only because, as Francesca Rhydderch notes, 'For such a small country, Wales has an immense border'.[9] Tacitly, Rhydderch might be referring to more than the country's perimeter, the 177 landlocked miles bordering England swelled by a further 1,680 miles (2,740 km) of coastline (*http://www.cartographic.org.uk*).

Arguably, Wales has been deeply incised by the so-called 'Marches', the contested territories held for lengthy periods by (often absent) 'Marcher lords' in the name of a remote English monarch. Frequently mapped onto the Welsh–English borderlands of the south and east, in fact the mobile, partitioning Marches reached as far as the western coast. Hence Tony Conran, in 1997, linking Wales's growing anglophone literature with the 'March':

> These days the March is not a geographical feature. It can be anywhere – through my backyard in Bangor, where my children are Welsh-speaking but I am not – through a Cardiff shop or a Llangollen office. Most people in Wales live lives that at some point or other are different because of this insidious March, snaking along between them and the complacency of being completely Welsh or completely English.[10]

Conran's elision of geographical, historical and linguistic division is typically shrewd. As Gillian Clarke tells David Lloyd, 'living in a land with two languages is a delicate situation. There's no moment of life in Wales that hasn't got that edge . . .'[11] If nothing else, the dynamism that both Clarke and Conran acknowledge resounds, as Tristan Hughes notes, in the 'double-edged' legacy of the bilingual

> political, social and cultural fault lines that run through and between and across [Wales's landscapes], [always] forcing us to think of ourselves as being either on one side of them or the other: insider or outsider, native or newcomer, custodian or usurper. And yet all the time those lines are becoming more fluid and amorphous, harder to fix . . .[12]

Situated by dint of birth, place of domicile, or cultural-political choice among Hughes's shifting fault lines, many poets discover in the tension-filled, Bhabha-like 'beyond' of Conran's 'insidious March' (comparable if not identical with Clarke's politically enfranchised 'far country'), a multidimensional space in which to sift the layered dis/continuities of both rural and urban, historic and mythologised, semi-autonomous, increasingly trans-cultural, contemporary Wales. As Katie Gramich and Catherine Brennan say of their fourteenth-century foremothers, the poets I read write, with confidence and purpose, as 'full participant[s] in the tradition, confident of [their] own craft and relishing what [they] depict as the privilege of [their] female Otherness'.[13] In doing so they invite us to read them, together and separately, as writing across or beyond the intersecting material, political and referential frontiers of their different cultural experiences. In 'rethinking the parameters of parameter', as Jo Gill puts it, writers like Anne Cluysenaar, Wendy

Mulford, Jo Shapcott, Zoë Skoulding, Deryn Rees-Jones, Sarah Corbett, Pascale Petit and perhaps above all Gwyneth Lewis and Menna Elfyn echo Clarke's affectionate sense of Wales as 'a small country, a place of coincidence and connection'.[14] At the same time, however, they endorse Daniel Williams's noticing how 'being both "inside and outside" . . . mutates into a position from which to speak, *beyond* the divisions, of the wider, international, relevance of Welsh cultural and political debates'.[15] From this vantage point, they spiritedly re-imagine 'what the geopolitical space [of Wales] may be, as a local or transnational reality'.[16] As Lewis remarks of the edge: 'It's offered me freedom, so I choose to stay.'[17]

The language(s) of landscape

Every piece of land is itself a text.[18]

As Dennis Cosgrove explains, any landscape is a construct of the perceiving eye; 'a way of seeing'; thus he warns against treating landscape 'in a vacuum, outside the context of a real historical world of productive human relations and those between people and the world they inhabit'.[19] Given the 'primary role that discourses of landscape play in the field of cultural contestation', and the tensions that still resonate inside and outside Wales's many kinds of border, the interest which English-language poets have taken in 'the relationship between language and the land in Wales' in the twentieth century should, perhaps, not surprise.[20] The divisive effects of this concern are both implied and dismissed by Stevenson, for whom the overlapping narratives enshrined in Wales's topology are always diminished by the natural theatre in which they are played out:

> The raised sedimentary mountains that encircle our cottage in Cwm Nantcol (geologically part of the Harlech Dome) are hundreds of million years old . . . In geological time, human history has occurred in a mere split-second – though in Wales, traces of it can be found everywhere. Roman remains are in many places still a visible presence. Over these the Arthurian myths, mixed with tales from the Mabinogion, throw a mythical haze from the Dark Ages. In the late thirteenth century, the Normans under Edward I finally overcame the native Britons (whose tribes gave the Paleozoic rock strata their geological names), and great square Norman castles – Harlech, Caernarfon, Conwy, Beaumaris – still grandly watch over empty harbours.

As she goes on to say of Cwm Nantcol, 'The place puts us in our place'.[21]

As I have shown elsewhere, in the late twentieth century, various women worked to make poetic space for their own 'ways of seeing' the acculturated landscapes of their contemporaneous environment(s).[22] For Stevenson, the 'timelessness and placelessness' of her environs is permissively 'wordless'.[23] Her Belgian-born peer Anne Cluysenaar finds in Wales's geology contrastingly eloquent subject matter. To the latter's scientific mind, the geological history of any landscape lends it a manifestly palimpsestic, deeply provisional referentiality. The opening poem of the neglected sequence 'Timeslips', written soon after Cluysenaar moved to her home in rural Usk, 'Landfall' meditates on the multiple 'edges' – dividing inanimate from animate, past from present/future, silence from expression – brought into productive contact in a fragment of fossil:

> tender flesh turned
> to stone: the gape of the shell
> where a tongue of tissue calcified
> to silence, its moment of sense
> suspended until our senses
> bent to meet it. (*Timeslips*, p. 89)

Despite its implicit articulacy, the fossil – and its geological context – seems to find voice only in the reconciling moment of sensual recognition. In fact the eleven poems of this powerful sequence repeatedly undo the edges they hunt out. With 'Landfall' warning 'how easily past might slide over present' (p. 90), 'In A Gap of Light' shrinks the gulf between the experiential limit of the primitive 'hunter's long-toed stride' – preserved in estuarine silt – and the speaker's own. The transcendent-seeming coalescence of ancient and contemporary ('Nowhere to be but here, / on a dark edge moving slowly / across a molten core') is arguably recorded, and can be teased out, in an individual's biological history or 'genetic footprint':

> What else they passed on is here
> in our own flesh . . .
> Stranded on a bench
> in the lab, a pale cloud
> floats free of the scalpel's tip. (*Timeslips*, p. 94)

'Quarry' resorts, discreetly, to synaesthesia in Cluysenaar's scrupulous construction of endpoint as meeting place:

> The long lines of their edges
> interlace in the haze, bare
> masses of sandstone, clouds
> of rock. (*Timeslips*, p. 102)

In this otherworldly environment, the passage of geological time – from glaciers to desert – is telescoped, its different realities converging with distorted beauty in the petrification ('broken off in mid air, / solid rivers') in which reality comes to seem paradoxical; witnessed from the bottom of the quarry, these rivers literally blur the 'edges' they inscribe between then and now, fixed and fluid, water and stone, in even the substance of which they are composed:

> It is mudstone,
> smooth, without taste. The river
> flows again, thickening, messageless
> on our tongues.

In this odd, anachronistic 'contact zone', where actual and geological time collide in the form of rock clouds, stone waves and 'messageless' fluvial tongues, the borders between human and non-human are finally subverted:

> As I watch,
> my brain is an estuary, shallow,
> dazzled with plankton, cells
> at the tide's mercy, idling.
>
> Matter watching itself. (*Timeslips*, p. 103)

As Cluysenaar points out, some of the finest geologists ('Murchison and Lyell and people like that') developed their work in and out of the Welsh landscape 'because of the mountains and the way the land has folded . . . It's a quite astonishing part of the planet from that point of view.' For her geology diminishes, insofar as it precedes, human history: 'Big geological changes . . . don't respect the existence of a place called Wales.'[24] This attitude prevails in the fifteen delicately turned lyrics of 'Through Time', one of several sequences to be found in *Migrations* (2011).[25] In 'At Pantymaes Abandoned Quarry', traces of pre-human history – 'centipede-double tracks' and mud wrinkles – textualise 'this fragment of land / whose pages you turn for our eyes' (*Migrations*, p. 30). 'On the beach, Ogmore-by-Sea' makes the tactility of rock still more palpably expressive, centralised margins subverting conventional visual relationships between different words and lines as the poem's diction, like the speaker's fingers, feels its way through the unstable chronology of the shoreline:

I pull off a glove
and slip my hand
into a gap.
My fingers move,
tip by tip, over stone.

Runways. Rucks. Burrows.

Braille of what bred us
reading its own
present . . . (*Migrations*, p. 42)

The exploratory mode of 'Through Time' is replayed in both its seriality, 'a metaphor for time, layers of time, linking back to each other, evidenced in landscape', and shifting stanzaic forms; the poet herself has explained that it turned out to affect its composition in ways which Cluysenaar half expects to extend, in turn, to her readers:

> Finding and then fulfilling the form led me to discover impressions and thoughts I hadn't been altogether conscious of. Linking lines back through assonance makes me feel that I am not so much moving forward as going deeper, through layers [;] . . . one doesn't have the control over the direction of the poem that one expected . . . For the reader, maybe stanzaic form can have analogous effects? Slowing the reader, encouraging layers of response?[26]

The temporal shifts enshrined in geology likewise attract Cluysenaar's friend Wendy Mulford. Based in Suffolk, Mulford is gaining recognition as the Wales-identified writer which, for reasons I explore at greater length in chapter 6, she has always felt herself to be. Hovering productively among several kinds of borderland, her still only partly published work 'Alltud' (its title the Welsh word meaning 'exile') meditatively layers time and public/private memory with the spiritual and mythic histories shaping, and shaped by, Wales's landscape.[27] In the formal-cum-spiritual terrain of this self-exploring text (to its author 'as much about psyche and spirit as it is about terrain or culture'), the part played by the poet in Wales and the part played by Wales in the poet coalesce, as Judaeo-Christian and pagan traditions intersect in topography, place-name and/or cultural tradition.[28] In its incantatory closing sections the Protean energies of Taliesin, the poet-speaker, the poem itself, and a mythopoeic/prehistoric Wales combine in the psalm-like sonorities of a literally unnameable consciousness:

Long before borders and nations were dreamed
I lay in the swamps and the silts, I fed from the ferns and the mosses
I am old as lava, unconformable as coal
My nature is shaped by crystal, by glacier
I am thrown into mountains, oxidated by iron
You shall never contain me for I AM
Old as the word on the day of Creation
I am tumultuous, I am solid, I am secret
I am wondrously made

Since the great glaciers of the Pleistocene
when the ice retreated and the rivers flowed
I was spewed out of the mouth of Severn . . .

No trace
of my provenance remains. ('Alltud', section 5, ll. 2–13, 21–2, ll. 159–60)

Recognising and refuting the invocational powers which Kenneth R. Smith once linked to 'the Welsh tradition, in riddle poems and in the mythological tales', as the excerpt suggests, the main impulse of 'Alltud' is manifestly self-inspecting.[29] Mulford's poetic consciousness is as exploratory as Cluysenaar's, but the formal/linguistic mysteries relished by this practising Catholic are laced with the kind of spirituality which Cluysenaar, for her part, tries to avoid specifying.[30] Mulford's writings, however, affirm that her faith – in all its manifold complexities – is also and always bound up with a sense of place, causing her co-author Sara Maitland to describe her work as mapping 'a geography of women's spiritual presence in the bedrock of the land'.[31] Interestingly, in fact, Mulford's deeply held religious beliefs have seemed only to sharpen her sense of the liminalities which feed so powerfully into her own (creative) imaginary; as Hooker says, *Virtuous Magic* constructs saints as 'boundary-transgressors', hagiography as 'a geography of the boundaries, of the borders and the unboundaried' and pilgrimage itself as 'a prising apart of closure, in pursuit at one and the same time of the unknown and the known'.[32] Mulford confirms:

> A 21st century Silurist operates from no certainties [where] a 17th c religious poet has a framework available to him/her . . . I feel myself increasingly writing out of the same consciousness that I inhabit when I'm at Mass, but I wouldn't say that makes me a Catholic poet . . . I see myself as maybe intermediary between the two positions.[33]

Another practising Catholic, Catherine Fisher proves an equally equivocal guide to the age-old border territory of her native Gwent, and its low-lying Levels. As I show in more detail in chapter 5, Fisher's guarded poems reveal in this sequestered region a suggestive contact zone, the dialogues of its legendary and historical pasts inscribed somehow dialogically on, in and between, the very features of the land itself:

> Boundary between voices, ways of speaking,
> tethered to England by a silver chain
> a second in the forging;
> a place
> to pass through, wary for the snares.
>
> A people not like any other people;
> Scornful of Welsh and Sais
> . . .
> ('Teyrnon Looks at Gwent Iscoed', *The Unexplored Ocean*, p. 37)

Elsewhere, the spirituality which lapsed-Catholic Hilary Llewellyn-Williams shares with Fisher, Mulford and Cluysenaar lends another very differently made oeuvre its trademark 'emphasis on mystery: the mystery of the Incarnation, Resurrection, the Mass and the sacraments . . . of life itself'. Her interest in the 'ancient precursors [of] and parallels to the Christian systems and symbols' propel Llewellyn-Williams towards themes ('the tree calendar, Hermetic philosophy, pagan religions, outlawed or forgotten knowledge') often rooted in a Nature she views as 'both more real and more mysterious than the humanly-constructed world'.[34]

Llewellyn-Williams's interest in the natural world informs her sense of her craft's transforming properties: 'Poetry, like magic ritual, universalises experience and gives it back to the world in a transformed state.'[35] These powers are appraised in the six-part sequence 'Sculpture at Margam', searching the overlap between idea and materiality in any art form. Framed by the economic, ecological and socio-historic contexts of the coastal country park which it treats, the sequence confirms Hooker's sense that its poet's mobilising of the antique 'wisdom buried in the land' works best when it is directed back into the resonances of the Wales in which she has spent most of her writing life.[36] The thematic and formal crux of 'Maze Stone', the opening text of the sequence, is the hermetic fertility symbol of the Green Man etched on 'a milestone on the road / to elsewhere'.[37] Like the labyrinthine sculpture over which its fingers seem literally to travel, the poem wreathes itself insinuatingly around, into and through the inscrutable 'leafy face' of the peculiar animus it honours. Text and sculpture co-produce the tactile mazy 'map' snaking into and out of the experiential borders separating subjectivity, artefact and environs from each other, 'round / and back and round / / to the centre space; right through, and out / the far side. Like a lens . . . an eye made of air, a doorway':

> This journey is endless.
> In and out of the stone,
> in and out of the trees –
> . . .
> Every turn, every path you take
> brings you here again. (*Animaculture*, pp. 35–6)

The apparently immutable energy of the pagan archetype is held in tension with the worn Christianity indexed in the roofless ruins of 'Capel Mair', where 'the seen and the unseen / meet' against the backdrop of sea, park and Port Talbot steel works. Antiquity alone relieves the comfortless theology figured in this neglected building, 'Old, old / older than church or Celtic battlements / / her shape in the land, river and tree and stone' (*Animaculture*, p. 39). The poem does not so much transform these mysteries as open up the experiential – always liminal – space they both stage and enshrine.

To all intents and purposes, the finely made miniatures of Jo Shapcott's 'Gladestry Quatrains' return us to the geo-cultural borders preoccupying Morton.[38] The sequence reveals Shapcott's intimacy with an area of Powys radiating out from the quiet rural market town of Kington, on the ancient boundary of Offa's Dyke, which she has visited regularly for years. Suffused with the rurality that conditions so much of Wales's perimeters, the poems probe the ambivalent relations between an undecideable terrain and the visitors wryly urged to 'warm your hands / on this border country, touch / its crust, finished, like bread' ('Radnorshire', *Tender Taxes*, p. 26). Openings into this inviting but resistant 'crust' can be hard to find. 'Gilwern Dingle' presents 'A lane between two meadows / not leading anywhere' (ibid. p. 50), while the anthropomorphising 'Road Not Available' uncovers a narcotic self-absorption in fields which 'endlessly remembering / / . . . drink their pasts further and further / down, . . .' (ibid., p. 45). For a poet who insists on the multiplicity of the poetic voice, 'Gladestry Quatrains' may seem biographical: Shapcott has often talked and written about her links with the Welsh borderlands of the Forest of Dean, where her parents originated.[39] The connection resonates in the self-consciously equivocal way these texts register their equally equivocal sense of relationship with their environs. Depicting the land conversing with the wind ('a linguist / who's known its old words for ages' and 'understands just how to say them'), 'Over the Col' concludes with the speaker blown riddlingly into 'an enormous step / backwards, to put me in my place' (ibid., p. 48). In 'Llan', language loss denies a Shapcott-like speaker the cultural entitlement of her parentage:

> Old border tongues trash
> this cwm, words and sounds
> I can make when my parents,
> rarely, let me eat their ashes.
> . . . (*Taxes*, p. 51)

Elsewhere, 'this border country' becomes an agent ('evading me') in the isolating effects of cultural displacement, its refusal of affiliation cast as betrayal, defensively partisan: 'though my own grandfathers / mined coal, coughed, spat / and died not far away',

> You round a corner and the hill
> has moved, the sky's gone AWOL
> and the ancestors, muttering in another tongue
> have dug themselves even further in. ('Wye Marches', *Taxes*, p. 49)

Shapcott's 'Gladestry Quatrains' ask to be mapped onto the socio-historical and linguistic geographies of the byways and boundary-lands of rural mid Wales. Read back into its parent collection, however, what Shapcott herself calls the 'uneasy pastoral' of the 'Quatrains' grows more suggestive. As its flyleaf explains, *Tender Taxes* is haunted by the modernist German poet Rainer Maria Rilke (1875–1926), specifically the two French-language collections (*Les Fenêtres* and *Les Roses*) written from his home in the bilingual Swiss canton of Valais, in the last years of his life. Shapcott's preface constructs her collection as 'a reader's book: a record of the way an author who was important to me . . . became as close as a profound friend, or an intimate enemy, or a lover'.[40] The relationship, played out through the atemporal poetic spaces of *Tender Taxes*, signifies on several levels. First, Shapcott honours both Rilke's virtuosic linguistic switching between his native German and the French in which he chose to write her source (inter-) text and his intercultural situation in Valais. However, written out of 'a place which has, literally, an edgier feel: the borders of Wales, where my family has its roots', so that the place-names 'change from Swiss to Welsh and English', Shapcott's 'uneasy pastoral' also troubles an exemplar in which 'intimations of death, or danger, or of the city in the distance' are oddly few, even though the poet's 'letters of that time paint a darker picture of the place and of his mood'.[41] Her remaking of Rilke in 'Gladestry Quatrains' respects but never simplifies the way the rural nuances poetic convention in Wales without overlooking its political-cultural complexities.[42] Yet importing Rilke into Gladestry conversely also takes Gladestry into Valais. Querying Rilke's poetic idealising of what would be his last home, 'Gladestry Quatrains' triangulates rural mid Wales's bilingual border regions with the transcultural complexities of landlocked (and, of course, tri-lingual) Switzerland, fixed in and mediating between the intercontinental cultural-political frameworks of an similarly rural central Europe.

Shapcott's probing of the geopolitical boundaries marking rural mid Wales seems to presume on a re-emergent nation's nascent Europeanism. She is one of a number of poets who discover in the tension-laden topology of post-millennial Wales an outward-facing, culturally spacious 'beyond' at ease with its increasingly networked, transcultural socio-historical moment. Chief among them, current editor of *Poetry Wales* Zoë Skoulding offers a more sustained unpicking of the cultural norms inflecting twenty-first-century Wales. Shifting smoothly from European centres of high culture like Venice, Paris and Budapest to the Asia (India and China) and Persia mediated in her grandfather's letters, Skoulding's opening collection *The Mirror Trade* testifies to the voracious reach of a poetics written from the littoral domain of the poet's home, overlooking the Menai Straits. Perhaps the most significant overlap with Shapcott's oeuvre, however, is the part played by Europe in Skoulding's refusal to construct Wales in culturally straightforward terms; her own practice, as discussed in chapter 6, is deeply inflected by the ideas of Michel de Certeau, Lefebvre and (to a lesser extent) the radical aesthetics of the European situationists. In productive dialogue with such figures, Skoulding's *Remains of a Future City* (2008) echoes Shapcott's semi-playful searching of the valency of the rural as cultural identifier, even if her own wryly historicised European urbs differs sharply from the unpeopled Wales/Switzerland Shapcott negotiates. 'The Old Walls' opens by musing 'The wall is who we are and they are not and / farther in the boundaries collapse . . .' (*Remains*, p. 13), while, in 'The New Bridge', 'the lines of the landscape / run through me to somewhere else' (ibid., p. 14). And yet these poems, like the work of the cultural geographer Edward Soja, resolutely depict the embodied 'distinctively spatial' subject, the self, as 'continuously engaged in the collective activity of producing spaces and places, territories and regions, environments and habitats'.[43]

'A space of splitting': body/language

> the very place of identification, caught in the tension of demand and desire, is a space of splitting [marked by] the production of an image of identity and the transformation of the subject in assuming that image.[44]

For women, the issue of cultural-political identification can be complicated by feminised allegories of nation, territory and language, not least because, as Leigh Gilmore learns from Audre Lorde's *Zami*, 'the imagined geography that links land to body also links parents to child'.[45] For Raymond Williams, the familial linkages of this 'geography' offer political reassurance: '"Nation" as a term is radically connected with "native". We are born into relationships which typically settle [us] in a place.'[46] However, sharpening socio-critical awareness of 'the body as a site of difference in representation' has come to trouble the fixities which console Williams, querying both the construction of his embodied subject and the apparent simplicities of its 'native' sense of place.[47]

As Tiffany Atkinson sees, 'produced and made meaningful only by the discursive frameworks which position them as objects of knowledge [bodies become] both radically unfixed and historically contingent'.[48] As such, Elizabeth Grosz decides, they can only 'extend the frameworks which attempt to contain them'.[49] Accordingly, Atkinson insists, bodies must also be understood 'not just [as] objects of enquiry *out there* [but also as] the very location of the thinker's here and now, a site of ongoing negotiation between subject and object, inside and outside, thought and sensation, personal and political, self and world'.[50] These mobilities explain and justify Grosz's 'looking at the outside of the body from the point of view of the inside, and looking at the inside of the body from the point of view of the outside' to expose the undecideable 'relation of introjections and projections . . . in which neither the body nor its environment can be assumed to form an organically unified eco-system'.[51] Such critical manoeuvres deepen the already complex relationship, at once intimate and distant, between material and referential versions of the human body: as Maggie Humm rightly notes, reading bodies can often be very like reading texts.[52] As both Atkinson herself and Samantha Wynne Rhydderch are keenly aware (see the readings included in my Afterword), the equivalence duly lends texts *about* bodies a particular resonance when they are read back into and across the borders of their own ethnographic hinterlands, and even more so when a text physically 'embodies' its transgression of another kind of cultural-political boundary: the aesthetic terrain of genre and/or poetic form.

Exposing the feminist agenda behind North American women's poetic reclamation of the female body, Alicia Ostriker historicises a theme which remains political in the very different cultural context of today's Wales.[53] Writing – from a rather nearer cultural topos – about her own and other women writers' determination to re-author, on their own political and aesthetic terms, 'the part they were once assigned as objects', the renowned Irish poet Eavan Boland leaves us in no doubt of the extent of the problem they faced: 'In pastorals, lyrics, elegies odes [women] were shepherdesses, mermaids, nymphs. The accoutrements of their persons became images within images; their jewels, silks, skins, eyes became tropes and figures, at once celebrated and silenced.'[54]

If Welsh literature is studded with the same gender-constraining constructions, the gendering of Wales's poetic history came about for different sociocultural reasons. As Jane Aaron has explained, the patriarchal character of the bard's powerful cultural influence, spanning Wales's often inaccessible-seeming territory, had to do with the mobility which the role required. A craft which was taught in the family, and picked up by wives and daughters along the way, was gendered chiefly by the practical difficulties which travelling posed to women whose working lives were focused perforce on the home.[55] However, literary and poetic objectifications of the female body have exasperated the poets I read here as much as any of their Irish, Scottish or even American counterparts. Boland's contemporary, Welsh-language poet Menna Elfyn, recalls her own early career: 'The more I wrote the more I realised that I was crossing a border because the bardic tradition was all male and I only knew of one other woman poet who was admired, Nesta Wyn Jones.'[56] Dissatisfied by what she perceived as the imaginative poverty of her native poetry ('there was so little about human life and living'), Elfyn began to write in ways which made space, figuratively and literally, for the meshing languages of her own physicality.[57] She says now, 'that was my passport to being a writer – to write from myself'.[58] In Ireland, coincidentally, Boland was also reaching into the

> visionary language . . . made by my body . . . When I stood on my front doorstep on a summer night, the buddleia and the lamplight glossing the hedge were not just visible to me. I saw them with my body. And the sight of my body was clear and different and intense.[59]

Writing about the emblematic form, biological function and contingent affects of a bodily reality she frequently summons as cultural-political metonym, Elfyn is among the poets Francesca Rhydderch notices exploiting the female body 'as a site from within which to create a rhetoric "of their own" [while] moving beyond the borders of that body in ways which stress [their creative] singularity'.[60] A powerful exemplar for her Welsh- and English-language female peers, Elfyn's construction of Wales as 'desire' opens the experiential and linguistic interstices – between self and other; parent and child; body and (sometimes national) space; between the word/text and the referent(s) it can never quite shape – among which her work, like that of others, situates itself.

From the outset, Elfyn's poetic imagination seems to have been compelled by the borders enshrined in her own body; its incipiently maternal function shadows her moving scrutiny of a female subjectivity learning the cyclical forces of her biology. For the voice of *Eucalyptus (Detholiad o Gerddi)*, the first collection in which English-language translations appeared beside Elfyn's Welsh-language originals, the menstruating, miscarrying and then gravely maternal body offers a rich new idiom; the searing sequence she published about miscarriage proved among the most significant of the borders she found herself traversing: 'in 1977, . . . nobody had written about that experience before in Welsh'.[61] In an unapologetically feminist recuperation of the sensibilities of the functioning female body, writing as both 'sexual petitioner and practitioner [in] a love poetry suffused with the ecstasy of female eroticism', Elfyn remakes the exclusive literary-historic conventions of poetic tradition, and of Welsh poetic tradition specifically, from within:[62]

> *Yn ysu wir*
> *am ddathlu yn fethlgnawdol,*
>
> *a tharo alaw wefusgar*
> *anadlu a charu a churo*
> *y gêm, sy'n hŷn na* 'human'.
>
> Truly I crave
> to celebrate tangled flesh,
>
> and my lips to sing out its tune,
> and breathe, and make love, and collide
> in the game that is older than 'human'. ('Siesta', *PN*, pp. 32, 33)[63]

As Peter Stallybrass and Allon White point out, the human body 'cannot be thought separately from the social formation, symbolic topography and the constitution of the subject'.[64] The bodily sensuality of Elfyn's voracious poetic imagination is likewise nuanced by the relational – familial and cultural – emphases by which it is grounded and encoded. The six texts of the extraordinary sequence '*Diwinyddiaeth Gwallt*'/'The Theology of Hair' (*PN*, pp. 50–9) explores the extents and limits of this trans-generational, trans-cultural signifier of female power. '*Dim ond Camedd*' / 'Nothing But Curves', its final line providing the title of its parent collection *Cusan Dyn Dall / Blind Man's Kiss* (2001), finds in lingerie a compliant signifier of patriarchy's sly colonising of the female body, its promise to make the wearer 'a homeland all to herself' exposed as a 'brand-new way of getting / the rounded breast into bed' (*PN*, pp. 100–3).[65] Throughout, however, Elfyn's unwaveringly political imaginary frames the maturing self and its creative energies in the securing, nested, geographies of home, homeland and 'horizon' sketched in '*Cysgu ar ei thraed*' / 'Asleep on Her Feet':

> *y llwybrau yn llygad-bell,*
> *gan synfyfyrio ar fy nhraed*
> *a rhoi ar gerdded – freuddwydion.*
>
> my eyes on long horizons,
> meditating on my own feet
> setting my dreams on their way. (*PN*, pp. 232, 233)

Poised, in the politically and aesthetically complex, and controversial, setting of the parallel text – which I shall look at in more detail in a moment – between the two linguistic versions of the Wales which like the performative mechanics of her writing she mediates and bridges, bodily and imaginatively, Elfyn's 'dreams' are typically, like her 'own feet', rooted in her homeland. For some of those who share her interest in the cultural troping of the often-appropriated form and languages of the desiring female body, Wales offers a more problematic context. Neither Pascale Petit nor Sarah Corbett claims to identify very closely with the cultural hinterland which has variously framed their route into publication and public recognition. These poets find poignant common ground in their vigorous subversion of the relational intimacies combining in what we might call the familial body. The younger of the two, Corbett rarely refers explicitly to the north Wales in which she spent the 'troubled' childhood described in the jacket blurb of *Other Beasts*

(2008); it obtains, more subtly, in the mostly rural backdrops against which she has doggedly tested the anatomical limits of a body in pursuit of fresh new ways to escape it. From her acclaimed first collection, *The Red Wardrobe*, Corbett's dismantling of the borders of human subjectivity finds her refusing, as in 'The Electric Dead', to 'distinguish / / between what is felt and what is imagined' (*RW*, p. 55). Taken literally, this refusal illumines a poetry reluctant to leave the empowering space it makes between palpable realities it seems hardly able to think about, and far-fetched possibilities it imagines in self-protective response. In a darkly mobile idiom, the tactile powers of shape-shifting – enshrined as much in the mythic ('Ocyrhoe Becomes a Horse'; 'Athena') as in the natural world of the hunting heron ('Night Flying') or the 'twisted body of a hawthorn' ('Dark Moon') – are sometimes vengefully redirected towards an often spectral mother, as in 'Bitter Fruit' (*RW*, pp. 11, 50, 54, 53, 17). The catastrophe of parental cruelty plays out in two equally unsettling characterisations: the viciously female voices of 'Black Crow Woman', 'Little Bitch' and the eponymous 'The Witch Bag' are not only outwardly vindictive; their venom is turned on themselves. Their tragic counterpart is the perhaps self-destructively disconnected mother of 'My Three Dead Daughters', her professions of maternal love shockingly ironised by the grave inadequacies they signify (*TWB*, pp. 12, 13, 7, 9–11).

Corbett's self-enlarging subjectivity permits her to sidestep Petit's more confessional re-imagining of her own traumatic journey into emotional and creative independence. In the latter's starkly transgressive poetics, bodies, especially parental ones, prove disquietingly unregulatable. In the corrupt transactions of abusive parenting, the child's most fundamental emotional and bodily needs are violated and denied; the proper moral and social distinctions between familial and sexual love are brutally dispensed with. To all intents and purposes, Kathryn Gray rightly assumes that Petit's 'work bears little trace of engagement with a coherent Welsh tradition'; interestingly, however, Gray's analysis seems to me to overlook why a ravenously intercontinental imaginary should strive quite deliberately to lose itself in the eco-cultural 'other' of South America, in the remote so-called 'Lost World' of Venezuela's Amazonian rainforest, and the myths and belief systems of the Pemon tribe which inhabits it.[66] Like the American 'confessional' poet Sharon Olds, whose work is a major influence, Petit treats the body as an endlessly renewable text which 'discovers meaning by making connections with other bodies and other discourses'.[67]

The lush fragile biosphere of the Amazon can provide a means of (re-) understanding by overwriting the emotional impoverishment of Petit's own early life. If this poetics takes more interest in cultural affiliation than Gray perhaps realises, its goal seems primarily to unfix both itself and its author:

> I was born in Paris, grew up in France and Wales. My happiest memories are of living with my grandmother in Mid-Wales (she was half Welsh/Irish and half Asian Indian). My memories of Paris are grim. When I was a teenager I lived with my mother in South Wales and that was awful. I don't have . . . any firm roots, I'm an outsider . . . I look out of Britain for my imagery and landscapes.[68]

Its taste for exotica rooted, she speculates, in the childhood games played 'in a forest-sized hedge in the fields behind my Welsh grandmother's house', Petit's insurgent poetics looks quite deliberately out of that early, elusive context, in order to open up and try on the array of transcontinental othernesses she uncovers in the terrain, flora and fauna, cultural history, mythologies and mores of Amazonia and its metonymic female strength.[69] More intimately, it traverses the clothes, skin and consciousnesses of other not always animate bodies and beings (a warao violin, a were-jaguar, a dugout canoe). In particular, the figures conflated in 'this beast named Motherfather' ('Motherfather', *TZF*, p. 19) and dominating *The Zoo Father* and *The Huntress* are also repeatedly, ruthlessly, reconstituted. *The Zoo Father* imagines the father as 'Lungfish', 'King Vulture', dolphin and whale; in the similarly febrile imagination of *The Huntress* the mother shifts from deity (Xipe Totec and Coatlicue) into rattle snake, mantis, river even 'stalagmite Madonna'.[70]

Circling the doubly insidious, and doubly occluded, outrage of parental abuse, Petit's freewheeling idiom – often graphic enough to risk seeming gratuitous – discards common notions of poetic propriety as freely as it refutes conventional versions of territorial and cultural alterity. Filtering the intimate horrors of her childhood through the exotic lens of Amazonia, Petit's poetry is no more 'confessional' than surreal; it occupies instead an invitingly penetrable space between the soberingly familiar and spectacularly strange. To western readers, the bodily violations described in 'Trophy' ('he closed your eye-holes, plugged / your nose and ears. Then he lit a fire. / He tipped your face upside-down, / turned it inside out and scraped off / the flesh with a machete . . . Your head shrank to the size of a fist. / You were cured, my perfect trophy father', *TZF*, pp. 28–9) and 'My Father's Body' ('I'd boil your skin / and iron it with river flames. / . . . I wouldn't stop until / you'd shrunk enough to be my doll. / I'd hang you from a hook / and stare at my naked Papa - / your miniature penis / that couldn't hurt a mouse', *TZF*, 32–3) seem more shocking for being practised on the body in death. Yet these ritualistic behaviours afford a kind of redemption which is, as far as Petit is concerned, not only private; in her view, 'the self's crises are those of society internalised'; accordingly, 'as long as there is brutality in society [her] personal is universal'.[71]

Recalling Grosz's theoretical manoeuvres, Petit's writing strategically turns ordinary boundaries and power relationships inside out and upside down, re-orchestrating the intersecting coordinates of space and time in a complicated blend of opposing emotions. In 'My Father's Lungs' a telescoped speaker examines her (dying) father's transparent forest-like body with spiky tenderness:

> I'm looking at those luminous trees
> growing in his rib cage,
> to replace his choked lungs.
> I'm piercing his body membrane,
> I'm so small now, it's like the skin of a sky
> I can fly through, into his chest. (*TZF*, p. 14)

Such texts confirm the controlling logic behind their interest in the limitless liminalities of metamorphosis. Reflecting on the origins of *The Zoo Father*, rooted in the weeks spent unexpectedly with her dying father in his cramped Paris flat, Petit confides that poetry offered a way out of a traumatically conflicted situation: 'by bringing the rainforest with its threatened lungs into his flat I was also bringing him and his oxygen machine into the vanishing jungle'.[72] In some ways the urge to defuse these tension-filled circumstances by refiguring them seems predictable, given Petit's rootless childhood: 'everything always shifted: I moved from country to country, from home to home, from carer to carer (or guardian), from school to school. Life was surreal.'[73] Creativity became a refuge: 'From teenage onwards, I knew my life was about creating alternative worlds where I could live luxuriously, like Keats' mansions in the mind.'[74] In those worlds, she could neutralise the threat posed by her psychologically disturbed mother: 'when I bring her into my created world I can change her into images I can control. I can stand up to her and for myself.'[75] Accordingly, this poetry takes self-protective interest in its own construction. An artist before she began writing, who seeks 'to shape [her poems] as one would a sculpture, to make them self-contained and physical', Petit's work offers 'sanctuary, not in its subject matter, but in its art-making': its capacity to transform 'the mess of experience into nest-like shapes of words'.[76]

Like Petit, Deryn Rees-Jones finds the sexually conscious body a rich source of materials, albeit for very different reasons. Rees-Jones retains a keen but edgy sense of connection with her father's native Wales, and the familial ties which caused her to feel 'growing up in Liverpool, that I was Welsh, because of my name'.[77] She tells Gillian Clarke that the phrase books she bought as a child

> in red and white and green with dragons on . . . stood for a part of me I couldn't get to know, but which I wanted all the same. Even my name, which marked me out as Welsh, which I would hear Welsh people pronounce in a way that none of my family or friends did, left me feeling a stranger to myself, but also gave a quality to language – and in some ways a self – that I had lost.[78]

The uncertainties appear more sporadically in Rees-Jones's than in Petit's oeuvre, in a poetics apparently glad to pay them attention. Take the week-long childhood visit to Wales, with the warm, wondering, memories of a bed shared 'with an aunt / and words I couldn't understand – iawn iawn iawn / / bechod iawn', savoured in 'Half-Term', collected in Rees-Jones's debut collection (*The Memory Tray*, p. 14). In 'Oral Tradition' a productively uncertain sense of cultural place is punningly paralleled in a tender contract inflected by bilingualism:

> Twinned from the start, suckled by the same wolf,
> except we were two foreign cities: familiar as our own
> four hands, and yet the more we looked the stranger –
>
> . . .
>
> I'll remember your words that first time, *That's enough*
> Our *paned o de / cupán té* exchange
> (*Signs Around a Dead Body*, p. 55)

The doubling is touchingly resolved, in the poem's closing moments, by its 'placing of ourselves in time, two specks of dust / on the earth's circumference, two compasses encompassing the years' (*Signs*, pp. 55–6). The emblematic confusion of Welsh/English/Irish in the poem summons the cultural-linguistic fulcrum of Rees-Jones's home city; the location in which the strands of her different cultural loyalties converge and mesh: 'I'd like to claim myself as a Liverpool writer – because I think I do represent something about the cross-fertilised, hybridised kind of identity that Liverpool represents.'[79]

Perhaps Rees-Jones's boldest poetic manoeuvre to date, *Quiver* (2004) is set in the city. The unnumbered lyrics of this three-part work, part sequence, part verse-novel, construct an accommodating aesthetic terrain in which to contextualise, tease apart and recuperate 'that simultaneous sense of belonging and estrangement [which] is a part of what it means for me to write'.[80] Lying somewhere between downsized epic, Arthurian quest and contemporary whodunnit, *Quiver* reworks the model of the two poetic murder-mysteries by Rees-Jones's friend Gwyneth Lewis, *Y Llofrudd Iaith* (1999) and the English version 'The Language Murderer' collected in *Keeping Mum* (2003), both of which I discuss in chapter 4. Rees-Jones's thematic is very differently accented, however: her chief subject is creativity, lightly pathologised in protagonist Welsh-Liverpudlian Fay Thomas, a poet with writer's block, and played out against the multiculturalism of Fay's happy seven-year relationship with her Chinese-Irish husband, Will. As the story behind the murder of Mara, Will's previous lover, unfolds, Fay's returning creativity is marked by the italicised lyrics scattered through the text, most significantly in the embedded Artemis/Actaeon legend which informs *Quiver*'s title, in both its part-erotic part-chivalric central trope, and in the hesitancies (quivering) of its mood and mode. By the end, Fay is expecting her first child; the work concludes on 'Afterthought', in which the 'soft osmosis' of a newborn daughter seems both to resolve and make sense of the poem's questing momentum:

> See! I have pressed the soft vowels of your imagination
> and made them part of me. They pull me open, stitch me up,
> your animal grunts and hungry gestures –
> so much a noise that might come from my own mouth,
>
> I can't tell us apart. When I do, daughter, I'll admit, I'm lost,
> my new body wandering the forest,
> dropping trails of bright stones
> till I find you again, a new friend in an old place. (*Quiver*, p. 86)

'Afterthought' returns us to Rees-Jones's central theme: body-as-language, as a generative hermeneutic zone in which emotional, ethical and moral, as well physical and pathological, discourses meet and mix. It is a theme this poet has herself explored – in her professional role as critic and scholar – in the work of her friend and near-contemporary

Gwyneth Lewis. For the determinedly bilingual Lewis, the creative process which *Quiver* searches is bound definitively into the problem of a native 'tongue'. As Rees-Jones puts it, in Lewis's politically vigilant, formally imaginative poetics, it is invariably the case that 'the body . . . works as a touchstone for truth'.[81]

For a poet whose Welshness has never been in doubt, the very utterance in which poetry comes alive necessitates political (because linguistic) choice of language. The difficulties – stretching familial and cultural loyalties – of making such a choice ring through the much discussed 'fetishistic quiz' of the now well-known lyric which sits, keystone-like, at the architectural core of Gwyneth Lewis's eleven-poem sequence 'Welsh Espionage'. In this poem – to which I return briefly in chapter 4 – the Welsh language becomes the reason for, and site of, conflict between a daughter gripped by her father's impromptu lesson and an absent (and, we learn later, disapproving) mother: 'Father and daughter on the bottom stair: / 'Dy benelin yw *elbow*, dy wallt di yw *hair*, / . . . Let's keep it from Mam, as a special surprise' ('v', *Chaotic Angels*, p. 43). For all the discussion it has prompted, commentators have tended to overlook the formal control, characteristic of Lewis's casual-seeming idiom, of the close-rhymed mostly end-stopped couplets (the italicised words even-handedly rendering both languages the alien term), and the facility for archaic conventions it seems always on the point of discarding: the visual and sonic patterning inherent in the Welsh words cheerfully jostling, yet also always working in fruitful tandem with the conventional literary symmetries of classical chiasmus ('Lips are *gwefusau*, *llygaid* are eyes'). In this very readable but complex poem, the body thus becomes an eloquently vulnerable incarnation of cultural-political as well as emotional uncertainty and negotiation, its unconscious gestural language(s) both embedding and troubling the cultural-political minefield of linguistic affiliation.[82]

As if developing on the figure of the child, ingenuous tabula rasa for her father's surreptitious political agenda, 'The Reference Library' (dedicated to the opening of a sixth-form library) urges its youthful addressees to prize and above all capitalise on the transformative potential of their own unknowingness:

> Throw the big tomes out,
> and the almanacs with their logorrhoea.
> Read first the lexicons of your own doubt,
> . . .

> for in your spines and not in those of books,
> lies the way to live well, the best library;
> for the erudition of your open looks
> shall turn old words to new theologies. (*CA*, p. 50)

Lewis herself recently speculated that 'the capacity to endure unease may be at the core of what it is to be a writer'.[83]

In Lewis's virtuosic *A Hospital Odyssey*, the ancient (Welsh as well as classical) poetic tradition of epic disciplines the thematic return to the pathological implications of body-as-language. Another female protagonist, the symbolically named Maris (recalling *mares*, Latin for 'sea'), is jolted by the sudden admission to hospital of her cancer-stricken lover Hardy into a baffling journey through the incompetence, neglectfulness and corruption of a hostilely corporate NHS to come to his aid. As the poem unfolds, and Maris learns more about the inner workings of the hospital liner on which she is trapped, Hardy's diseased body becomes a charged metaphor: for his relationship with the volatile, often unsure Maris, for the blithe spirit of Nye Bevan, and for the literary traditions on which, convention demands, the poem must call. At times the Lewis-like poet/narrator becomes as much victim as potential healer of Hardy's cancer; similarly the text symbolises a clinical world it exposes as paradoxically both death-dealing and restorative. Book 5 begins:

> I've said already that I won't feel well
> till this poem's finished and I find what I mean
> about health and loving . . .
> . . .
> Words are my health,
> the struggle to hear and transcribe the tune
> behind what I'm given by word of mouth,
> it's the only work that can make me immune
> to lying. May my language gene
>
> grant me haemoglobin and many platelets,
> potency deep inside bone marrow.
> My safety lies with other poets
> who've shown the way they took through shadows.
> Milton, Villon, be with me now. (*AHO*, p. 59)

Like Rees-Jones in 'Afterthought', and like Petit and Corbett too, Lewis's study of body-as-language, aestheticised in the textual, visual/

aurally realised form of the poetic construct, is itself reflexively *embodied*. Crucially, for all these poets, the aesthetic-linguistic effort to re-present or re-produce the multiple boundaries which a body's (many) languages may stage can never take such borders for granted. Angela Leighton herself finally concludes that 'form', in all its profusion, is perhaps best glossed in terms of deferral:

> Although it looks like a fixed shape, a permanent configuration or ideal, whether in eternity, in the mind, or on the page, in fact form is mobile, versatile. It remains open to the senses, distortions, to the push-and-pull of opposites or cognates. . . . [F]orm makes mischief and keeps its signification moveable[:] . . . it is, and is not, the object it represents.[84]

Leighton's construction of the 'in-between' nature of form, always in the process of becoming, poised between continuing manoeuvre and finished artefact, helps to explain why, for writers like Lewis and in a very different way Elfyn, poetic form becomes so articulate a means – site, or *embodiment* – of political and ethnographic expression. Lewis's bilingualism explicitly regulates her practice, her publications so far strictly alternating between Welsh and English: 'for me both languages are the same, even though they look quite separate. They're part of a larger language.' Lewis goes on to figure the relationship between her two languages as 'two models of social order if you like, and I favour a kind of benign anarchy in this sense rather than prescriptiveness'.[85]

Elfyn resolves the issue of language choice – one she understands in equally political terms – rather differently: 'The whole way I see life is through my Welsh language . . . I think a language chooses you, and I have to be true to that.'[86] However, like most Welsh speakers in contemporary Wales, in practice Elfyn is of necessity bilingual, which seems partly why her sense of cultural/linguistic place turns out to be surprisingly fragile:

> Although I write in Welsh and speak Welsh at home, and my kids are Welsh-speaking and I live in the 'Welshest' part of Welsh-speaking Wales apparently (Llandysul), . . . I sense myself as an outsider even within my Welsh language community. I was brought up in the Swansea valleys and went to a school where there was no Welsh at all; so I would be speaking English in school, and Welsh at home and in Chapel. . . . Although I knew I was Welsh and was proud of being Welsh, I also wanted to prove to everyone that I could speak English as well as the next person . . . And because I was brought up in the Manse, where we were taught by my dad that there was a Welsh word for every

English word, I wouldn't use Anglicised words in my Welsh; so I would speak a kind of pure Welsh, which put me out of sorts with my friends.[87]

Doris Sommer asks, 'How is one to identify, when one is more than one?'[88] The particular complexities of Elfyn's language use were sharpened by the defect – requiring surgery in childhood – which prevented her from pronouncing the rolled 'r' on which many Welsh words depend. In '*Nam Lleferydd* / Malediction' inarticulacy renders the speaker pitifully impotent, '*rhyw greadur mewn magl yn ei gwendid, / yn nadu, heb im dafod chwaith i rwydo'r byd*'; 'a creature snared in its own weakness, / whimpering without a tongue to net the world' (*PN*, pp. 128–9). The poet recalls: 'I used to hate the fact that, living in a Welsh culture, I couldn't speak the words I wanted to in an eloquent way.'[89]

In functioning as a cultural, even ethnic, signifier, eloquence remains for this poet an instrument both aesthetic and political. The bilingual critic Lisa Lewis makes sense of 'the mixed blessing of [her own] double consciousness' as[90]

treading a continuum of translation. Or perhaps a palimpsest is a better word – as though one language is inscribed on top of the other, endlessly, so that the mind as it translates thinks not of either/or but of unfolding layers . . . The choice is not between two words, but two entire worlds. And I am of both and embody both.[91]

For this bilingual commentator, the internalised 'continuum' she describes replays and is replayed in the implicitly political social processes – 'we need . . . to point beyond ourselves, to locate ourselves in a wider discourse' – which for her etch 'deep longing in the activity of translation, of wanting to be heard'.[92] The explanation illumines the private and public logic of Elfyn's mature and sometimes controversial poetics: in which the culturally subversive intertwining of Welsh and English in Welsh culture is put to powerful use through the translation process.

In conversation, Elfyn views her turn to translation in pragmatic terms: 'I wanted to connect with the English-speaking majority, who through no fault of their own didn't speak Welsh . . .'[93] Elsewhere, she puts the shift down partly to changing thematic concerns: 'the subject matter of my poems in the eighties . . . meant a gradual moving away from identifying myself as solely a Welsh-language writer'; 'saving the world took second place now to . . . wanting my words in English to be every bit as powerful as I hoped they might be in Welsh'.[94] The consequences of this decision are indexed in the criticism directed, mostly by Welsh speakers, at the parallel texts Elfyn began to produce with the help of an illustrious cast of translators: 'I was opening a gate or a door they didn't want opened. Now everybody's translating or writing books in Welsh and English and nobody says anything, but at the time what I was trying to do was seen as a kind of betrayal.'[95] The distrust – opprobrium in some quarters – which the translations excited among her own language community could not dissuade Elfyn from pursuing a transactional poetics which she resolutely refuses to understand in singular terms: 'I've been liberated into writing dense and difficult poems because I have such wonderful translators . . . to know that they are there has strengthened my resolve to be more daring, more forthright.'[96] Her 'resolve' echoes the excitement Sommer ascribes to bilingualism: 'Everyone can experience language as arbitrary and slippery; but bilinguals can hardly avoid the (aestheticizing) risk/thrill of slippery speech.'[97]

The cultural-political and aesthetic significance of what Michael Cronin calls 'the nomadic ethic of translation', the 'dilemmatic' act of linguistic re-engineering and traversal which Homi Bhabha famously characterises as 'resulting from living on borderlines', has not been overlooked in either of Wales's linguistic communities.[98] Grahame Davies has summarised the ways in which the act of translation – literary or otherwise – can be constructed by the Welsh-language community in Wales. As he explains, what some understand as a 'final act of colonial appropriation . . . cherry-picking, asset-stripping, strip-mining' he has himself come to see more positively: 'the bridge of translation has opened up new territory for me to cross over into a different world'.[99]

The cultural-political implications of Elfyn's facing-page texts have been unpicked by Tudur Hallam. The significance of the poems' adjacence to their linguistic-textual Other(s), each text inextricably part of its pair's hermeneutic apparatus and topography, is not lost on this Welsh speaker: 'when the text to be translated and the translating text share the same physical space, to the extent that the cultural border between them merges into a fruitful non-existence', the effect is to corrode the original. The translating text becomes 'a creation which maintains the possibility of being read, of being translated [while] its predecessor, the original, is reduced to . . . the translating text's pretext, its trace, its ghostly past [,] . . . and thus forfeits its expectant referential power'.[100] The complexities of the material environs in which Elfyn's parallel texts share – the self-doubling aesthetic space(s) which they help produce and are themselves produced by – inform Hallam's uneasy recognition of the 'distance [they open] between author and translator [and] between translating and translated texts'. For him, the multiple contingencies of the texts' 'non-identical co-existence, conjoined in their signification' do not so much admit expressive possibility as 'the translated *cerdd*'s misplacement and the translating poem's conquest'. Hallam's self-confessed sense of *hiraeth* for 'the translated poem's . . . uniqueness, its separate source, its locality, its people', seems unsurprising: its translation imperils the survival of his own first language. As Jane Aaron says, 'if all minority language speech acts, or written acts, were immediately translated into a majority language, there would very soon be no minority languages'.[101]

Amid these tensions, for me Elfyn's linguistically permissive, proliferating poetics also remakes the normative hierarchy of author over petitioning translator as symbiotic, 'troubling . . . the entire edifice of conceptual complicities which maintain the power of . . . creation over reproduction, male over female'.[102] Elfyn herself seems to savour the dialogue for the collegiality which her translators ('my first audience, my keepers') offer a habitual solitary.[103] As a child, 'my best friend was me, and trying to write. I always felt that, from a very early age . . . And having come from a very lonely place, my translators I suppose are my poetic community, they're the ones I trust.'[104] However, the collegiality is also to be prized for its impact on the compositional process, when an idea emerges which 'wasn't in the original . . . and even though I think the poem is finished and they have the finished version, that extra draft is sometimes needed. . . . And that's why I also allow them to take risks with the translations'.[105] The dialogic process of this composition-by-negotiation works, in Cronin's words, as 'an unmooring, a setting of the text adrift' which, involving 'the patient, careful transfer of literature from one language to another [can] create [an] enduring infrastructure for aesthetic exchange'.[106] For Elfyn, this exchange both justifies and underwrites her controversial resolve to '[push] poetry in Welsh to a place where it hasn't been before.'.[107] She argues:

> Welsh is diminishing in its quality, in the sense of what I can achieve in writing poetry in Welsh. And enriching the language is becoming more problematic as it declines in another sense. Being translated has given me a new freedom, to be able to push the limits of the language; to write the way I want to write . . .[108]

Interestingly, of course, the enriching effects partly depend on the way in which translation exposes even as it confounds the epistemological presumptions which harden the relationship between author, text, word and referent. Referential instabilities, for Elfyn, can only freshen her idiom: 'It's that sense of still being radical and still pushing boundaries and still being restless . . . it's another way of thinking and it makes you more agile.'[109] Elfyn's parallel texts make available to her English-language audience a sometimes breathtaking degree of formal and intellectual agility. Her linguistic self-consciousness takes an Elizabethan-seeming pleasure in its own wit: '*Cusan Hances* / Handkerchief Kiss', for example, retorts to R. S. Thomas's disdaining of poetic translation (as 'kissing through a handkerchief') by delicately eroticising it:

Minnau, sy'n ymaflyd cerdd ar ddalen
gan ddwyn i gôl gariadon-geiriau.

A mynnaf hyn. A fo gerdd bid hances
ac ar fy ngwefus

sws dan len.

As for me, I hug those poems between pages
that bring back the word-lovers.

Let the poem carry a handkerchief
and leave on my lip

its veiled kiss. (*PN*, pp. 176–7)

Part promise, part denial, this 'veiled' conclusion reveals Elfyn at her irrepressibly subversive best. As M. Wynn Thomas observes, 'invading and appropriating a male genre, she makes inventive play with several of its key conventions, including that of the *llatai*, or love messenger'.[110] In its remaking of the patriarchal conventions and formalities of her native poetry, this light-footed but intensely serious poem speaks to the embedded chauvinisms of her sociocultural context(s): 'promiscuity in language is not a bad thing when you consider it's the only spiritual freedom we have left'.[111] Her words reiterate how deeply the 'desire' Elfyn associates with Wales meshes with language use.

Desire suffuses the self-conscious verbal play of '*Geiriau Lluosog am Gariad* / Ten Words for Love and Longing' (*PN*, pp. 278–81), and not only in the glossings of which its title warns. Resting performatively on the inter- and intra-lingual translations which are its theme and substance (each fugal reworking of each new linguistic term recuperating the metaphor-rich traditions of Welsh-language poetry), the poem's own approach is twice ironised in its English-language version. First, this text never translates its italicised Welsh lexicon: guessing at the root-signifier of each new explanation, the faltering non-Welsh speaker is deftly co-opted into the poem's aesthetic. This flexing attitude to its own semantic reach is affirmed in an endnote: 'The original poem in Welsh is 30 words for love but in the act of translating this has been changed to 10' (*PN*, p. 296). In the losses it yokes to a love which is not only sexual, a self-dismantling text thus becomes a kind of love poem to the linguistic-cultural horizons it frames, semantically, textually, aesthetically and politically, twice over:

Gan adael,
Angerdd ac adnabod,
Yn adladd mewn hen ydlan,
Tywysen noethlwm fel hiraeth,
Alaeth a phrofedigaeth,

Cariad: curiad, ac agoriad.

Leaving
angerdd and *adnabod,*
the aftermath in an old granary
a bare stalk winnowed by a long grief
of *hiraeth* and mourning,

Love: the knock on the heart's door, the door's opening. (*PN*, pp. 280–1)

This text stages – in its trans-lingual, trans-paginary facing-texts – the mobile desiring processes, linguistic and poetic, in and out of which it came into being, and which must, Derrida-like, always be deferred. Bhabha's reflection on the dilemmatic effects of translation seems apposite: 'The desire for the Other is doubled by the desire in language, which *splits the difference* between Self and Other so that both positions are partial; neither is sufficient unto itself.'[112]

'Ten Words' reiterates that for Elfyn articulacy should never preclude openness. As M. Wynn Thomas notes:

> For her, the concept [of openness] is cognate with ideas of (ad)venturing, of risk of vulnerability, of exposure, of psychic excursion, of acknowledging

> otherness – all of which relate in their turn to the way she apprehends her Welshness, her religious faith, and her womanliness . . . Most obviously, she is fascinated by boundaries, limits, liminal situations, neighbourliness.[113]

Thomas is right. Elfyn is determined to expand the border-crossing part she can play, as Welsh-language user and female poet, in the complex cultural-political imaginary of her dual-language home. Her self-doubling facing-text poems, poised between the cultural and aesthetic interstices of their co-production, reiterate the political and creative desires which intersect in her sense of Wales itself: 'I like the idea of poems being questions.'[114] Her own work seems to confirm Ian Gregson's claim, made in reference to dialogic poetry, 'that the lived experience of the self can only be expressed through determined efforts to evoke the otherness with which the self continuously interacts'.[115] Hallam is disarming about Elfyn's textual 'border-crossing': 'I would rather have both the *bardd* and the poet for myself.'[116] Yet Elfyn confides: 'I find the word "poet" easier on the tongue than the equivalent Welsh "bard"; it's somehow easier to live up to.' She cites Afrikaans writer Antje Krog: 'I carry a past with me. I do not want to become English . . . In English I wanted to stay the Other.'[117] She also summons John Berger, urging writers towards 'the horizon where . . . nothing is ever very distinct and all questions are open'.[118] Both sources confirm the disposition of the various kinds of poetry I have been exploring here: which undoes, by interrogating, eroding and/or transcending the geological, socio-historical and textual/linguistic markers and boundaries which might circumscribe it. In refusing those confines, such texts collectively imagine a reorienting Wales, its altering sense of geopolitical selfhood anchored in its newly transcultural purview.

2

'Not without strangeness': Ruth Bidgood's Unhomely Mid Wales

The uncanny . . . shows itself to be a strange land of borders and othernesses ceaselessly constructed and deconstructed.[1]

> Certainly this is an excellent beauty,
> not without strangeness. After the stumbling
> down rarely-trodden rides, the last yards
> forced through prickly spruce, these dark walls
> suddenly rearing in the close dim glade
> startle and delight. This is no longer
> a house, though it keeps some of that shape.
> Fern, fronding lintel, frilling wall,
> has joined with stone in symbiosis.
> This is a thing both made and grown.
> If it outlasts the forest, it will lose
> that weird fertility, shadowy dignity.
> But for a while yet it yearns upward
> from its hidden ground, a votive candle of dark.[2]

The enigmatic 'Strangeness' takes its starting point from the epigraph that Bidgood borrows from Francis Bacon: 'There is no excellent beauty that hath no strangeness in the proportion.' Partly as a result of this frame, an already sonnet-like poem begins to seem more than accidentally Elizabethan in its pursuit, through remote 'ride' and 'dim glade', of a prey which arguably seems, again in line with lyric convention, only the more desirable for its elusiveness. And yet in one very obvious way the text itself seems only distantly related to the literary model it discreetly invokes: the 'turn' having shifted to the end-stopped seventh line, 'Strangeness' falls naturally into two evenly balanced (seven-line) parts, the second obliquely recalling the formal intricacies of the conventional sestet in its fragmenting of the seven lines into couplets and a singleton. Just as the poem thus unostentatiously reworks the traditional form it summons, so the ruinous building, in dereliction 'a thing both made and grown', is an odd theme for a courtly love song. In formal terms, utterance and uttered seem as strange as each other; the poem no more constitutes a sonnet than the 'fronding lintel' and 'frilling wall' now represent a house, even if both constructs, emerging as somehow metonymic of each other as well as of their generic antecedents, 'kee[p] some of that shape'.

The structures of 'Strangeness' are at once familiar and unfamiliar: neither poem nor building is what it seems, the compromised fabric and aesthetic identity of each figured in what remains of the house. A further layer of suggestiveness inheres in the 'weird fertility' which the poetic construct, in its own strangenesses, works to honour and preserve. Indeed, in its deft and delicate excavation of what is normally 'hidden ground' the poem discreetly echoes Freud's essay 'Das Unheimliche', which explores and plays on Schelling's sense that 'everything is *unheimlich* that ought to have remained . . . secret and hidden but has come to light'.[3] In this, 'Strangeness' reflects perhaps the principal preoccupation of Ruth Bidgood's lengthy poetic career; as one of her most percipient critics, Jeremy Hooker, has said, 'again and again, in her poems, she brings life out of the dead'.[4]

As Nicholas Royle's seminal *The Uncanny* notes, it was the Russian formalist Victor Schlovsky who first identified, in poetry in particular, the creative potency of 'making strange' or defamiliarisation: 'The technique of art is to make objects "*unfamiliar*" . . . Art removes objects from the automatism of perception.'[5] In Freud's wake, Royle spells out how the generative intersection of the strange and familiar which Schlovsky spotted underpins the condition of the uncanny: 'It can take the form of something familiar unexpectedly arising in a strange and unfamiliar context, or of something strange and unfamiliar unexpectedly arising in a familiar context.'[6] Various theorists have used this mobile theory to examine the unstable cultural-political significations of the idea of 'home', and particularly in connection with the idea of nationhood. Of particular relevance for me in this chapter is Donna Heiland, for whom the postcolonial nation, Gothically, embeds 'an uncanny doubling that . . . makes clear the uncertain ground on which terms like 'nation', mother country and 'colony' really stand'. Heiland returns us to Bhabha, whose cultural and psychological reading of home 'as a place that can be both familiar and utterly strange' she finds illuminating those doubling 'situations that ask people to "negotiate the powers of cultural difference"'.[7]

Amid the many manifestations of a problematically slippery signifier, as Rosemary Marangoly George notices, the idea of 'home' is founded on 'a pattern of select inclusions and exclusions. Home is a way of establishing differences.'[8] This is what makes the 'dream' of home 'dangerous, particularly in post-colonial settings, because it . . . exacerbates the inability of constituted subjects – or nations – to accept their own internal differences and divisions'.[9] These dangers explain why Bhabha recommends troubling the culture- and time-bound notion of home from the vantage point 'of "the beyond": [which] captures something of the estranging sense of the relocation of the home and the world – the unhomeliness – that is the condition of the extra-territorial and cross-cultural initiations'.[10]

It is perhaps naively, then, that Kenneth R. Smith assumes that 'the cultural deposits of the Welsh have been layered in places, named and known . . . in house and field, which testify to the fate of the nation'.[11] The subject of this chapter, herself a distinguished local historian who has written extensively in poetry and prose about all kinds of Welsh places, including houses and even fields, both named and not, might well have bridled at Smith's confidently reductive locating of Wales's national heritage in the 'named and known'. Having authored (in addition to some ten collections of poetry) two books and numerous essays and pamphlets about the environs of her home near Llanwrtyd Wells in north Breconshire, Bidgood has said: 'I've never written a word or a line that didn't express the value I set on Wales as my country'.[12] Nevertheless, she warns, 'Bound up with my feeling for the place is a preoccupation with the strangeness of time, and a baffled but not unrewarding sense of the mystery surrounding and penetrating our lives'.[13] In this way, the suggestively uncertain, often ruinous even occluded mid-Walian topoi explored – constructed – by her quietly intelligent poetics might be said to mark, Bhabhaesquely, 'neither a new horizon, nor a leaving behind of the past'; but perhaps especially 'a sense of disorientation, a disturbance of direction, in the beyond'.[14]

For Heiland, Bhabha's gender-sensitive emphasis on the disturbing liminalities of cultural identity affirms that 'the unhomely life develops from the same pattern of doubling that is at the heart of uncanny experience, and from the same root interest in "home" as a place that can be both familiar and utterly strange'.[15] The idea of alterity certainly resonates with the work of a poet always drawn to the uncanny-seeming spaces and features of the area of mid Wales in which she has lived since the 1970s. Bidgood has until recently avoided explicitly presuming on her own sense of place in her rural home. However in 'Meeting the Bus', from *Time Being* (winner of 2011 Wales Book of the Year

Award), a suggestively Bidgood-like speaker contemplates 'the tug of those small joining / filaments I've grown, / that tell me I'm no stranger, but placed and known' (*Time Being*, p. 17). As Hooker has said of Glyn Jones, even as this poet 'defamiliarises' her much loved and deeply known locality 'by [her] way of seeing [she also] sees and feels as a native who honours [her] people, the people of the place'.[16] However, in a highly sophisticated and still under-critiqued poetics, as Anthony Vidler promises, the presence of the uncanny is what comes to link Bidgood's tireless 'speculation on the peculiarly unstable nature of "house and home" [with] questions of social and individual estrangement, alienation, exile and homelessness'.[17]

This chapter argues that the kinds of strangeness Bidgood uncovers in the topographical features, historic sites, lost or ruined buildings and scattered communities of rural mid Wales charge her sense of the generative unhomeliness of her own cultural and aesthetic situation. Her poems give, in oblique half-gestures, onto other vague and vestigial worlds, only ever partly mapped on a shifting geography of the never quite there, in the limpid and reflective style that 'Viewpoint' adopts:

> An hour ago, across the valley,
> we'd been on a known slope,
> where a pile of stones could rebuild itself
> into a house we remembered
> from forty years ago; where bridleways
> were mapped and understood;
> where lines of runaway trees,
> once hedgerows, delineated
> fields we could trace and name;
> where the man at my side
> had run as a child, and today
> seemed ghosted by that small shadow.
> . . .
>
> Now in afternoon sun
> we drank, delighted, the blend
> of known and unknown, of our own
> commingled years, of stories told
> and stories waiting to be found. (*Time Being*, pp. 9–10)

In the gentle pressure which an understated idiom exerts on such un/familiar sites, Bidgood's work seems to me in its unostentatious way both to express and produce the layered cultural geography of her environs. This now elderly writer's voracious creative imagination shapes poems which might themselves be read, in form as well as theme, as reflexive textual geographies, individually and collectively mapping and framing, yet never managing to confine, the im/permanent interpenetration of manmade and natural in the secretive places and elusive ideas they try but always somehow fail to represent.

'Little to say of home'

Where the Scottish poet and critic Robert Crawford has asked 'Where is home?', Bidgood seems more inclined to begin by asking '*What* is home?' We might normally expect to find home/liness made most immediately and reassuringly available in the domestic sphere, yet Bidgood's houses rarely seem very homely. 'Journeys' relives a childhood train trip 'through landscapes of anticipation' to 'a grey house / at the edge of trees'. This tantalising sketch is never filled out: circled and retreated from with all the speed of the approach, the house remains a baffling space in the text's central lines:

> This was the destination
> I at once wanted, hung out
> Into ear-aching wind to hanker after,
> Was hurried away from,
> Forgot for years. (*NSP*, p. 100)

Shifting between past and present in the form of a speaker ('a child in that loved house') both identified with and differing from the other two children in the text, the doublings of this dreamlike text renders the 'destination' itself uncannily familiar and ('hurried away from') estranged and estranging.

Less shy of house and home than 'Journeys' implies, the domestic interiors about which Bidgood writes are all too often unnerving. Discovered in an appositely 'central room . . . / over the great hearth' of a part-restored 'cruck house', 'Green Man at the Bwlch' casts a different light on Bidgood's insistently unhomely houses. Under scrutiny this ancient totem turns into an oddly alluring double, its 'mouth-borne branches' transformed into 'an abyss, like Nietzsche's, / into which if I look long / I find it looking into me' (*RBSP*, p. 42). The (self-)troubling moment echoes Kristeva:

> strange is the experience of the abyss separating me from the other who shocks me . . . Confronting the foreigner whom I reject and with whom at the same

> time I identify, I lose my boundaries, I no longer have a container . . . I lose my composure . . . The uncanny strangeness allows for many variations: they all repeat the difficulty I have in situating myself with respect to the other.[18]

The 'kingdom of possibilities' over which this implacable mask presides argues Bidgood's fascinated appreciation of the uncanny interplay between self and other, while obliquely affirming the role played by history in the complex relations linking place with identity.

As Melanie van der Hoorn has remarked, even after destruction, 'the social life of a piece of architecture . . . can continue to live in fragmented form and act as an intermediary onto which people can project their memories . . . or experiences [of the place it used to occupy]'.[19] The local history reflected everywhere in Bidgood's poetry is often mediated by manmade structures, ranging from ancient monuments, rural churches, abbeys and castles, to the abandoned quarries and mine buildings in 'Carreg-y-Frân' (*The Given Time*, p. 23), 'Heol y Mwyn (Mine Road)' (*RBSP*, p. 106) and 'Slate Quarry, Penceulan' (*RBSP*, p. 137). However, the architectural ruin, usually isolated, empty, rundown or ruinous domestic houses – invariably mediating all the onward 'social' (and signifying) life which van der Hoon anticipates – predominates. Sometimes these are or were notable buildings in their own right: Bidgood, like any local historian, knows that the manorial estates of the landed gentry and (sometimes) the grander residences of the aristocracy leave fuller records than less prosperous establishments. However: 'I've never been drawn to writing about the stately home and its family. What attracts me is the human dimension of life as lived by ordinary people.'[20] Accordingly, the still-preserved, manifestly humble remains of an abandoned 'Shepherd's Cottage' give pause: 'I lean on the sill, seeing what they saw / Who lived here, hearing what they heard' (*NSP*, p. 18). In Smith's rather reductive view, 'The tendency in Wales is to conserve the past as a means of maintaining a Welsh consciousness'.[21] Bidgood seems to agree: 'By writing local history I hoped to be a remembrancer . . . to celebrate in my own way the life of my "especial scene".'[22] She uses an old-fashioned term ('remembrancer') for a role she understands as custodial, even curatorial: 'somebody who was conscious of the fact that they were trying to save the past in the present'.[23] The work of the historian invariably overlaps with the poet's, even if 'the treatment is so utterly different'; yet the two spheres of activity, so different in discipline (the historian's reliance on fact conflicting with the 'latitude' allowed by the poetic) can complement each other, if only in their habits of thought: 'I tend to be drawn to people and houses that very little is known about and where source material is hard to get.'[24] Elsewhere she qualifies this:

> my work on local history builds up a picture, the story of the place, and I feel that to be important . . . It's in the human pattern-making that the poetry and the history come together – they're both ways of spotting the patterns that are there and setting them out so that they can mean something to somebody else as well.[25]

The implication that pattern-making generates certainty is disingenuous in the context of 'Question', for example, a richly inconclusive study of 'Bronfelen, tawny hill', on which there *may* once have been the site of a house. If such a building ever existed, nothing – not even anecdotal memory – of the original structure remains beyond the twice-repeated question ('"Was there a house here?"') which haunts poem and hill alike. It seems to be the question itself, keeping the possibility of the house's presence uncertainly alive, which finally renders the hill 'A boundary place / between known and known; a place of blurred identity; / an acreage that's lost / the filaments tying it once / to something recognisable' (*NSP*, p. 243).

'Question' is not unusual in constructing Bidgood's 'especial scene' as equivocally unhomely. As 'The Given Time', title poem of her very first collection (1972), demonstrates, uncertainty proliferates when the structural 'filaments' which Bronfelen lacks survive in some form. In appropriately halting phrasing, the speaker struggles to make out a ruin which is 'Hardly a shape even – a darkness, / irregularity, among the ordered trees – '. The vagueness both invites and denies the kind of identifying relation the speaker seems, similarly, both to hope for and dread: 'Silent, it poses questions, / Troubles me with half-answers, glimpses, echoes' (*NSP*, p. 13). As in 'Question', the tensions generated by this mysterious place lock speaker, text and reader into an inviting but also baffling hermeneutic complex; as Christopher Woodward puts it, with sombre grace, 'When we contemplate ruins we contemplate our own future'.[26]

Thematically and textually, poems like 'The Given Time' and 'Question' affirm the inherent uncanniness of ruination. In one of few critical studies of ruin poetry, Anne Janovitz argues that architectural decay attracts poets for its metonymic (and Bhabha-like) collapsing of history into topos, time into space: 'insofar as the ruin gives evidence of ineluctable genesis and decay, it challenges the structure of the present, and threatens to eradicate temporal difference, swallowing up the present into an unforeseeable yet inevitable repetition of the past'.[27] For

Bidgood, likewise, 'The Given Time' proves that 'I don't attempt to escape into the past, despite my interest in it, or believe it is possible to do so'.[28] In fact, 'It's time rather than simply the past which is a preoccupation. As far back as I can remember, I've felt our picture of time as . . . a line disappearing into distance, is misleading.'[29] Implicitly, the words defend and justify 'remembrancing' as a cultural project. The speaker meditating on the decaying 'Shepherd's Cottage' is firmly positioned outside the building, bearing witness through its glassless windows to a construction which is and is not historic: 'And memory plays tricks, reminding me / Of things I cannot have known – ' (*NSP*, p. 18). This comment summons David Punter, teasing out the definitive strain of uncanniness which Coleridge's 'Rime of the Ancient Mariner' locates in

> that peculiar kind of repetition in which origin cannot be found [; that] lends itself to odd moments of recognition, odd moments of not merely feeling that we have been here before, but that we genuinely recognise something even though we may have no ascertainable means of doing so.[30]

The poem also echoes Thomas McFarland for whom 'The phenomenology of the fragment is the phenomenology of human awareness . . . incompleteness, fragmentation, and ruin – the diasparactive triad – are at the very centre of life'.[31] Indeed, McFarland, Punter, Janovitz and Woodward all endorse Bidgood's conviction that ruins, like 'filaments' inherently partial despite their connective role, both stimulate and embody imaginative energy. Poems like 'The Given Time' and 'Shepherd's Cottage' only confirm the creative and cultural potential of what McFarland dubs the 'diasparactive' agency of ruination.

Bidgood's construction of ruins as texts to be read (into) implicitly supports Janovitz's account of the ruin as a cultural signifier in which topos and history mesh and merge: 'The ruined structure suggests the close connection between land and history, and marks how deeply the natural world is imbued with cultural values. But insofar as the [building] is in decay, it also suggests an opposing movement, the "naturalizing" of culture by time.'[32] In Janovitz's model the (Romantic) ruin poem, typically about decaying public edifices like churches and castles, helped entrench a particular sense of 'British' nationhood at a particular time. Dealing with more contemporary writers, Guy Rotella pertinently finds them helping us 'to consider how the human impulse to build to last . . . might co-exist with relativism, multiculturalism, and diversity'.[33] In similarly broad-minded spirit, the unhomeliness of Bidgood's often ruined (and, in their own understated ways, monumentalising) and mostly domestic buildings figure a liminal space more reminiscent of Bhabha's generatively undecidable 'beyond', in their subtle inscription and occupation of

> a revisionary time, a return to the present to redescribe our cultural contemporaneity; to reinscribe our human, historic commonality; *to touch the future on its hither side*. In that sense, then, the intervening space 'beyond' becomes a space of intervention in the here and now.[34]

Above all in Bidgood's poems, the beyond – like the ruins that offer it one kind of signification or form – can paradoxically aid the individual's effort to locate him/herself in a resistant or uncertain sociocultural milieu. In 'Neighbour' a nearby 'trace of walls – Caeglas' proves explicitly unhomely in and of itself:

> Dark day, dark trees conferred
> a chilly mystery, estranging stone,
> creating sombre shapes with little to say of home.

The unease permeates the speaker's private domestic world 'At night, downstream'. Amid the interpenetration of inner and outer, past and present, the poem stages the eerie communion between its speaker and the vanished neighbours represented in and by 'Caeglas' in a snatch of refrain:

> Even in this I was included,
> as the same wind thrummed on my roof,
> cried on my hearth, as on my dark
> neighbour's; even in this. (*NSP*, p. 218)

As Kristeva observes, 'By recognizing our uncanny strangeness we shall neither suffer from it nor enjoy it from the outside. The foreigner is within me, hence we are all foreigners. If I am a foreigner, there are no foreigners.'[35]

'The calling of kindred': home as community

> It may be that the uncanny is a feeling that happens only to oneself, within oneself, but it is never one's 'own': its meaning or significance may have to do, most of all, with what is not oneself, with others, with the world itself. It may thus be construed as a foreign body within oneself, even the experience of oneself as a foreign body.[36]

The title poem of *Kindred* (1986), Bidgood's fifth collection, opens – disorientingly – *in medias res*, its apparently hiking speaker self-confessedly 'still a mile or two / from the source'. This air of guarded detachment deepens in the closing stanza, as

> Round the next curve of the stream
> low broken walls delineate a life
> almost beyond my imagining.
> Something calls, with a voice
> seeming at first as alien
> as the stream's, yet inescapable,
> and after a while more like
> the calling of kindred,
> or my own voice echoing
> from a far-off encompassing wall. (*NSP*, p. 105)

Poem and speaker alike seem to pause to bear witness to both 'the broken walls' and the vanished 'life' that they commemorate (significantly '*almost* beyond' the possibility of imagination). After the speech-like sound of the stream, the 'call' which conflates otherness ('alien') and ubiquity ('inescapable') is disturbing. As near and far, familiar and unfamiliar, real and imagined coalesce, the poem's eponymous signifier grows increasingly resonant.

Defined by the *OED* as 'being of kin, relationship by blood or descent'; 'family, clan, tribe'; and 'allied in nature, character or properties', the word 'kindred' elides familial and communal in a collective identity (interestingly, one that can extend to embrace an entire nation's people) bespeaking if nothing else rootedness. In the context of Wales, the term's comforting associations are formalised with interestingly ambivalent effects. As Gwyn Alf Williams explains, the Welsh for 'kindred' (*cenedl*) enshrines a powerful self-regulating mechanism of sociocultural connection and (judicial) constraint dating from the eleventh century:

> The central institution was the *cenedl*, a structured, measurable kindred group. It was decided by male descent. A woman had her own kin, which she did not lose on marriage, and there were complex regulations relating to a mother's kin. But a woman existed in the *braint* [status] of her husband. The law invented a kindred focused on the individual which moved outwards in concentric circles from that individual. The law, in effect, was a community law, enforced through kindreds.[37]

Partly thanks to this history, as Alwyn Rees has shown, in rural Welsh communities the idea of kindred, as played out in kinship networks, remained an important means of social (if diminishingly patriarchal) coherence well into the twentieth century: 'The community has many of the attributes of a large family . . . Every person counts as part of the social organism.' He finds these links both intensified and more diffused among the dispersed settlements of upland areas:

> isolated farms are not outlying members of a nucleated community, but entities in themselves, and their integration into social groups depends on the direct relationships between them rather than upon their convergence on a single centre. The traditional social unit does not consist of the environs of a town or village; it is *cefn gwlad*, the neighbourhood in the countryside.

And, after the manner of centuries, 'the doors of the homes remain wide open to welcome those who have come from afar'.[38]

These ancient social frameworks seem to shadow the ambiguous 'far-off encompassing wall' of 'Kindred'. Insofar as it 'encompasses', the wall gestures at a social context which, being uncertainly 'far-off' seems to admit as much as it restricts, and signals 'the value, the uniqueness, of each community, each *bro*'.[39] But to encompass is also to encircle, close in and off, as the speaker is by the reverberating 'call'. Thus the speaker's generative sense of cultural dis/connection is retraced to the contours of a landscape which both offers and denies connection, which seems to embrace and license, refuse and exclude at the same time. In this way 'Kindred' obliquely inscribes Bidgood's own productively ambivalent sense of cultural place. Born in 1922 'in the mining village of Seven Sisters in Glamorganshire', to a 'Welsh-speaking Welshman from Crynant' and a West Country schoolteacher who refused to let her daughter learn Welsh, the poet's deeply rooted 'love of Wales and . . . conviction of Welshness' was imbibed from her 'gentle and kindly' father, but it took many years to resolve the much resented cultural uncertainty which her monoglot upbringing bequeathed:

> I don't remember a time when I didn't want to identify fully with Wales. I didn't want to be half English at all. Now, though, I accept that I'm a mixed-[nationality] person, and I feel there's a positive side to that. When I was young I wanted things to be more clear-cut, and it caused me trouble – sorrow even – to be a mixture.[40]

Bidgood left Wales for Oxford before the Second World War, which she spent coding in Egypt. Afterwards she returned to London to work, where she met and married her physicist husband. The couple lived in Surrey, where Bidgood spent the next twenty years or so at home raising her three children, and feeling out of place:

> Despite sporadic attempts to identify with the English side of myself . . . I never felt part of the life of the place which for many years was our family home. Increasingly I wanted to come back, not to my native Glamorganshire, but to mid-Wales.

Eventually, in 1964, Bidgood and her husband bought the holiday cottage in the tiny parish of Abergwesyn, north Breconshire, in which her self reinvention began: 'It was in 1965, I think, that I started to write both poems and local history articles, which later led on to more serious research.'[41] Divorce ensured her return to Abergwesyn for good, in 1974.

In retrospect, it seems appropriate this writer should have made her final home in arguably Wales's most indeterminate and estranged (estranging) region. Despite efforts to redefine it, the territory known as mid Wales has traditionally stretched the length of what is now Powys, from Rhayader in the north to the southernmost borders of old Radnorshire.[42] Bidgood first visited Radnorshire as a schoolgirl; years later she said: 'Mid-Wales had even then seemed familiar, my proper place.'[43] Today she is emphatic that, despite her south-Walian roots, 'the bond with Mid-Wales is very strong . . . although I've never deluded myself that it's the same as that of the old families of the area'.[44] Her own cultural origins notwithstanding, the region of mid Wales has from the first been deeply identified with this poet's idiom, even muse:

> I think it would be fair to call me a poet of place, in that many of my poems . . . were occasioned by the houses, villages, lakes and hills of mid-Wales, especially those of my own area of north Breconshire (now in Powys).[45]

She savours Abergwesyn's isolation, partly because so few authors choose to 'write about a really remote countryside. That has its voice. That too has to be heard.'[46] This literary-cultural purpose is interestingly nuanced by the sense of cultural dis/connection which echoes in 'Kindred': 'I've always felt that however inadequate I might be as a voice for mid-Wales, it was up to me to speak, all the more because I was an incomer. I had to give, not just take.' Later she confides:

> I have never wanted to escape from the world by coming here, and if I had I'd have been disappointed. Sometimes people talk of 'the world outside' this remote village. To me this is meaningless. This *is* the world . . . it can happen that only part of all one feels to be important has the special power to spark off poems. For me that part of experience has been this 'hole in the heart of Wales'.[47]

On another occasion, she warns that 'though I don't always write about the area I live in I do always write out of it'.[48] In this, Jarvis honours a poet he wryly dubs 'outsider-native' as *Bardd gwlad*, for an oeuvre always concerned with, and ultimately written on behalf of, 'a community in its place'.[49]

From the outset Abergwesyn charged and helped refine Bidgood's interested respect and affection for her environs: 'the local history really started from walking off the road and up side-valleys and finding that they had lots of ruined houses which started me wondering about the life that had happened and was lived there'.[50] In some ways, Smith is right to highlight the pervasive dereliction of Bidgood's 'especial scene': 'The dilapidated houses and gardens which Bidgood finds in the Welsh hills are reflections of the crumbling society and culture.'[51] Again, however, his portrait is reductive: Bidgood's own foreword to her study of Abergwesyn, *Parishes of the Buzzard* (2000), pronounces the village 'still alive, though its churches, schools and inns are gone, its every valley holds ruined houses and disused fields, and many of its farms and sheepwalks have been lost to forest and reservoir'. It goes on:

> Abergwesyn has seen many changes this century: the shift of balance in population and language towards English-speaking incomers who, mainly, have arrested depopulation, the planting of the forests, the drowning of a large part of the upper Tywi valley . . . the coming of tourism on a larger scale than ever before. Its people have known the divided mind which made them welcome the work brought by the Forestry Commission . . . yet weep for the vanishing of old farms 'planted to the door': the split heart that welcomes all newcomers of good will yet feels the pain of the loss of the old days, the Welsh way of life, the hard work . . . and the vigorous enjoyments that went some way to sweeten labour. Under the surface of new life old tides run. Those native to the place share knowledge, attitudes, responses not easily come at by the most welcome of incomers. In many ways this is still a secret land, that remembers more than it tells.[52]

Something of this ambivalence is suggested in an interview: 'as soon as I came back to Wales, immediately there was the call of the land and the ruins – drawing me up side-valleys into the *remains* of communities'.[53] Imbuing 'the land' itself with the 'call' of the vestigial and incomplete, her comments reiterate her sense of locality as lacuna, partly in rendering the area's physical and social topography as invitingly fractured. In a piece of semantic cunning, the noun-verb 'remains' signifies the extent to which the small scattered communities of upland mid Wales both mark and continue to survive the erosive pressure of sociocultural and economic change. Bidgood's consciousness of the imbrication of absence and presence marks her gentle interrogation of the complex cultural history of her remote locality. The elegaic 'All Souls' depicts 'a conversation of lights' between the farms studding the valley sides, with implied relief that 'higher in darkness answer still, though each now speaks / for others that lie dumb'. The 'latecomer' speaker is also (again like Bidgood) plainly embedded in this shadowed community, capable of mapping each set of lights onto an intercourse where presence and absence overwrite each other, name by vulnerable name:

> Light at Tŷmawr above me, muted by trees,
> is all the voice Brongwesyn has,
> that once called clearly enough
> into the upper valley's night.
> From the hill Clyn ahead
> Glangwesyn's lively shout of light
> celebrates old Nant Henfron, will not let
> Cenfaes and Blaennant be voiceless.
> I am a latecomer, but offer
> speech to the nameless, those
> who are hardly a memory, those
> whose words were always faint . . . (*NSP*, p. 71)

Bidgood seems to confirm the figurative nature of a poem like this when she confides: 'Since I came to live here, the age-old symbols of light and dark have had new force for me. It comes from walking in a night with no street lamps, and seeing the few lights against the huge dark.'[54] That symbolism functions with particular suggestiveness in the six-part long poem 'Valley-before-Night' (*NSP*, pp. 149–58), about the Upper Camarch valley, one of Bidgood's favourite local haunts. Running parallel with the valley containing the main road to Abergwesyn village and reliant for some decades on a Forestry Commission track, the valley is remote even for this parish. Known locally, a prefatory note reports, as *Cwm-cyn-Nos* (literally 'the-before-night-valley') the valley once comprised 'a community of some sixteen farms' but, 'Most of the houses are ruined or demolished. When this poem was written Llednant was still farmed and Coedtrefan was occupied – Robin, Hazel, Tomos and Gwyn [their portraits comprising the poem's four central sections] were the only children who lived in the valley' (*NSP*, p. 149). Framing the life of a close-knit but diminishing community, their common history, beliefs and traditional practices expose in the Camarch a disturbingly unhomely topos. Preserved in the informal retellings which the poem embeds, the valley's troubled past is insistently (to cite Bhabha) 'renew[ed] and refigur[ed] as a contingent "in-between" space, that innovates and interrupts the performance of the present' with interestingly undecideable results.

Bidgood was struck by the valley on her very first visit: 'One day I walked up behind Pantycelyn chapel to the pass and looked down into the Camarch valley and it just seemed so remote and weird. I thought it was somehow creepy but in a way that intrigued me, not a way that put me off.'[55] Then, 'as I found out more about it from local people's conversation, I realised it was a valley that had very dark stories in it . . .'.[56] The poem makes an ominously fractured start out of remnants of those conversations:

> 'Why Cwm-cyn-Nos?' No-one's answer
> seemed complete. 'It was best
> to be at home in that valley, or out of it,
> before night', one said, adding 'perhaps'. (*NSP*, p. 149)

From here on, day and night, and their symbolic cognates darkness and light, death and life, seem to contend over a place in which past and present, nature and culture, historical event and local legend, homeliness and unhomeliness casually permeate and compound each other:

> Griffin Thomas of Cefn Gilfach went to Rhaeadr market to buy iron pots for his son's marriage-gift. Returning over the moors in heavy summer rain, at the ford over the Camarch below his house he was swept away by a sudden wild up-swelling of the river.
>
> Coming home late one evening from shepherding, William Arthur of Blaencwm saw a light dance on the river between Carregronw and Fedw, and hurried on. Near that spot the next day was found the body of Griffin Thomas. (*NSP*, p. 150)

Underpinning the text's narrative fragments is its sense of a self-sufficient community's foreshortening existence: 'Who heard the *cyheuraeth* for the doomed farms? / Who heard the *cyheuraeth* pass along the valley?' (*NSP*, p. 156).[57] The poem confirms Bidgood as 'remembrancer',

> trying to keep in the present what was valuable about the past. I think with the Camarch valley I felt that something valuable had gone, that these were places where real farm life and community had gone, and that I wanted in the poem to keep that.[58]

The four twentieth-century youngsters, Robin, Hazel, toddler Tomos and the 'happy, humorous' baby Gwyn, offer a refreshingly energetic counterpoint to a place perhaps in thrall to its own moribundity, even if none of them seems entirely impervious to its menaces. The delicate meshing of past with present (in the children's different stories) seems to offer to stem, even as it points up, the sociocultural darkness which the text suggests oppresses the community at large. Bidgood comments that 'on the whole people move here to live and work and bring up children in the area, which is nice, but they are all from "off"'.[59] Visiting 'the shepherd Evan', the speaker recognizes the old man's recollection of 'a girl on a palomino / . . . my daughter. / I felt filaments of time / bind me to her memory and his, all of us into the valley story' (*NSP*, p. 152). The local custom of *dechreunos*, described in the closing section of the poem, has much the same effect.

According to Bidgood, *dechreunos* originated in domestic economy:

> T. Harri Jones [has referred to] 'grudged candlelight'. The candlelight was grudged because it was a terrible job in the autumn making the candles to last through the winter. Once you'd got them you wanted them to last. In this area there was a custom that in each valley, every evening, most people wouldn't light up their houses at all: they would simply bank the fire up and meet at one house, which would light all of its candles. This was *dechreunos*. They would spend a few hours there . . . And then they would go back to their own homes for their bowl of cawl, or whatever, and stoke the fire for a little bit of light so they didn't have to light their own candles, and go to bed early . . .[60]

In the poem, the custom seems talismanic for both thematic and cultural reasons. As social tradition, it permits an embattled little community to gather in a self-consciously collective moment carved out almost defensively against an hostile-seeming environment. The sociocultural space and symbolic illumination afforded by *dechreunos* is manifestly sharpened by local belief and superstition. In closing, the poem draws hopeful attention to the valley's remaining family perpetuating the custom simply by inhabiting Coedtrefan. The light-filled farmhouse indicates the tensions of its unhomely environs, while signifying and safeguarding the children's richly liminal situation, between forest(ry) and farm(ing), future and past, living and dead, even visible/light and invisible/dark, without fully realising it:

> Along darkening paths they came.
> Each time the door was opened,
> against outflowing of light
> a shape of darkness moved in,
> silhouette vanishing into light.

Coedtrefan keeps *dechreunos*
for people of invisible houses. ('Valley-before-Night', *NSP*, p. 158)

'Valley-before-Night' constitutes a palpably uncanny/unhomely cultural topos: the 'heritage' or the 'especial scene' which the text literally and figuratively 'brings to light' constitutes a demonstrably provisional cultural space, and remains somehow the more recognisable and compelling for that.[61] In Rosemary Marangoly George's words: 'Home is a place to escape to and escape from . . . It is not a neutral place. It is community. Communities are not counter-constructions but only extensions of home, providing the same comforts and terrors on a larger scale.'[62] Valley, poem, and the practice of *dechreunos* which the text seems somehow to stage as well as interrogate, all affirm Bhabha's observation that

> To be unhomed is not to be homeless . . . The recesses of the domestic space become sites for history's most intricate invasions. In that displacement, the borders between home and world become confused; and, uncannily, the private and the public become part of each other, forcing upon us a vision that is as divided as it is disorienting.[63]

The 'divided' and 'disorienting' vision which pervades 'Valley-before-Night' bears directly on Bidgood herself: the four children of Coedtrefan are her own, now adult, grandchildren; their parents still live in the lower reaches of the valley.[64] Poignantly, the remembered girl on the palomino is Bidgood's now dead daughter Janet. As Royle warns:

> It is impossible to think of the uncanny without this involving a sense of what is autobiographical, self-centred, based in one's own experience. But it is also impossible to conceive of the uncanny without a sense of ghostliness, a sense of strangeness given to dissolving all assurances about the identity of a self. The uncanny is perhaps the most and least subjective experience, the most and least autobiographical event.[65]

Bhabha offers a pertinent corollary: 'The unhomely moment relates the traumatic ambivalences of a personal psychic history to the wider disjunctions of political experience.'[66] As Bidgood ruefully told her contemporary, the poet Sally Roberts-Jones, in interview,

> Some people . . . would think writing out of an area like this would line me up with those who would keep Wales parochial and small minded and shut away from the big world . . . I don't think living intensely in one's own small area means that one is not a citizen of the world – perhaps one is all the more a citizen of the world for loving and getting involved with one small place.[67]

Her comment perhaps explains the faintly talismanic quality of 'Valley-before-Night', a quality which would seem unlikely to surprise Royle: 'The uncanny . . . always engages a performative dimension . . . something unpredictable and additionally strange happening in and to what is being stated, described or defined.'[68]

'Structures, tangible/broken are speech enough': aesthetics and the 'inbetween'

> Above all, the uncanny is intimately entwined with language, with how we conceive and represent what is happening without ourselves, to ourselves, to the world, when uncanny strangeness is at issue . . . its happening is always a kind of un-happening. Its 'un-' unsettles time and space, order and sense.[69]

As Katie Gramich and Catherine Brennan reveal, women poets in Wales have been writing about their domestic circumstances at least since Felicia Hemans began constructing 'the domestic as site of fulfillment and frustration for the female subject'.[70] Bidgood's probing of the inclusive/exclusive, un/homely trope of the private house, though rarely gendered, often reflects on the domestic lives and experiences of the 'ordinary' women of mid Wales: 'I'm not anti-feminist and I have nothing against my own gender . . . I like women and I think we have got something special to give very often.'[71] However, she has been careful to prevent her work from appearing in women-only anthologies: 'I don't like being put into a little box labelled "Women Poets" without the slightest idea of how I stand in relation to "Poets". It seems to me to be a limiting thing.'[72] Her views notwithstanding, Hooker includes Bidgood among the poets whose gender assures 'ambivalence in their relationship with the community, which they can hardly be said to speak to and for, after the manner of the folk poet'.[73] Conversely, like the other poets I treat, Bidgood's gender seems to sharpen her engagement, through the aesthetic space of the *cerdd* (or poem) itself, with the poetic traditions it might be expected to embody.

Bidgood's abiding sense of her un/homely cultural context nuances her aesthetic perhaps most obviously in the poetic sequence, a form she has long enjoyed. The seven poems comprising 'Guerinou', for example, search the separate valleys of the converging branches of the River Grwyne, which drains into the Usk north of Abergavenny. Bidgood took the title from

> Raymond Williams. He said it was the old name for an area of the Black Mountains which includes the Grwyne Fawr and Grwyne Fechan valleys . . . I don't know it well at all but my visits there made me very interested in it . . . Grwyne Fechan is benign, it seems to me, and Grwyne Fawr rather malign . . . One might expect two valleys close together in the same area to have much in common. When the opposite seems true, there's the thrill of the unexpected, surely?[74]

This remote, mesmerisingly dual (and apparently polarised) topos – well suited to the linking/dividing economies of the sequence – like the Camarch valley yields an array of uncanny signifiers, including isolated, empty and ruined buildings, woods and darkness, and a morbidly violent history ('Incident in Vengeance Wood') which seems to bear oppressively on the present ('Patricio 2001'). The sequence is scattered with the unhomely houses exemplified most powerfully by the unsettling un/inhabited form of 'Tŷ'n-y-Llŵyn', and the ruin of 'The Hermitage', luring its visitors 'without fully knowing why'

> miles
> in search of a broken house, unsure
> who built or named it, obsessed
> with an idea of hiddenness,
> an unreliable story. (*NSP*, p. 264)

Here again, ruination and rumour both stimulate and obstruct the ('presumptio[us]') urge to pursue the 'hiddenness' each locus promises. However, 'Guerinou' differs from 'Valley-before-Night' in self-consciously discovering in the aesthetic a space in which to interrogate cultural identity. For Janovitz, the ruin-like genre of the poetic fragment is definitively framed by its staging of 'the relation between its own incompletion and the greater whole to which it alludes, and which it both aspires to and struggles against'.[75] This astute gloss constructs in the intrinsically incomplete lyric fragment an inherently uncanny form, simultaneously refracting and refusing the unattainable wholeness out of whose destruction it came. The poetic fragments collected in the dis/connective textual and aesthetic topos of the sequence self-evidently replay the tensions which Janovitz teases out and which reverberate in the 'offerings' assembled at the start of 'Guerinou':

> There seem so many of them, despite
> the hiddenness of the place; as if
> in a time of fear and shattering
> these humble shapes are once more
> valid – raw letters spelling out

> helplessness, not yet
> reshuffled into words of power. ('Patricio 2001', *NSP*, p. 257)

Obliquely politicised ('in a time of fear') these 'humble shapes' reflexively stage what Janovitz calls 'the problem of finding an adequation between what one wants to figure in language and what one can figure in language'.[76] 'Patricio 2001' makes an eloquent prelude to 'The Hermitage', and the woman rumoured to have occupied it. Bidgood explains:

> There's no proof at all that she existed, there's just a very strong tradition that John McNamara of Llangoed – now a posh hotel on the way down the Wye valley – kept a mistress in the Grwyne Fechan valley and used to ride over one of the high passes of the mountain to visit her. And I imagined her, in a sort of echo of Tennyson's Mariana in the Moated Grange, being snowed up there. If you don't actually know anything you can imagine what you like.[77]

'McNamara's Mistress' is a duly wretched figure in the alcoholism which offers her refuge, her maudlin prediction of her own historical obliteration ('it's as if / there's no story of me as if nobody / will ever make me one') obliquely signalling its awareness of the paradoxically ruinous nature of poetic – and by implication aesthetic – expression.

In an idiom always more inclined to hint at than belabour the riches of language and/or situation, Bidgood's negotiations with the conventions of poetic form are typically light-footed. Her interest in the marginalised generic form of the 'found poem' may seem contrastingly hard to miss, especially since their republication in *Hearing Voices* (2008). These texts merit attention, not least in their conscious exploiting of the inherent uncanninesses of the poetic construct itself. The explanatory introduction which prefaces *Hearing Voices* helps to confirm this impression: in it, Bidgood defines as 'found' poems those comprising 'passages from . . . any prose source which without their writer's knowledge or intention make themselves known as poems'. Her words foreground the contingent nature of the creative process in which she is involved: it seems as if she wants to permit the 'passages' themselves to author and direct their own reinvention, and the creative opportunities flowing from that. The poet seems less agent than passive channel through which excerpts 'make themselves known as poems', even if the process through which they find poetic life manifestly depends on her:

> their rhythm . . . unity and . . . emotional charge have encouraged me to 'lift' them from their setting and edit them into lines of verse which I hope bring out

> their poetic qualities. Editing [may involve] abbreviating, cutting unnecessary repetition but in a true found poem one should not invent or add. (*Hearing Voices* [6])

Bidgood's part-authorial, part-editorial relationship with these ruin-like texts is plainly as uncertain as the ambivalent web of relations stitching the finished poem into the yoked contexts and conventions of both its source and its new literary-poetic life. It is also manifestly even self-consciously uncanny, in reanimating precisely the textual 'corpse' David Punter describes:

> in our most everyday encounters with language we are always coming on to a scene that is peopled with foreigners, strangers, strange words [;] . . . in every poem we read, we experience also a haunting, the present absence of some other story [recounted in] the stony voice of an inscription, and it is our privilege and our risk to breathe life into this animated corpse which is text.[78]

The poems comprising the second half of the collection ('partly inventions [which] make use of "found" material') both simplify and further destablise that relationship. Fetched from the historical archive into the poem's prolific hermeneutic life, the borrowed materials signify as much in the nature and contexts of their (estranged) sources as in the voices they conflate. In their pan-historical, cross-generic heteroglossia, both kinds of poem quietly challenge the literary conventions with which each negotiates. Interestingly, the first section is more woman centred. Whether author or mute recipients of their source documents, the experiences of wives, sisters, mothers and daughters resonate in and through their poetic reincarnations: Alice Owen's spirited rejection of her petitioning mother ('Grievance', *HV*, 20–1), the wayward and anonymous sister whom Edward Bache must 'advise . . . / not to throw yourself away' and Elizabeth Lochard's disarming 'Grumbles to her Sister' (*HV*, 30–1, 28–9).

In offering such lively women some very belated cultural representation, *Hearing Voices* (like 'Valley-Before-Night', among others) arguably captures its author in mildly political mood, critiquing the implicitly gendered politics of literary convention. In Bidgood's found poems, the text itself frames and enacts the conversing, mutually alienated, haunted and haunting co-authorial presences of poet and her source, converging in their quasi-collaborative, self-estranging and unhomely reorchestration of the poetic text which emerges from its prose original. These uncertainties proliferate in the complex linguistic and textual topos of 'Chancery: Opening Music', embedded in the closing 'Sources' section, in which the discourses of the law, music and poetry are weighed against each other, the contingent realities of the 'true, found poem' displaced by a more traditional voice, navigating the creative parallels between unread historical source ('Long parchments and limp inky scraps / corded together') and the 'stiff pages' of unplayed piano music. The interpolated, fragmentary 'found' (perhaps also partly imagined) exchanges between the embattled 'widow' and 'the Commissioners' – rehearsing the unheard story of the Chancery source – are viewed like a kind of score. They not only enshrine the particular 'music' which the poem elicits from the dry-seeming language of seventeenth- and eighteenth-century probate; they await the attention of Bidgood's quietly keyed-up but typically self-deprecating speaker: the 'halting interpretation / of tentative harmonies, broken phrasing, / less-than-perfect cadences' which the poem performatively offers (*HV*, p. 47) Thus, in its final swerve, does a complex text gravely arrive – like Janovitz's ruin poems – at its central cohering intention: the surreptitious problematising of the extent to which language is ever capable of relaying or realising experience.

Inhabiting and mediating the perhaps surprising overlap between music making and legislative manoeuvring, this poem like the collection as a whole registers its sense of its own creative potential. Hovering between conventional and new forms of authorship, between traditionally imagined and 'found' materials, it directs us into a politically charged literary 'beyond' in which its creative energies can be allowed full rein. The kinds of uncanny fragmentation in which Bidgood's found poems characteristically trade, invariably help to unpick and unsettle the kinds of cultural and aesthetic traditions by which readers – critical or not – like to use to situate and understand, but also by the same token often confine, a poet. Hooker has constructed Bidgood's as a poetry 'haunted by a lost function, in whose absence it has gained another'.[79] His sketch holds delicately true of an understated oeuvre's persistent, subversive interrogating of its own textual and thematic possibilities and expectations, as well as its compellingly unhomely cultural environs.

3

Frontier Country: Christine Evans

Christine Evans divides her time between her home on the southernmost tip of the Llŷn peninsula in north-west Wales and Bardsey Island, which lies off the same coastline. In the BBC film made to mark an appearance at the Hay Literary Festival, the Yorkshire-born Evans confides: 'To live surrounded by the sea – coming as I did from the middle of England – has been a revelation. The light for one thing, and the constant sense of an almost living presence, whispering or roaring.'[1] More than a little of this sense of wonder is preserved in 'Waves', in which we find ourselves navigating the uncertain space between land and sea, the 'innocent' breaking waves ('with a strength at back / that . . . drowns / heartbeat / with its own') conditioning a terrain always, self-effacingly, in motion:

> Shore and sky wiped clean, over and over,
> by the pulse and roar and pounding
> like a great loom . . .
> This is frontier country:
> to walk here is to feel
> perception quicken . . . (*IDH*, p. 14)

The relentless way in which this fluidly marginal place throws the surety of borders and limits into question seems both generative and menacing. The text situates the self, perilously yet invitingly, on the watershed between known and unknown, order and chaos:

> Stand still
> and the whole slow world spins
> round you . . .
> offering completion
> unravelling /
> control.

Thus the poem reinterrogates the connections between the centralised but also dissipated self and its 'slow world', its ponderous orbit likewise somehow both definitive and indeterminate ('unravelling control'). The effect recalls Homi Bhabha, whose 'postmodern subject, like the postmodern landscape it occupies in a relation of mutual reinforcement, has lost its traditional form of closed interiority encapsulated in a boundary . . .'[2]

As for Ruth Bidgood, and the poets discussed in chapter 1, or indeed any of the poets treated in this study, the problematic nature of the boundary – whether topographical, geographical or psycho-social – offers Evans a rich thematic seam. Given her ambiguous sense of relationship with the landscapes of her own island/mainland domicile, it perhaps should not surprise us to find that the part played by the coastal boundary in the construction of cultural identity has long been a particular concern in Evans's subtle, habitually self-searching poetics. What Doreen Massey has called the 'n-dimensional space of identity' remains for Susan Stanford Friedman 'unthinkable without some sort of imagined or literal boundary'. As the latter points out, 'Borders protect, but they also confine'; conversely, in 'insisting on separation at the same time as they acknowledge connection', Friedman notes, borders 'also specify the liminal space in between, the interstitial site of interaction, interconnection and exchange . . .'[3] This uncertain space might equate with Bhabha's so-called 'third space', 'where the negotiation of incommensurable differences creates a tension peculiar to borderline existences . . .'[4] It seems helpful here, as it was in chapter 1, to keep Massey's ideas in mind:

> the particularity of any place is, in these terms, constructed not by placing boundaries around it and defining its identity through counter-position to the other which lies beyond, but precisely (in part) through the specificity of the mix of links and interconnections to that *beyond*.[5]

Rooted in and emerging from a physical and social territory which is for geological and cultural reasons manifestly dual, Evans's poetry may be suggestively read beside and through both Massey and Bhabha, even as it illuminates the confines of the essentially masculine literary tradition with which it converses and contends. Although its publication in *Island of Dark Horses* (1995) seems to locate 'Waves' on Bardsey, the poem was in fact written on and about Pen Llŷn.[6] As the text itself hints, moreover, in Evans's liminal poetics, the shorelines separating and connecting Bardsey and Llŷn from their cultural hinterlands typically situate the partly 'complet[ed]', partly 'unravell[ed]' and frequently gendered self in a richly equivocal sociocultural 'frontier country'. Evans's interrogation of the uncertain relationship between island and peninsula, and with their separate/linked territories, charges what turns out to be her deeply provisional sense of relationship with Wales, in and through her twin cultural communities. As for Anne Cluysenaar, Ruth Bidgood and (as we shall see in succeeding chapters) other poets including Gwyneth Lewis, the sequential poem offers Evans a usefully flexible textual space in which to tease out some of the complexities which flow from her particular cultural situation.

Land

In 1967 when Evans was 23, her Welsh-born father died unexpectedly. His eldest daughter, then working in north London, promptly moved her mother and three younger siblings from their home in the Yorkshire Dales with her to his home town of Pwllheli, where she had landed a post teaching English at the grammar school: 'It was somewhere for [us] to start again. With hindsight I see it was naively optimistic, to think one can uproot a family and plant them again.'[7] The move worked out for Evans herself, however: 'In my first summer here, a teaching colleague invited me to stay on Enlli, Bardsey Island, and my fate was sealed. Reader, I married the boatman.'[8] Evans's husband ('the son of a farmer who preferred the sea') was born on Bardsey: the island is as central to his *cynefin* as Aberdaron, memorably characterised by Justin Wintle as 'a seaside parish almost at the end of the remote and magical Llŷn peninsula, at the extreme north-west of the Welsh mainland'.[9] Bardsey remains at the core of Evans's life in Uwchmynydd, the hamlet outside Aberdaron where the couple have lived since their marriage; the family can spend up to five months a year on the island. And, although she is often hailed as one of a line of poets associated with Bardsey, Evans has in fact written just as much about her mainland home.

The connections between Pen Llŷn and Ynys Enlli are implied in the ambiguous title of Evans's first full collection, *Looking Inland* (1983). Its perspective tethered no more firmly to mainland than island, the volume gestures at their proximity. Mary Chitty estimates that:

> The shortest distance from the mainland is about two miles, but [Bardsey] Sound is notorious for its difficult currents and the sea route can be up to six miles. The island is about one and three quarters of a mile long and three quarters of a mile wide and is shaped like . . . an animal with a large oblong head near the mainland, a narrow waist, and a tail stretching out into the sea. She turns her back on the mainland: for the 'slug-like' form of Bardsey mountain

> firmly shuts off and hides from the mainland shore the lower fertile western plain. [Yet] those who climb Mynydd Mawr at the end of the Llŷn peninsula can look along this western expanse to the lighthouse, white on the southern and most exposed part of the island.[10]

For all Bardsey's nearness, Chitty prepares us for a place resolutely independent of its closest land mass, at once protectively self-enclosing and self-extending in its western projection away from the shelter of mainland Wales into the Irish sea. The self-sufficiency which Chitty depicts is reiterated by Evans in 'Unseen Island', a relatively early study in which Bardsey is constructed – interestingly, by a speaker anchored firmly on the mainland – as a locus of particular and compelling clarification:

> So like a compass I am pointing
> always where you lie –
> elusive, shimmering –
>
> but no mirage:
> my unblurring. (*LI*, p. 15)

Evans, who freely concedes the personal character of much of her poetry, has said that arriving on Bardsey felt to her 'like discovery, a green place where I could take root and grow'.[11] Her own 'unblurring' seems to have been partly prompted by the highly tuned simplicity of the island's traditional way of life, after a childhood which slid into chaos after her father discovered the fact of his illegitimacy in the wake of his own father's death. Amid what became his prolonged absences, for his reserved and clever daughter an increasingly straitened home life revolved – until she began the university education she had set her heart on – around the demanding and unpredictable figure of her mother. Bardsey by contrast appeared to be 'a place where everything seemed in balance', while her new family's farmstead Tŷ Pella offered

> the orderliness I craved; the safety within a family. My mother-in-law washed on Mondays, baked bread three times a week, had dinner on the table at noon every day. The men moved between the farm and the sea, following the weather and the tide. It was predictable, within a natural pattern. I was intoxicated by it all at first.[12]

The remarks confirm how Bardsey's beguiling rhythms are governed – that is, both sustained and threatened – by the sea which circumscribes its curving form. Identifying this paradox as the 'fundamental tension in the idea of the island', Gillian Beer defers to *The Oxford English Dictionary*:

> 'Isle' in its earliest forms derived from a word for water and meant 'watery' or 'watered'. In Old English 'land' was added to it to make a compound: 'is-land': water-surrounded land. The idea of water is thus . . . as essential as that of earth. The two elements, earth and water, are set in play . . . . The land is surrounded by water; the water fills the shores. The island, to be fruitful, can never be intact.[13]

The defining presence of the sea underwrites Evans's poetic portrayal of the island in 'Defensive, secure, compacted, even paradisal' terms.[14] In 'Unseen Island' ('nowhere / more steeped in calm, / more resonant of growing'), Bardsey proves an intensely self-nourishing environment: 'I am played to a tune / I scarcely recognise / / easy as water, but earthed' (*LI*, pp. 4–6, 8–10).[15] In a later work, 'Enlli', the process of self-examination seems literally 'earthed':

> Small fields that run all one way
> to the sea, inviting feet
> to make new paths to their own
> discovered places. (*IDH*, pp. 7–8)

Meanwhile, the ameliorating influence of the sea nurtures the island's diverse flora and fauna, and supports the farming on which its residents have depended down the centuries. Indeed, as 'Broc Môr' (its title translating roughly as 'Sea Debris') only half-humorously testifies, even Bardsey's beaches are generative: 'Mornings, still, the islanders "walk round", / working the shore for a first finding / for what the sea has left' (*IDH*, p. 56).

Yet Evans overlooks neither the vulnerabilities of Bardsey's exposed position nor the treachery of its seas. Despite the changeable beauty savoured in 'Watchers' (p. 63), poems like 'Storm', 'Sounding', 'Through the Weather Window' and, perhaps most forcefully, 'Crossing from the Island' dramatise the potential of 'weather and tide' to menace the island and its residents. Matthew Jarvis and others notice how, by extension, 'plump and secret Enlli' lends Evans a powerful trope in which as Beer promises 'centrality is emphasized and the enclosure of land within surrounding shores is the controlling meaning'.[16] 'Broc Môr' is one of various poems which seem to endorse Jarvis's view that Evans's Bardsey exerts a 'gravitational pull; it is the centre towards which things will tend'.[17] 'Sounding' conjures the powerfully centripetal/centrifugal of the 'double echo' of the foghorn, its boom intensifying a sense of isolation which the speaker seems both to cherish and resent ('Like a mantra, tugs awareness back / Continually to the centre') (*IDH*, p. 30). In the words of 'Terce', the third section of the title sequence concluding *Island of Dark Horses*,

> This is a real place, small enough
> to see whole, big enough to lose
> our own importance. Brings us back
> to our senses. (*IDH*, p. 80)

On the other hand – in an irony never lost on Evans, who learned to swim only after years of hazardous shuttling across the sound – the sea is the chief agent and medium of connection between any island and the rest of the world.[18] In Beer's words 'a vast extension of the island, allowing for the psychic size of the body politic to expand', the sea makes possible the cultural fluidity which poems like 'Broc Môr' and 'Island of Dark Horses' encourage us to identify with Enlli, frequently through the trope of the island's lighthouse.[19]

Completed in 1821, and at an imposing 30 metres the tallest in the British Isles, Bardsey's famous lighthouse comes to seem – like its sonic proxy the foghorn – a peculiarly powerful signifier for Evans, primarily in its ambiguities. The building metonymically fuses the known and the unknown: it testifies to – advertises and illuminates – the hazardous nature of a coastline both dangerous and deceptive enough to warrant its construction. Its sole purpose is to dramatise a peril which is always contingent, and (ideally anyway) only ever potential. Likewise, the safety it figures is counter-intuitive: however helpful its presence, no lighthouse can ever offer refuge, as such. Just as it has been designed to make the latent or hidden in some way actual and visible, so it protects, ironically, by warning away, refusing, shrugging off.[20] Evans uses Bardsey's lighthouse to map these ambiguities onto the island's long and complicated cultural history. In the opening section of 'Island of Dark Horses' (named 'Lauds' after the first religious office of the day, in a gesture at Enlli's monastic history), the lighthouse becomes a cohering focus for the multiple ethnic strands which came to be woven into the island's earliest constructions:

> *Andros*, Pliny called it; *Edri*
> to ancient Greek mapdrawers of the western edge.
> *Ynys yn y lli* or Viking Bardr's raidplace –
>
> . . .
>
> A world of waves and pouring air
> the lighthouse's long steady stroke
> in the flux of the sea. (*Selected Poems*, p. 121)

As a later section makes clear, this layered sociocultural history is both renovated and threatened by this powerful building, partly thanks to the role it played in enriching the island's linguistic diversity: 'the light-house families . . . came from all over Britain, a lot of them from Tower Hill or Essex or Devon, [yet was itself] built by Cornish stonemasons at a time when the community on the island would have been almost exclusively Welsh speaking'.[21]

'Island of Dark Horses' fixes on the lighthouse as an equivocal agent of cultural change: it serves as a historic but also contemporaneous focal point for both the potentially destructive forces of Anglocentric cultural expansion and Bardsey's anciently heterogeneous sense of cultural identity, in 'pointing out' the migrant 'birds of passage' (or 'many-coloured fragments') which the island has attracted from the outset:

> scarce one breath of Saxon till the lighthouse
> sweeping the night skies four times a minute
> changed the focus, pointing out. Making a haven
> a trough in the rock that brought
> a hundred years' prosperity. And attracting
> birds of passage, eager or exhausted strangers.
>
> In the shell sand the many-coloured fragments
> tossed up here for a time
> rub against each other, silent, still evolving. (*IDH*, pp. 78–9)

Thus it is that in Evans's poetic treatments of her island home, and more or less just as Doreen Massey posits, Bardsey's 'global' context comes almost inexorably to be assimilated into the (admittedly sea-bound but far from exclusive) 'local' which this remarkable outcrop of land encompasses, 'in the very process of the formation of the local'.[22]

In Evans's inward-/outward-looking poetics, sea and lighthouse become oddly metaphoric of each other, working independently but in tandem, rhythmically and remorselessly, to entrench but always as we have seen to diffuse the island's inherent insularity. Each separates and connects, dramatising Bardsey's isolated position while confirming and safeguarding its ancient cosmopolitanism. 'Songline' opens *Island of Dark Horses* by affirming the intrinsically restorative nature of a place at once familiar and extraordinary in its quietly global reach:

> Under my own apple tree
> in a warm walled garden

on an island
at the extremity of a green peninsula
in an amniotic sea

I sit and read
of nomads

so all night I hear herds
grunt and shuffle,
breathe earth and leather
under a roof of antlers
and embroidered flowers.

Behind, the grasses wither.
Beyond, the passes
may be blocked with snow.
Here is sweet water, a ripening
green now. I wake

to light-filled island air
and it is so. (*IDH*, p. 7)

Its self-sufficiency figured in the speaker's Edenic but far from conventionally spiritual walled garden, the gateway-like island of 'Songline', anchored in its suggestively 'amniotic sea', is rendered a richly uncertain, self-interrogating cultural locus of dispersal and centring.

As 'Waves' reminds us, the 'frontier country' of any shoreline exposes the otherwise hidden bedrock in which two apparently physically discrete territories are fused. In 'Llŷn' the northern coastline of the peninsula is carefully distinguished from that of Aberdaron, its most outlying village, where 'the clays / of the southern shore slide palely under' (*IDH*, p. 71). A sketch of Uwchmynydd confirms Evans's sense of the connectedness of island and mainland:

> I rarely walk here without a sense of the massive spasms that shaped the land, the pulse of an ancient sea-bed that can still split and heave upwards and outwards from the great molten core . . . Geologists call this promontory and Enlli a 'mélange': it is a jumble of rubble, as if some giant toddler had rolled the rocks in his hands like plasticine so that purple jasper, creamy chert, red and green and black-grape mudstone all squeezes together in a grey base, with slabs of sandstone and limestone in dogged lumps.[23]

In this wryly affectionate portrait of the community where she has lived now for some forty years, Evans constructs the peninsula in a suggestively dual way:

> On the map of Wales, it is the tip of a finger pointing to Enlli; from the three-seater Cessna droning its way over the cold volcanoes, the fertile sweeps and wooded folds . . . at 15,000 feet, it is a last defiant fist, four rocky knuckles clenched against the sea.[24]

In part this double-edged construction affirms R. S. Thomas's declaration that 'It is the sea that makes the Llŷn Peninsula what it is'.[25] As 'promontory' rather than island, Llŷn's remote but still connected position seems to guarantee the cultural authenticity which Thomas ascribes a place 'not very different from what it has been for centuries, a Welsh-speaking peninsula with the sea on all sides of it'.[26] Evans herself likewise delights in her coastal home: 'Once I came to live and work in Pen Llŷn my life was filled up with astonishing scenery; I could do my walking from home – and have hardly needed to travel anywhere else.'[27] On the other hand she views the peninsula with more ambivalence than her literary predecessor; 'Mynydd Rhiw', an early poem located on the mountain dominating Aberdaron and its environs, introduces us to 'Taid', 'Forking more loose hay up to a load / Precarious already. "Lots of room / Above, you'll never bang your head."' (*LI*, p. 23).[28] The words reverberate in a text which constructs a frontier-like peninsula as hovering vertiginously between permission and prohibition:

> Just to be here
> Shrinks us into where, not who, we are:
>
> Out on a limb,
> At the extremity of a digit,
> Poised on a ridge in a fingernail
> We grow dizzy at the scale of things. (*LI*, p. 23)

Many of Evans's poems – composed on a tape recorder on the daily drive along the length of the peninsula to and from school – savour the contours of an empty, manifestly separate landscape. Mostly it is the farthest tip of the peninsula towards which such poems tend. 'Driving Home' notes, with quiet exultation, 'Behind me, all the hills of Gwynedd / Drown . . . / Ahead, the swooping road that races darkness / Down this last finger to the sea.' (*LI*, p. 48). In 'Peninsular', the same journey takes the speaker, significantly, 'away / from the womb-connections' of the rest of the country. During what begins to seem like a process of cultural maturation, 'mainland' Wales recedes before 'thinning horizons / where distance smooths / the shadow of named places' (*CP*, pp. 9–10). Among the finest of these studies, 'Llŷn' is similarly conscious of spaciousness: 'Skies tower here, and we are small.' In one eloquently compressed moment, the isthmus is deftly pathologised as 'a flap of land in a dark throat', an adjunct-like growth which if it is uncertainly attached to its context (perhaps Wales, but just as possibly the sea), like the epiglottis crucially gives that 'throat' voice. Before closing, 'Llŷn' turns outwards to survey its southwestern horizons:

> after dark
> like busy star-systems, the lights
> of Harlech, Aberystwyth, Abergwaun
> wink and beckon. The sun's gone down
> red as a wound behind Wicklow.
> A creaking of sail away
> Cernyw and Llydaw wait.
> Once, here was where what mattered
> happened. A small place
> at the foot of cliffs of falling light;
> horizons that look empty.
> If we let ourselves believe it,
> fringes. (*IDH*, pp. 71–2)

The degree to which Ireland haunts the coastline where, as Chitty says, 'the Welsh hand is extended towards Ireland', is treated in more detail in chapter 5.[29] Here, yoking the scattered lights of the Welsh coastal towns to the silhouetted Wicklow hills, the 'older world' at which 'Llŷn' gestures reiterates Massey's conviction that places 'are constructed through the specificity of their interaction with other places rather than by counterposition to them'.[30] For Katie Gramich, amid the historicising Welsh 'for Cornwall (Cernyw) and Brittany (Llydaw) . . . the first-person plural "we" in the penultimate line suggests a sense of shared and defiant national identity, a refusal to be written off as marginal or peripheral'.[31] To me the same gesture subverts the process – the construction of a 'defiant' national identity – which Gramich discerns here. Poised on the very 'fringes' of Wales's westernmost border, the poem's perspective seems deliberately wide angled. Just as the text moves beyond the time when 'here was what mattered / happened', the Welsh words ironically bind speaker, peninsula and nation alike into a broader cultural history, its existing and/or historical borders subsumed in the ancient cultural kinship it revives with those erstwhile trading partners, Cornwall and Brittany, their historic cultural autonomy still more occluded and distant than Wales's. In line with Massey's construction of places as 'open and porous networks' of 'social relations', the poem's final lines view in those 'fringes' a permissively mobile and self-fragmenting form of frontier.[32] If, as Gramich has argued, 'Evans sees Enlli and the Llŷn peninsula very much as part of Wales', it is from both sides of its richly unstable, self-interrogating cultural border(s).[33]

Community

For Edward Relph, 'landscape is not merely an aesthetic background to life [but] a setting that both expresses and conditions cultural attitudes'.[34] R. S. Thomas would have concurred; for him, approaching retirement, Pen Llŷn offered cultural anchorage, a haven from which to ponder and protest his sense of Welsh identity, 'a peninsula where I can be inward with all the tension of the age'.[35] Amid the changing demographics of the twenty-first century, Evans's environs seem to retain a special sense of cultural identity: 'There are more incomers now, and a high proportion of elderly residents, but young people are resisting the need to move away, and Uwchmynydd has kept its Welsh character.'[36] However, for all her intense affection for her adopted home, Evans's more complex apprehension of her coastal locality 'conditions' her problematising of the insularity in which Thomas found such regenerative solace.

Relph's formulation pre-empts Massey's recognition that 'Space is . . . a complex web of relations of domination and subordination, of solidity and co-operation'.[37] Marriage into the heart of 'a small community that is one of the last toe-holds of a traditional culture' propelled Evans into the equivocal situation from which she still writes today, as (the blurb of *Looking Inland* explains) 'both a part of her community and an outsider raised in England, an observer'; from this position, the newcomer quickly noticed the signs of Massey's socio-spatial relations: 'I was struck most by [the] patterns, the invisible web of relationships and deferential conventions.'[38] On one level at least she seems likely to have disliked the distinctiveness which accompanied her sense of cultural peculiarity. Describing herself as a 'withdrawn' and 'solitary' child, she reveals that a poem now entitled '"Adjusting the Focus" (it was called "Small" for a long time) began with a sense of feeling . . .

what it felt like to be me . . . about trying to make myself small and quiet and be unnoticed'.[39] This instinct might explain why the near-exhilaration of 'Mynydd Rhiw' should convulse so suddenly into self-conscious and self-reproving anti-climax: 'We must go down. / . . . It is not easy for my kind / To be detached, to stand up high' (*LI*, p. 23). Troubling its own association of the airy landscape of the peninsula with sociocultural freedom, this text finds elevation both permitting (imaginative) independence and imperilling social survival. Beverly J. Stoeltje warns 'The very nature of the "frontier", in any geographical setting, implies a process of adaptation in the settlement of that frontier, and interaction of the settling people with the physical environment [and] with each other'.[40] Whether or not we want to align the voice of 'Mynydd Rhiw' with the self-searching figure who would become Christine Evans poet, the speaker of this poem seems to feel that to stand apart from 'my kind' – to call attention to oneself, to announce otherness – is to fail to adapt, or fit in. Evans's poems repeatedly return to the need to cooperate in a locus where the need for community is intensified by its coastal frontiers. In 'Peninsular' the landform which is Pen Llŷn is constructed as providing both 'the taste / of meaning otherwise' and the social context for that experience: 'Space and time stretch out / to show us to ourselves / as local examples' (*CP*, p. 9), the landscape a refuge for those who must 'move closer to share warmth',

> knowing where the road ends
> where the land sinks
> beyond the island (*CP*, p. 10)

As these lines also suggest, a sense of community can transcend physical boundaries. This is ironic given that, as Chitty says, 'Islands attract . . . most of all those who for any reason want to put a moat between themselves and the workaday world, its claims and its distractions'.[41] The centring insularity which is so attractively evident from the coast of Llŷn has always underpinned Enlli's allure, not least for latter-day visitors like 'Viv', drawn by 'a seamless ripening that took her in / and whispered here might be the place / for the bright strands to converge'('Keeping in Touch', *IDH*, pp. 65–6). In 'Off Camera', to the 'islanders returned by helicopter / to their birthplace for the day', Bardsey emerges as

> the enduring pole
> they measure progress from.
> It is the mainland, they point out, themselves,
> that have moved on. (*IDH*, p. 26)

By the same token, 'Island of Dark Horses' insists:

> we must not let these clarities
> crystallize into the one place
> rooted at the centre of the world
> lest we make exiles of our mainland selves (*IDH*, p. 89)

Evans has always found aspects of her Gwynedd domicile restrictive: 'A small community can be security and also straitjacket, and there's little privacy because its focus tends to be inward-looking. Petty concerns assume too much time and importance; attitudes get accepted and easily harden into prejudice.'[42] She remembers: 'The hardest thing was learning what was and what was not acceptable – talking about emotions, or elaborating wild ideas; behaving out of the ordinary. I came to think of it as rural convention, the strength of the group rather than encouraging individual expression.'[43] In an early poem, kindly visitors provoke ambivalence:

> Only small, swarthy men with the friendly smell on them;
> Yet walls press close and the room seems cluttered.
> I am glad to go and make obligatory tea
> As their voices sway, slow with the seasons,
> And, ponderously, come to the point. ('Callers', *LI*, p. 8)

The 'slow' voices themselves gesture at another quiet threat to a shaping literary imagination:

> I'm part of a family and a community with very practical people who perhaps don't see the need for artistic expression or perhaps even think that it shouldn't be necessary . . . My father-in-law . . . had tremendous respect for education. The word and the number. But in his case it was as tools. [So] I have a sort of shame about writing, I think. I hide it. I do it privately.[44]

Such conservatism was not unfamiliar to the young Evans: 'I grew up very much in a working-class family where, despite my father's interest in the arts, reading . . . had to be a hidden activity, a secret activity, and . . . – certainly my mother wouldn't have encouraged writing.'[45] The circumscriptions of life in the remotest part of Welsh-speaking Wales were only compounded for the non-Welsh-speaking newcomer, especially one who had been appointed to her teaching post chiefly 'because I was monoglot English'.[46] 'Second Language' can be read as apologising for what seems, to its teacher-speaker, the desecration of the rare cultural heritage of a class 'grown in the delicate light / of an old walled garden that was once the world' (*CP*, p. 60). At ease with a 'language [which] fills the mouth like fruit' these pupils seem too easily 'beguil[ed]'; the speaker fears that to teach them linguistic strangeness, as required of her, is to condemn them to an equally unjustifiable form of cultural alienation:

> In their calm faces I can find no clues
> that they are still at ease in their own skins
> that dredging for this voice has drowned no other
> and my teaching has not made them strangers. (*CP*, p. 61)

As I have noted, in all its disadvantages, women can find estrangement enfranchising. Insider and outsider in Llŷn and Bardsey alike, Evans can and does exploit all of the perspectives of her uncertain situation in her writing. The speaker of 'Meeting the Boat' is too familiar with the rigours of island life to be patient of the women with 'clammy, over-eager hands', to whom 'the island, all of us, are in soft focus' ('On Retreat'). More scorn is reserved for those stranded 'on the beach without their wives / or suitcases. Ankle-deep, they stand bemused or bray / for contact' (*IDH*, p. 9). The tourists' situation is drawn in terms both martial and cooperative: 'In turn, each has to improvise a way / To make a meeting with our mustered forces. / Then we will form a chain to land the luggage' (p. 10). As the sea which brought them to Bardsey ironically hampers their arrival, so the very isolation the visitors seek is shown to depend on the communal spirit and kindliness of their 'mustered' hosts. 'Island of Dark Horses' is similarly stern: 'On an island there is no isolation: / in a web of mutual dependence, privacy / is an illusion' (*IDH*, p. 84).

In contrast, the speaker of 'Pulpit Enlli' feels sufficiently detached from the island community to mock an edifice which, with its 'gilt cherubs heavy as fungus / engorged and smug', seems as absurd as its history: '1870: fourteen families / told to choose: stone harbour / or chapel, . . .' The families are not blamed for their decision: 'how could they see into a time / when it was no longer God's will to have grown two strong men from every house . . . ?' Rather, the poem indicts the cultural myopia which shadows the still harbourless Enlli, and 'A tiny community of individuals / thrown together as on a voyage –'

> freed from seeing ourselves reflected
> except as close-ups in each other's eyes
> so shadows of all the others we have been
> sidle close . . . ('Terce', *IDH*, p. 81)

Evans constructs Llŷn's 'frugal way of life, crofting rather than farming, on a handful of small, salt-scorched fields' with equal ambivalence.

On one hand its special practices seem fragile, as 'Summer in the Village' makes clear:

> Shell Gifts, Crab Sandwiches, To Let,
> the signs solicit by the gates, left open
> where the milk churns used to stand;
> and the cash trickles in.

The speaker is left lamenting how, amid the 'second homes', 'all that was community seeps out' (*LI*, p. 13).[47] Yet Evans is herself knowingly implicated in the process of cultural attrition: 'Llŷn gave me the confidence and the context to be a writer, but [also] the guilt (as an English incomer being one of R. S. [Thomas]'s nails in the coffin of the Welsh language, and the more successful I am, the further I'm driven in), the constriction I sometimes feel.'[48] For all the 'powerful North Wales allegiance' which Gramich discerns in her work, Evans remains resolutely careful of seeming to over-determine her place in her adopted national context: 'I came to the Welsh landscape as an adult, so I never took it for granted. Some things an outsider can see more clearly – and although I have been here a long time now . . . – I am still an outsider. . . . Yet I have felt from the first more at home here than anywhere.'[49]

Writing

Evans is clear that her sense of linguistic and cultural estrangement has charged and refined her poetic development: 'there was no encouragement to me to learn Welsh for at least the first five or six seven years. . . . [I]t gave me that sense of isolation. . . I think that writers . . . need to have spent some time alone, to be solitary, to be aware of their own separate identity and perhaps living in Wales has emphasised that.'[50]

According to Benedict Nightingale, the notoriously chauvinistic R. S. Thomas perhaps mischievously declared that 'The trouble is that the Welsh welcome newcomers; perhaps they are too open-handed'.[51] Thomas's august presence has arguably haunted Evans's idiom from the moment his friend, Bardsey boatman Wil Tŷ Pella, persuaded his English daughter-in-law to show the elder poet some early work 'in about 1969, 1970. I'd written before then but I'd never thought about writing for an audience other than myself.'[52] Evans recounts the meeting in 'Bonanza', the opening poem of *Looking Inland*:

> 'Words,' he told me, trying to be helpful,
> 'respond through craft and concentrated effort.

> A recluse alone can have the time
> for the ceaseless innovation
> and the hours of contemplation.'
> So that was the end of that. (*LI*, p. 7)

Evans's immediate response, 'burning with shame that my thoughts were so ordinary, and clearly lacking in talent', was to stop writing until, she recalls, 'quite abruptly, out of the euphoria of giving birth and feeling like a proper woman, secure in that role, I began writing about the community I was living in'.[53] In the now well-known words of 'Bonanza',

> In between
> washing some nappies, preparing a lesson, kneading the bread
> and lambing a speckle-faced ewe,
> I stumbled over a poem; and now they spring up
> haphazard as mushrooms after August rain. (*LI*, p. 7)

Paradoxically, perhaps, the whole of Evans's oeuvre can be read as stemming from this early poetic retort to a writer who helped to affirm her sense of cultural and poetic separateness. In part, her challenge was issued on behalf of her local community: 'I actually wrote a whole collection [a set of unpublished pieces entitled *Call Us Peasants*], a poem a day, for a month, between Christmas and February 1976, and all of them about local people . . . as a riposte to his dour joyless Welsh peasants.' However, the unapologetically autobiographical lyric 'Bonanza', for Evans a key text in what we might want to call her poetic biography, the story of her journey into poetic expression, just as deliberately grounds a ripening poetic sensibility in the definitively female experience of motherhood. In her view, this poem

> deals with R. S. Thomas telling me more or less that what I thought about as a young woman was of no interest. It wasn't poetic enough. I would object to that. And when I did start writing, well, that poem is defiance isn't it?[54]

Arguably in fact, a quiet defiance still fuels a poetics which has never been reluctant to gender itself, still less fastidious about its interest in female sexuality and female-centred experience. In *Poetry Wales*'s 1987 'Symposium on Gender and Poetry', Evans retraces poetry's 'reaching-out towards narratives of ordinary lives' to the cultural influence of women: 'We have always been story tellers, users and developers of language to explain or while away tedious occupations.'[55] Like many of her generation, with the exception of more politically active and activist figures like Wendy Mulford and Menna Elfyn, say,

Evans is generally inclined to fight shy of political labels ('I wouldn't identify myself as a feminist'); nevertheless, she insists, 'Gender is important to me because I have a woman's body and the body is where we live'.[56] Intriguingly, indeed, for this writer it seems that female experience – whatever her twenty-first-century readers might think – specifically offers 'an extension of [poetic] subject matter', not least because 'the traditional role keeps a housewife/mother in touch with sensuous rather than cerebral reality, an environment with its own richnesses and satisfactions'.[57]

From the first, Evans's highly self-conscious poetic oeuvre has summoned that sensuous environment to a poetic process which is often more distant from the biography I have recounted here than it can sometimes seem, and not only in female-centred works like the long early poem 'Falling Back' ('about a woman *like* my sister'; author's emphasis), 'Mrs Crusoe' and 'Out Of Season'.[58] However, Evans frames the part played by gender in writing in typically scrupulous terms:

> I do write differently because I am female, influenced no doubt by hormonal rhythms and social conditioning (as I am by my working-class background and connections, by my physical surroundings and all the quirks of taste and temperament that make me who I am) but I don't accept that imagination is subject to limitations of gender. It can grope towards other species or states of being . . .[59]

She discovers a sometimes subversively regenerative power in the female imagination in particular (see 'Tree Wife', 'Meanwhile, In Another Part of the Island . . .', 'Whale Dream', and 'In Women's Thanatological'), although her own reading has taught her that that power is not always benevolent. Sylvia Plath, for example, 'I find both inspiring because of her use of language and very threatening because of her . . . flirting with death'.[60] The speaker of Evans's 'Winter Visiting' expels Plath's spectre in a series of parodic side-swipes at the older poet's imaginative menace:

> I must shake them out, your brilliance,
> Your stings. No, no, no—
> I cannot cope with you.
> Back into the cold you go. (*LI*, p. 18)

A more productive figure has been Gillian Clarke, whose work Evans encountered when her own first collection was being considered for publication 'It was a poem called "Babysitting" . . . I remember a sort of burning sensation because that was how I was trying to write.'[61] Dedicated to Clarke, the dream-like 'Between Waking' pays tribute to the 'steel-wimpled' Oracle-like figure at its heart:

> A lifetime's images of light
> drown between her eyes and mine.
>
> . . .
>
> A woman poet in a crystal cave.
> Silence and sootfall.
> A last eye being closed.
>
> I pray to find myself again
> between wakings. (*CP*, p. 18)

Although Evans has never overlooked or trivialised the significance of gender issues in her poetry, she equally resists the over-determination of her writing. She argues that while the question of gender may limit experience, it cannot be assumed to confine the energies of the imagination. Much like Clarke, in the heat of composing *Letter from a Far Country* and the powerful poems which followed it, Evans prefers to discern the effect of gender on poetic form, and specifically in her own and other women's inclination to treat experience 'not as disjointed phenomena but fragments of an organic and continuous whole'.[62] Thus, 'Weaning' equates a shaping poem with a newborn baby, its vigilant author, 'intent / lest any word should wake / stirring in the close warm quiet', absorbed in a physical process which is both maternal ('The fat of my life / is burnt up, suckling them. I am / all bone, charged') and self-nourishing: 'in myself, each time, / there is a minor alteration. / / It feels like growing' (*LI*, p. 27). The words replay the attentiveness for which Evans herself strives, in her effort 'to allow the poem to find its own shape, in contrast to ideas tacked down by end-rhyme, the relative safety of iambic pentameter, the linguistic games and deliberate technical constraints of much recent successful work'.[63] For Evans, it would seem that poetic expression offers a means of facilitating as well as charting self-growth, for all the undeniable mobility and contingencies which are enshrined in the human subject. Arguably this explains the poet's fondness for the 'fragment[ed]' but 'organic' textual space of the (long) lyric sequence, a form she has spent her career testing and refining.

Evans's most recent and most innovative foray into this aesthetic territory takes the self-consciously self-circling form of the long sequence 'Burning the Candle', published, like her very first book *Falling Back*, as a stand-alone volume. However, where its forerunner is exclusively given over to its long title poem, *Burning The Candle* juxtaposes with its seven-part, twenty-nine-page title sequence five further elements: the candid near-daily journal charting the poem's rapid genesis over the four week period in the late spring of 2007 leading up to the family's summer migration to Bardsey; the fourteen 'spin-off' poems which came into being along the way; a short manual-like closing section entitled '7 Steps: Or how I worked towards the long poem', apparently aimed at other practising but presumably less experienced writers; and a 'Selective Bibliography'. Although formal and thematic links might be made between it and any of the lyric sequences which Evans has produced, in the very self-consciousness of its multi-part construction *Burning The Candle* opens a newly performative textual space in Wales's contemporary poetics.

In theme as well as form, this work's closest forerunner is arguably *Cometary Phases* (1989), another seven-part free-verse sequence which traces the imperceptibly changing relationship between growing boy and watchful self-restraining mother against the vastness of the solar system they scan together for traces of the visiting Halley's Comet. The latter work shares much with *Burning the Candle* in its prizing and probing of the chaotically human in the apparently empirical domain of scientific knowledge and enterprise, a theme quietly confirmed in the chorus-like dream sequences which help regulate both poems. They find similarly common ground in the protective will to tease the personal out of the impersonal institutions and cyclical impulses (temporal and natural) which at once secure and threaten the special characteristics of human life and society. Both finally summon a troping vision in which apparent binaries like dark and light, flux and stasis, growth and death commingle and alter each others' effects and significations. Indeed, it is possible to read the reflective closing sections of the earlier poem, in which the speaker is left meditating, in her sleeping house, on her dying fire (one last ember turning to ash 'a moon-version of mothwing gold / a mineral incandescence'), as uncannily prefiguring the imaginative and philosophical terrain of the second sequence (*Cometary Phases*, p. 106).

The longer of the two sequences, *Candle* reaches thematically well beyond the daily miracle of human growth and development which galvanises *Cometary Phases*. The later text rummages both more widely and more inventively among the recalcitrant synthesising powers of the human intelligence; in the book's preface, Nigel Jenkins draws an analogy between the fluid modalities of what he calls an 'epic of the mind' and 'those of the symphony'.[64] More pertinent for me is the inescapably reflexive nature of a work the very architecture of which has the effect of calling its own aesthetic project relentlessly into question. The figures populating this accommodating text – whether the discreetly tragic muse-like presence of Betty, around the moment of whose death ('the light abruptly freezing in her eyes', p. 10) the whole poem is constructed, 'D' (Evans's 'gentle father') and an eclectic constellation of interlocutors including nineteenth-century scientist Michael Faraday, modernist poet David Jones, the poet David Constantine and the attentive tutor of the watercolour class – lend 'Burning the Candle' the kind of discursive but also importantly interrogative momentum at which Jenkins gestures, when he describes it as 'something of a pilgrimage'.[65]

In its deliberate trying of the uneasy frontier between writing and reading, ratifying as it mines its own textual disorderliness – the insouciant yoking of lyric to discursive voice, the ordinarily separate worlds of poetic utterance and review – this self-inspecting text quietly turns itself into a new kind of literary artefact. Grafting the critical apparatus of the working journal onto the lyric sections with which it converses, each a record of the other's slow gestation, Evans makes visible, physically teases out, the collaborative dialogue, the compact, on which – in this publishing format – each element's identity depends. The text's architecture thus stages, brings literally to light, the often hidden degree to which poem and critical reflection may intersect and fertilise each other in the creative process. In doing so, paradoxically Evans succeeds in both approving and troubling the assumption that any poetic – any aesthetic – construct can be adequately understood on anything other than its own (in this case manifestly, spatially/textually, complex) phenomenological terms. The paradoxes are played out in the negative theology which imbues the poem's title and the thematic resonances of its imaginative lodestone, the burning candle which propels us from the anti-climactic moment of Bessie's death, to Faraday's humanistic 'taper', to the atom bomb, to the 'sarcophagus' of Chernobyl, 'a monstrous melted candle stump' and its unnamed 'spacewalker' curators (p. 20), to the dying victims ('wicks', p.22) of the Stalinist Gulag, to the Tilley lamp and self-immolating moths of Evans's own bedroom in Bardsey, to the 'candling' of an egg in a primary school classroom, to the 'sunset flaring' across Bardsey Sound from the anchorite's window (p. 34).

The eponymous combusting candle provides an aptly creative/destructive figure for Evans's aesthetic project. The 'freezing' (p. 10) 'incandescence' (p. 36) in the dying Bessie's eyes is doubly catalysing, in generating the parallel, similarly cerebral, similarly (oxymoronically) energising and yet draining labour out of which poem and journal emerge, separately and together, and in turn the larger text which their dialogue constructs, compounds, and causes to spill out of its generic housings. As 'The Way Light Falls' puts it: 'Light binds all unconnected things / as in a full-made poem, a brimming-over / of everything we know and are' (p. 12). The words justify the central, focal presence of the scientist Michael Faraday, 'the blacksmith's son' who 'inspired me to begin with' (p. 60) with the aphoristic 'Man's life is like to a taper burning' (p. 44). Faraday, and his *The Chemical History of A Candle* (1861) which emerges among several contenders as perhaps the poem's most productive intertext, charge the book, first with the artless yet spiritual-seeming devotion to scientific practice ('He preached the candle's peaceful flame / as the surest safest way to knowledge', p. 18), and then, more poignantly, in the slow disintegration of his mental faculties in his last years:

> Forgetting in sequence, as we all do,
> until 'Red' was all that he could point to
> . . .
> I wonder if he was still held
> in the certainty of being saved: that death
> as he said once, was not extinguishing the light
> but putting out the candle in the dawn.
>
> The last coherent message in his notebook:
> 'Let the imagination go.' ('The Blacksmith's Son', *BtC*, p. 18)

In its wondering, unwavering respect for Faraday's final message, and in the endless questions threading through it, the poem (and its co-conspirator, the journal) remains exquisitely compelled by all that it cannot begin to know, about itself, its subject, its array of interlocutors and intertexts, and – metatextually – even the processes of its own genesis. Hence the importance of the dream sequences, and the many other moments – to which speaker and poem alike seem helplessly drawn – on which the unknowable impinges. This is why we find the sparking match, poised 'between twin points of vermilion', illumining the 'spell' – like nature of its own combustion:

> a focus glows –
> as if thought could gather to a quick –
> like the instant before the anaesthetic works
> to snatch consciousness away, that stretched second
> when you feel swirled towards the mystery. ('The Scritch of the Match', *BtC*, p. 27)

If this moment, coming in the later stages of the poem, is prefigured in the lecturing Faraday, bewitched by the confluence of being and dissolution in his own experiment ('the solid substance / flowing upward to the flame, / that, melted into fluid, still holds / itself together!'), it also betrays Evans's intensely humane interest in the anti-scientific 'mystery' which binds the apparently inanimate kindled taper – 'at its heart / a gleaming carbon ember, still unburned' (*BtC*, p. 17) – into surprising, even somehow impossible, relation with any form of sentient life. Thus the book's title proves powerfully metonymic of the contingent creative-and-critical dialogue/cross-hatching out of which *Burning the Candle* grows: the provisional, self-troubling, phatic processes of the poem and the journal's slow conjoined coalescence into being, and at the same time the philosophical knowledge that each betrays of its inevitable failure fully or authentically to represent those processes.

For these reasons, *Burning the Candle* (which proved difficult to publish) crosses a new kind of aesthetic and culturally-inflected frontier reminiscent of and consonant with the kinds of geopolitical frontier which Evans has long been exploring. Although the poem never belabours its bilingual cultural context, it does not overlook the enriching linguistic resources to which knowledge of Welsh gives access. The interaction of discursive with poetic, eroding the formal/aesthetic limits which circumscribe/define each, seems to me an aesthetic refraction of Evans's ongoing negotiations with the cultural domain in and out of which she writes. In the poem, the central image of Bessie's dying gaze is revived in the linguistic drama of the opening section's closing lines, circling back to 'that eyelight / hearth-fire, brain's last brightness / glittering in the pupils, its candles, / *canhwyllau llygaid*, quite snuffed out' (*BtC*, p. 11).[66] The journal reveals that this idea was in fact very late to develop; the serendipitous discovery of a beautifully apposite phrase seems to have occurred at the very end of the text's composition (*BtC*, p. 89).

It is in the consonance between journal and poem that the reader is offered a chance to decouple, mediate and/or sift Evans's expert, compassionate balancing of creative and discursive modes, as national and cultural agendas slip in and out of focus. For Gramich, Christine Evans's maturing poetics 'shift[s]; the voice of the poems becomes more securely that of a native, not an incomer'.[67] I take the opposite view, even if this writer's ever-fruitful sense of cultural alienation paradoxically seems only to have deepened her sense of affection for, and loyalty to, her awkwardly double, culturally resistant place of domicile:

> I do feel that coming to Wales has helped me to feel at home and develop a stronger sense of self. I don't identify myself as Welsh. I'm very proud of the fact that one side of my family is Welsh but it's not a qualification. . . . [T]he thing that Wales did more than anything else, apart from making me feel at home, was give me a sense of otherness. How do you define your sense of self unless you have something to measure it by?[68]

In 1972, not so long after the meeting which Evans records in 'Bonanza', the poet Harri Webb was moved to honour, without any apparent irony, R. S. Thomas who 'has given us a country in which it is necessary to be a man. I don't think we could ask for better guidance'.[69] In light of Webb's eulogy, Evans's abiding sense of suspicion 'towards community because I have never felt part of one', like her stringent complicating of the creative/poetic act in the genre-busting *Burning The Candle*, seems relevant to her equivocal, blurred sense of national context: 'To be honest I don't see myself as a Welsh writer. I don't really see myself as writing from within any community of poets . . . I write as I do because I am a woman and because I live where I do.'[70]

4

'A kind of authentic lie': Gwyneth Lewis's English-Language Sequences[1]

'Part of poetry's power is that it enables you, literally, to speak beyond your own ego.'[2]

In interview, Gwyneth Lewis has insisted: 'I don't think of myself as a "confessional" writer in poetry.'[3] Critics have long recognised the significance of the genre now known as life writing in Welsh literary culture. This chapter reads Lewis's resisting of the 'confessional' tag against her culturally sensitive deployment of the hybrid genre of the lyric sequence. Arguably, it is only in her often playful conflation and simultaneous dismantling of the boundaries between the 'real' and the 'represented' self, between the 'genuine' and the 'fake', or the truthful and the fictive, that Lewis can lay artistic claim to her own assertion that 'Poetry [is] about telling things as they are'.[4] Like so many of her peers, this proudly bilingual writer is acutely conscious that, in the bifurcated cultural-political and linguistic landscape of Wales, 'telling things as they are' can be complicated. In response, Lewis opts for what Hélène Cixous might call the 'deranging' (with the effect as the theorist also argues of a 'wonderful expansion') of the conventionally self-sufficient formal terrain of the lyric.[5] In her forging – the pun is apposite – of a generically hybrid, *self-protectively* in/authentic poetics, Lewis's exacting oeuvre enacts the 'ceaseless displacement' for which Cixous looks. In doing so, her work shares and refracts the determination of the other writers I have explored here to address the complexities of their own ethnographic situation in and through the aesthetic. As Cixous asserts, 'there is no invention possible . . . without there being in the inventing subject an abundance of the other, of variety . . . the springing up of selves one didn't know'.[6] In the grip of Lewis's fiercely creative intelligence, once again we find (as with both Bidgood and Evans, albeit at the same time rather differently from each of them) the uncertain formal terrain of the lyric sequence opening on to an undecideable kind of interpretative horizon, where richness of possibility – of verbal play and semantic manoeuvre, of geopolitical affiliation, of mobile subjectivity – is always what matters above all.

In 1999, Lewis suffered a bout of serious depression. The experience gave rise three years later to a book entitled *Sunbathing in the Rain: A Cheerful Book on Depression*. Part memoir, part journal, part self-help manual, this conversational and often very funny work remains, for all its generic uncertainties, a highly autobiographical piece of writing. At the same time, however, it retains a purposefully professional air, not least in its searching of the origins and faltering development of Gwyneth Lewis *poet*. Through this often fragmentary alternative narrative – unwinding within the more explicit story of a sensitive individual's psychological collapse and struggle towards self-restoration – the book artfully calls attention to the way in which a poetic identity can be understood to have been shaped and strengthened by its subject's life and experiences, while dramatising its own propensity to problematise and/or float free of those experiences. A sometimes searing account serves both to uncover and undermine the endless generative links between the two main spheres of any writer's existence: the private and the public. Above all, perhaps, it argues the self-consciousness of Lewis's creative imagination:

> For me, poetry has always been about looking at life from a slightly off-centre point of view. One day when I was still a toddler, my mother had left me asleep in my cot and was doing her housework downstairs. The phone rang and it was the neighbour who lived behind us telling her that I was out on the window ledge of the back bedroom.
>
> I had somehow managed to open the big window to our 1950s Wimpey house and was treading the slate ledge outside, looking in, arms and legs stretched out into an X against the glass . . . I've never lost the sense of magic about leaning out of a window and looking back into the room you've left. It gives the objects inside, which are suffused with your smell, and a part of your dream life, a new objectivity. For a fraction of a second, you're able to see your own life without yourself in it.
>
> That's what poetry has always been to me – a way of giving yourself a point of view outside your own seeing. (*SR*, pp. 41–2)

At once centralising and sidelining the diminutive watcher spread-eagled against the window, this fragment seems both to confirm and call into question the figure of the author and her life story in the shaping of a maturing poetics. The remarks about poetry which frame this retelling of the incident make it more resonant still. First, there are the creative implications of the self-inspecting process described and explained here, in which real and imaginary intensify, fuse with and come to transform each other: the 'magic' in which the realms of the intensely personal, both physical ('suffused with your smell') and interior ('your dream life'), are rendered transfiguringly 'new'. However, if this process revolves in some way around the central perceiving singular self, any over-determining of that perception is denied in the liminality of the window ledge, and the privileging of a 'point of view *outside* your own seeing'. If the process of writing poetry affords the poet some kind of intuitive access to her own 'life', the defamiliarised and defamiliarising position she adopts seems far from simplistically narcissistic; the signifier 'you' remains both intimately self-referential and invitingly compound. If the interior scene remains interesting primarily for having been inhabited by the newly departed perceiving 'you', the objects in view authenticatingly 'suffused with your smell', in fact only 'your' *absence* seems to guarantee that freshening perception its powerful 'new objectivity'. In a mischievous inversion of gaze theory, it is, therefore, the *vacancy* left by the watcher's own recent presence which somehow comes equivocally to represent the colonised and colonising subject of creative, desiring preoccupation.

Holding as it does then and now, safety and danger, ordering/limiting presence and absence (dream) in creative equilibrium, the anecdote seems to conceive poetic utterance in particular as a peculiarly indeterminate process: in the simplest analysis it is '*about* looking'; later it becomes '*a way of* giving'. Each construction inscribes poetic articulation as active and open ended. Indeed, as a whole, like the excerpt, *Sunbathing* persistently reveals life writing as a richly uncertain and performative genre, self-consciously constructing as much as it 'confesses', or – from another angle – refusing as much as it promises.

Poetry as fabrication: 'How to Knit a Poem'

In the 1980s, Lewis was at Oxford, doing doctoral work on eighteenth-century forgery. 'I discovered that "forgery" was a highly politicised term in the period, a way of labelling ideas as beyond the pale. Basically if you liked an idea it was genuine, if you didn't it must be "forged".'[7] During a period of incipient crisis, as she battled a growing drink problem, Lewis was also seeking with increasing urgency to construct a stable and stabilising sense of poetic identity for herself:

> The irony of my preoccupation with authenticity didn't strike me at the time. My fascination with distinguishing between the genuine and the fabricated must, however, have been the echo of an internal struggle. What kind of poetry should come out of me? Was there a genuine Gwyneth? Which parts of me could be said to be fake? (*SR*, p. 149)

Implicitly, these words suggest that biography and creative – or professional – maturation are productively synergistic. The remarks embed an emergent poetics so deeply in the author, via the intimate signifier of her first name, that each seems to authenticate the other. The 'genuineness' of the one who claims to be a poet appears to reflect and be reflected in the writing which claims to be poetry. 'Genuine' or 'fake' – however problematic those terms begin to seem – the 'Gwyneth' of the extract ends up apparently constructed and authorised primarily in and by the poetry 'com[ing] out of [her]', and vice versa.

The 'internal struggle' Lewis describes refers to the agonising decision facing her youthful self: which of her two native languages to deploy in her poetry. In typically vivid prose, this accomplished poet has explained:

> I was brought up speaking a language which predates the Roman invasion of Britain. When I'm frightened I swear in ancient Brythonic idioms. Yet I'm a city dweller, and surf the net using the language of the Saxons who pushed the Welsh into the hills of western Britain in the sixth century.[8]

In interview, she has clarified the literary import of the linguistic confusions stemming from her own background:

> I remember visiting North Wales in that period and being told by a Welsh speaker that I wasn't Welsh because I came from South Wales. And I wanted to be a poet. Now that was *devastating* . . . But it's only been recently that bilingualism has been accepted as a benign condition . . . It's still regarded in some quarters as a betrayal of the Welsh language, because immediately you enter into a relationship with the English, it's taking the place of the Welsh.[9]

More courageously, then, than it might at first seem, Lewis eventually resolved her dilemma by opting for what she cheerfully calls 'a double life', wielding both languages ('Both English and Welsh are so delightful, how could I choose between them?') in a poetics which has been appraising and interrogating the cultural legacy of Wales from both sides of its linguistic divide ever since.[10] Elsewhere, she has remarked more soberly, 'It's impossible to overestimate how important Welsh-language poetry has been for my work'; in the same interview, she observes that bilingualism

> has given me a crash course in the nature of language, its limits and the incredible distances we can travel in it, against all expectations. I've never got over the feeling that writing in two languages is a hazardous activity, culturally and psychologically. But this lack of comfort might be a big asset for a poet.[11]

Much as *Sunbathing* promises, Lewis's poetry can frequently be found addressing materials which plainly seem to derive from her own life experiences: the decline into alcoholism ('The Hedge'), the loss of a sister-in-law to cancer ('Zero Gravity'), the cultural and linguistic tensions inscribed in a sense of Welsh identity and background ('Welsh Espionage') and perhaps most intimately of all the experience of therapeutic psychiatric treatment for depression ('Keeping Mum') are among the elements of her own biography to find their way into a spiritedly inclusive oeuvre. Yet, for all that they seem driven by what 'Welsh Espionage' ambiguously calls 'the terrible urge to tell it all. / Yes, the treason of telling it all', the same poems tirelessly extend and extemporise upon such materials until their sources come to seem barely if at all discernible (*CA*, p. 41).

In some ways, 'treachery' emerges as the keynote of Lewis's assured if uncomfortably equivocal poetics, always charged by its invitingly dangerous sense of the productively dialectical and contingent relation between truth/authenticity and the fictive/forged. *Sunbathing* warns that 'Depression is a disease of the imagination. This means that the depressive suffers from a faulty mechanism in the way he or she pictures reality, is a forger of his or her own life.' The same work argues, however, that '[the writing] process requires you to abandon your fictions and face up to your own truths . . . What works in poetry is the truth.' But the doctoral student seems unable to resist noting that 'Forgeries sometimes tell the truth, though they're not authentic in themselves'. Thus while Lewis will concede that 'Writing helps me understand my life', she is also careful to warn her readers that 'it's not a cheap form of therapy'.[12] The fact that recent re-evaluations of so-called 'confessional' poetry might concur bears interestingly upon her own poetically self-conscious troubling of the distinctions between authentic and forged, or 'genuine' and 'fabricated'.

Working in the wake of Leigh Gilmore and others, Jo Gill rehearses how the discourse of confessional poetics has long relied on the reductive assumption, first made by M. L. Rosenthal, that the 'I' of the confessional lyric unvaryingly represents that of its typically unfortunate author.[13] Not a little of this delimiting presumption has survived to the present day, as Jo Shapcott has rather resentfully complained:

'People expect poets to write about themselves and their history. Even when it's not about you, they'll read your poem as if it is. Novelists are allowed to make things up and take things anywhere they want.'[14] Reflecting on the 'post-humanist development of a diverse and challenging range of critical theories and practices', Gill's skilful recuperation of the extraordinary poetic oeuvre left by Sylvia Plath's friend and fellow American Anne Sexton – like Plath herself widely considered a central figure of the so-called 'confessional' school of poetry – argues the case for the critical overhauling of 'confessionalism as a whole'. In her own belatedly 'full and fair' treatment of Sexton's work, Gill boldly reproves the unself-conscious authoritarianism of the pathologising frameworks by which a deeply self-referential poetry has hitherto been confined. Readily untethered from its problematically circumspect author, as Gill's scholarship proves, Sexton's writing takes on a fresh and powerful contingency:

> Throughout [her writing] Sexton deflects critical emphasis from an evaluation of the putative authenticity of the confessional voice to an understanding of its potential inauthenticity – its tangentiality to the poet's subjective experience. Yet in a supreme double bluff, having established the equal validity of confessional truth and confessional artifice (the autobiographical and persona 'I's), Sexton undercuts the reliability of this distinction, suggesting that . . . [t]ruth and artifice are not so much equally valid as equally equivocal, and her own authority to determine such questions about her own work, her own value as witness, are thrown into doubt.[15]

The performative nature of confession underpins an account which cheerfully acknowledges its debts to Gilmore's triangulation of lyric speaker, text and reader, in her influential study of autobiography and female self-representation (1994). As Gilmore observes, 'One *confesses* in order to tell the *truth*'. Neatly, she theorises truth 'as a conceptual problem that may be addressed . . . through an apparatus of truth production: the legal or spiritual confession or testimonial, the presentation of evidence, the specialised form of . . . questioning'.[16] This definition echoes Michel Foucault, whose detailed unpacking of confession as ritual ('generated and sustained . . . by the discursive relationship between speaker, text and reader – penitent, confession and confessor') Gill borrows to demonstrate Sexton's transgressively self-conscious awareness of 'the fictive nature of confession', and powerful 'sense of her own writing self as constructed and artificial'.[17]

The history of critical disdain for 'confessional' writing with which Gill is contending explains why a generation of women poets like

Lewis have sought so earnestly to resist the reductive conflation of the lyric 'I' and its author and evade the indictment of narcissism. Among Lewis's most explicitly self-referential works, the lyric sequence 'How to knit a poem' reflects suggestively on Gill's dismissal of traditional readings of the confessional voice of poetry (*ST*, pp. 46–54). Completed late in 2006 and broadcast in the UK on BBC Radio 4 just before Christmas, as its title promises this poem teases out and examines the nature of the parallels between the writing of a poem and knitting. (When she wrote the sequence, Lewis was herself an enthusiastic but still relatively inexperienced knitter.) The title poem opens the twelve-part sequence by revealing, with impudent self-consciousness, that

> The whole thing starts with a single knot
> And needles. Word and pen. Tie a loop
> In nothing. Look at it. Cast on, repeat
>
> The procedure till you have a line
> That you can work with.
> It's pattern made of relation alone,
>
> Patience, the rhythm of empty bights
> Create a fabric that can be worn,
> If you're lucky, practised. Never too late
>
> To catch dropped stitches, each hole a clue
> To something that's bothering you,
> I link mine with ribbons, pretend
>
> I meant them to happen. You make a net
> Of meaning to carry round
> Mindfully . . . ('How to Knit a Poem', *ST*, p. 46)

To begin with, this text suggests that what the poet/poem prizes most about both knitting and composing poetry is the way that each contrives by the very processual nature of its fabrication to transform absence into presence, effectively by the process of knotting or patterning alone, in such a way that 'empty bights / Create a fabric'. Telling the story of its own gradual genesis, the text itself dwells rather disingenuously at the same time on the inexplicitly rewarding demands that its gradual emergence makes upon the author/knitter: 'each hole a clue / To something that's bothering you'. Disingenuous because, of course, while the poet/knitter is clearly profoundly implicated in the bothersome 'something' under construction, these words also recall very powerfully the pressures exerted by this, and indeed by any poetic text, upon its reader. After all, the text depends for its continuing existence and identity, let alone its poetic and conceptual validities, upon persuading its reader into a special and highly self-aware kind of hermeneutic activity, into knowingly participating – through the desirous act of reading – in its authorship, in its making of its own story: in the production of its truths. Thus, in a 'you' which accommodatingly conflates poet/author, knitter and reader, the poem collapses the distinctions between those categories: each is turned simultaneously into an investigator of linguistic inference, reading into and filling out, from their very differently informed perspectives, the 'empty bights' comprising the textual 'fabric' which is being literally woven, *fabricated*, before our very eyes. An almost theatrical emphasis is placed on the self-fashioning nature of poetic 'truth production', which takes shape literally in this poem as 'a net / Of meaning' founded upon 'pattern made of relation alone' and realised formally in the airy arrangement of its seven sometimes rhyming sometimes para-rhymed (proestic) tercets.

Lyric sequence as cultural artefact: 'Welsh Espionage'

'How to Knit a Poem' dramatises the narrative potential of the poetic text partly by constructing the lyric sequence, to which it acts as an acutely self-aware preface, as an ongoing process in which the reader is insistently and inescapably implicated. Remarking, guilelessly, that 'It's the kind of work / That keeps you together. The armpit's tight', the poem turns coyly but not unironically to the reader in conclusion: 'But tell me honestly: How do I look?' (*ST*, p. 46). If nothing else, in this disarmingly intimate close – a direct invitation which explicitly frustrates, to tweak Frank Kermode's inimitable phrase, any 'sense of [the] ending' we may have expected, chiefly by pointing us on into the narrative body of the ensuing sequence – the poem reflexively flaunts the narratistic tendencies which undermine, open up and complicate its lyric status.

M. L. Rosenthal, Roland Greene and others have argued that the special attribute of the lyric sequence is its suggestive problematising of its own generic nature, blurring the boundaries between narrative and lyric. As Greene notes, in the first place the form at once reinforces and complicates the defining singularity and experiential coherence traditionally inscribed in the lyric text. It both 'enables the sensation of enacting a lyric utterance as if it were our own speech', and yet at the same time its structural multiplicities ensure that 'its polyvocal realization, its spatiality, its patchworking of heterogeneous fragments . . . contribut[e] to a composite fiction'.[18] For Lewis, the very linearity inherent in the form's sequentiality turns out to be significant: '

> Every book is a sequence. I construct it like that. It's important to me that there should be a logic from the beginning of a book to the end of it . . . The sequence is my kind of pacing, if you like . . . And it's quite a self-conscious thing. I plan it.

Even then, in a revealing endorsement of Greene's second point, she goes on to admit: 'I don't know exactly where I'm going to end up. Usually I know how long it's going to be, and I do know what's going to happen, but I don't know consciously. So it's quite an adventure really.'[19]

In part, of course, the prodigality which Greene emphasises derives from the spaciousness of the sequence, in which the textual 'bights' comprising the whole work, whether stanza section or part, are both linked and yet remain separate, punctuated by the spaces and sometimes numerals or titles which mark them off like chapters in a novel. As we have already seen in sequences written by Christine Evans and Ruth Bidgood, and as Lewis's own comments themselves imply, the spaciousness of the sequence above all affords the poet a peculiar textual licence: sequentiality makes for a formal control which permits flux even non-linearity, if necessary, within fixity. Textual constraints and patterns can be restricted to the smaller units of organisation – lines and stanzas – or scaled up, extending into the conventional economies and ordering of the (ostensibly lyric) part or section, and even beyond into the larger structural space of the whole sequence. In an interesting reading of 'Cofiant', a powerful sequence by Lewis's contemporary, the anglophone Welsh poet Gillian Clarke, Michael Thurston confirms that the text's elongated but self-interrupting form 'offers at once a greater scope and duration than the single lyric and the continual complication of the lyric's closure effects'.[20]

Thurston's example is significant partly for its cultural focus. Clarke is today one of Wales's most influential and highly regarded literary figures; and, much like Lewis, the work of the elder poet has from the first testified to her creative enjoyment of the lyric sequence.[21]

Interestingly, Lewis retraces her own lengthy preoccupation with the genre to having 'learned to write poetic sequences in English by composing Welsh-language *pryddestau* [long poems not in the strict metres]'.[22] This habit was instilled by the poetry competitions held in the annual Welsh-language festival of culture and arts known as the National Eisteddfod:

> It started off because the Eisteddfod competition quite often demands a sequence. So you would be set a sequence of 200 lines on the subject of energy or increasing, or melody or whatever . . . It was quite interesting. You learn suddenly how to start constructing a long poem. I never won any of those prizes, but I did learn how to take a long breath and pace myself.[23]

An instructive discussion by the English-language poet Gladys Mary Coles corroborates and elaborates on the connection that Lewis implicitly makes here between the sequence as a poetic form and the creative traditions of her native culture. Arguing that 'classification [of] "narrative" is often understood and applied too narrowly', Coles herself draws a distinction between narrative 'which is chronological [and] linear in its story-progression, and the kind which is not '"story-led" [but] non-linear, oblique in its development'. Pertinently she notes that 'particularly in Welsh poetry, narrative has tended to be non-direct, oblique rather than linear', reflecting a generic inclination which she reads as linking Wales's ancient poetic history – 'the earliest bards, the *Cynfeirdd*' – with its newest literary inheritors, through 'traditions which today are perpetuated (consciously or unconsciously) in the work of [contemporary] Welsh poets writing in English'.[24]

Her own background having left her sharply sensitised to the complexities of cultural identification, Lewis appears to scent cultural as well as creative opportunity in the 'non-linear, oblique' narrative space of the lyric sequence. Appearing almost exactly halfway through her very first English-language collection *Parables and Faxes* (1995), 'Welsh Espionage' is one of her most explicitly political early poems. From the outset this slippery text constructs cultural identity as an elusive and frustratingly – which is also to say enfranchisingly – secretive terrain. In what purports to be an investigative commentary the poem's eleven separate lyrics can be read, in part through the deflections on which they all depend, as problematising the very idea of any territorially, historically and/or linguistically fixed or definable version of Welshness. On the face of it, the sequence is a fractured version of a quest narrative, mediated and complicated by a series of different perspectives: the apparently but not necessarily consistent 'I' of the speaker who introduces and concludes the sequence both inheres and is dissolved in the second- or third-person voice in use elsewhere in the poem. These shifts in perspective render the political stance of an already fractured text still less certain; they also heighten an increasingly oppressive atmosphere of what is often sexual suspicion. The apparently sanguine lover/partner of the opening poem is slow to adopt the interrogative stance of the dreams rehearsed in the poem; the final line's crucial question ('Tell me now, darling, whom did you betray?') does not seem rhetorical even if it remains unanswered (*CA*, p. 41).

Lewis has herself revealed that 'Fiddling with words has always been the most natural way for me to respond to life, as it gives me an added perspective on my problems, a view which is wider than my own' (*SR*, p. xix). It is partly her determination to preserve and protect that breadth of perspective which prompts her to understand language as inscribing threat as well as opportunity. In 'Welsh Espionage' the parading of language's subtly self-protective nature, particularly its capacity to insulate against as well as instigate and register cultural change, seems no more surprising than the poem's carefully recondite air. The work frames at its centre a text in which the gaps and slippages inherent in language emphatically frustrate any over-determining of cultural identity. The much anthologised section V boldly reads into a secretive language lesson a form of cultural abuse, not least in the tensions to which it gives rise:

> Welsh was the mother tongue, English was his.
> He taught her the body by fetishist quiz,
> father and daughter on the bottom stair:
> dy benylin yw *elbow*, dy wallt di yw *hair*
> . . .
> Each part he touched in their secret game
> thrilled as she whispered its English name.
>
> The mother was livid when she was told. (*CA*, p. 43)

The child is left understandably conflicted: 'Was it such a bad thing to be Daddy's girl?'[25]

The materials of this crucial poem – which I also touched on in chapter 1 – plainly originate in the poet's own childhood experience: as she has explained in more than one source, she remembers learning English in exactly this way from her father when her mother was hospitalised for the birth of her younger sister.[26] Partly as a result, however, and read on a larger scale – amid the formal satisfactions of an ironically showy array of perfectly achieved rhyme-schemes – the 'story' of the sequence as a whole offers little in the way of reassurance about how far language can simplify or distil the links between culture and identity. In a sense, instead, the text reproaches the pressures placed on Lewis herself to privilege one of her native languages (Welsh) over the other (English) in her poetry. In interview she muses, 'I don't think it works that way, in poetry certainly. It seems to me that linguistic inventiveness is stimulated by the rubbing together of two languages. And the more you do of both the better.'[27]

Arguably, then, Lewis is speaking for poetic as well as socio-historical culture when she confides: 'I am fascinated by the ways in which the language we speak guides the way we think, but I'm very resistant to that conditioning, always wanting us to be broader beings than our culture allows us to be.'[28] Textually, linguistically and – as it turns out, even culturally – commodious, the sequential lyric gives this dynamic poet the means of unsettling any fixed or proscriptive sense of selfhood and identity partly in the interdependence of freedom and discipline it enshrines:

> It's like making a documentary film; . . . the trick of it always is to get a narrative like a thread through a labyrinth so you can follow it, but then hang your metaphorical observations from that line . . . And quite a lot of the time you don't know what the hell you're doing while you're doing it.[29]

Echoing the central conceit of a poem in which the figure of the fictional detective is continually reconfigured, these remarks seem only to confirm that for Lewis it is at least partly the very nature of sequential composition, in all the generic indeterminacies it foregrounds, which seems to kick-start and help stimulate the generative and somehow ungovernable interaction between known and unknown in her poetry. She has said:

> the reason I like sequences is that narrative provides an anchor for . . . alterations of perspective and, therefore, a safe place from which to shape-shift. I never quite know where I'm going to end up, which is both frightening and, creatively, very worthwhile.[30]

Again recalling the anecdote in *Sunbathing*, the form seems to afford a way (a 'technique') of holding safety and threat, stasis and variety, known and unknown, in a productive (*truthful*) tension.

Language and silence: 'Keeping Mum'

The urge to understand or, to put it slightly differently, the determination to gain 'a point of view outside your own seeing', seems always to have been central to a poetic imagination which, 'Welsh Espionage' hints, takes a self-conscious interest in its own hermeneutic potential. In fact, the synecdochic trope of detection, and its cognates – crime, villain, victim, detective, and the collection and processing of evidence and clues (all, to echo Foucault, Gilmore and Gill, 'techniques for producing truth') – are everywhere in play in Lewis's work. *Sunbathing* is itself constructed as its author reflects

> almost like a police investigation: 'Every serious episode of depression is a murder mystery. Your old self is gone and in its place is a ghost . . . Your job is to find out which part of you has died and why it had to be killed.' In it I recounted as honestly as I could the emotional history which had led me to such a terrible impasse.[31]

Sunbathing's often unsparing investigation of Lewis' own psychodramas repeatedly connects depression with the activity of writing poetry. Indeed, the poet's illness has left her convinced that, like a kind of latter-day negative capability, it is 'essential' to writing,

> if by depression, you mean the feeling of not knowing the meaning of anything . . . You need to look at the world out of focus for a while in order to see it in a new fresh way when it finally resolves into a clear image . . . This not knowing, far from being an enemy to writing, is the guarantor of its quality. (*SR*, p. 195)

The 'new fresh way' of seeing which she savours here reopens the complex web of creative and aesthetic relations between author and text, life and writing, and the generative intersection of what is 'there' – is one might say 'clear', in focus, even 'genuine' – and what is permissively not. As the anecdote in *Sunbathing* warns, this extends of course to the construction of selfhood.

Lewis's discovery, in poetry, of the power 'to speak beyond her own ego' validates her figuring of the author as *ingenue*, a kind of self-surprisingly naive reader.[32] Conversely, however, she also uncovers in an Iser-like reader an ungovernably multiplicitous and independent-minded authorial force with its own complex ways of re/conceiving the poetic utterance. To some extent this is why Lewis's readers are rarely encouraged to construct the 'truths' they find themselves hunting in her poems as singular or stable: the clues and codes inscribed in her texts prove endlessly and powerfully contingent. In fact, partly in their vulnerability to manipulation, misinterpretation and/or reinterpretation (in 'How to Knit a Poem' the speaker disguises mistakes in order to 'pretend / I meant them to happen'), the kinds of truths fabricated in Lewis's poetry invariably demand to be understood as provisional, shifting and arbitrary.

Lewis's third major collection, *Keeping Mum* was published in 2003, a year after *Sunbathing in the Rain.* The second of the volume's three constituent works, the title-sequence is positioned immediately after 'The Language Murderer' (subtitled 'A Police File'), an English-language version of Lewis's famous Welsh-language poem, *Y Llofrudd Iaith*, which appeared in 1999. Like its Welsh forerunner, 'The Language Murderer' is a poetic whodunnit set, as its prologue recounts, 'in a West Wales village, where an old lady, my embodiment of the Welsh language, has been found dead'. In theme and title the sequence, therefore, explicitly and literally bespeaks Lewis's fears for the survival of her first language. She describes 'having seen my grandparents' village changing from being virtually monoglot Welsh to being a rural community [with] more in common with the Lake District or the Yorkshire Dales than with its own past in the Cambrian Mountains. If the language is dying', she goes on in this very candid preface to one of her most significant collections, 'it seems important to know who or what killed it' (*CA*, pp. 143–4).

According to its preface, then, 'The Language Murderer' is predicated upon the author's own compulsion to know 'who and what' to blame for a linguistic dereliction which implicitly presages catastrophic cultural decline and dissolution. The preface goes on: 'The prospect of losing a whole culture is an existential nightmare for a Welsh-speaker, fraught with questions of one's own responsibility in preserving collective values without becoming a parrot for the past' (*CA*, p. 143). The reluctance to 'parrot' can explain the shifts and slippages of a poem in which, just as Ruth McElroy remarks of its Welsh precursor, 'Lewis appropriates the detective genre only to demonstrate once again her reluctance to solve any problem for once and for all'.[33] In the English version, the voice of the (half-Japanese half-Welsh) investigating detective weaves in and out of the contesting stories of a cast of witnesses, mostly made up of the victim's neighbours, friends and relatives, each of whom represents, as convention demands, a plausible villain. As the poem's multiplicitous 'I' slips and slides confusingly between speakers, their different testimonies (each one staging a kind of cultural confession in and of itself) vie for attention. As the first of these simultaneously self-revealing and self-concealing lyrics, the playfully self-conscious 'A Poet's Confession' makes an appropriately uncertain opening for an almost promiscuously undecideable text:

> 'I did it. I killed my mother tongue.
> I shouldn't have left her
> there on her own.
> All I wanted was a bit of fun
> with another body
> but now that she's gone—
> it's a terrible silence.
>
> . . .
>
> Without her reproaches.
> I feel so numb,
> not free, as I'd thought . . .
>
> Tell my lawyer to come.
> Until he's with me,
> I'm keeping mum.' (*CA*, p. 146)

A complex text begins conversationally *in medias res*, in self-consciously direct (but as its speech marks warn also, like all the lyrics in this sequence, reported) speech, with a silence it invites us disconcertingly and enfranchisingly to fill; in time-honoured fashion, this detective story provides its readers with a mystery to solve. At the same time, however, this sequence is far from the straightforward whodunnit it pretends to be partly because it opens with this 'confession'. In a sense as a result, this narrative is constructed in reverse: it starts by anticipating its own denouement: our pre-existing knowledge of both the (poet) perpetrator and the motive ('fun') undercuts the narrative impulse. And yet this so-called confession could hardly be less satisfactory; as it continues, the text – like the rest of the sequence it initiates – simultaneously mocks and exploits both our sense of knowledge and our desire to know more, partly in subsiding into a silence which is as open-endedly permissive as it is incriminating. If in its duplicitously confessional nature the poem recalls the figure of Anne Sexton in more than one way, 'The Language Murderer' remains preoccupied with the problematic even treacherous ways in which nation and selfhood appear to converge and conflate in language, not least in the metonymic trope of the 'mother-tongue'.

Inevitably, given its central trope, the links between gender and language combine in the chief emphases running through the sequence's eleven constituent lyrics, identified this time by title. Recounted apparently by the victim's daughter, in faintly defensive but also shame-faced mood, 'Home Cooking' offers a superbly double-edged perspective on domesticity, a theme Lewis rarely treats ('Well you see my experience of domesticity is that it is dangerous').[34] In its oblique reconstruction of the 'Welsh Mam', the poem both celebrates and reproves a model of female domestication it finds dismayingly untrustworthy. The text is worth quoting in full:

> I thought she was magic. Like the time
> we went to pick *llysiau duon bach*
> up on the mountain. I rolled the fruit
> carefully between finger and thumb,
> pleased with the patina that made them look
> like mineral berries sweated out
> of bitter bedrock. I heard a shout
>
> and my mother said she'd see us back
> at the house. We were ling-di-long,
> stopped at the quarry to throw stones . . .
> When we got in, a cooling rack
> held two steaming pies, the washing-up done.
> I was stunned and couldn't work out
> how her time had gone slower. 'Short cut,'
>
> they told me. But a lift
> was the real answer. Then I knew
> that mothers didn't live in straight lines.
> Her world was folded, she had a gift
> for swiftness, sweetness and for telling lies.
> My faith in directness was undermined.
> I was always the plodder, a long way behind. (*CA*, p. 150)

Here, if motherhood is admired it is also wryly problematised; language ends up as a tool for producing half-truths which seem despite their 'magic' more troubling than inspirational. A cultural conspiracy which constructs women as effortlessly effective both condemns them to home and hearth, and implicates them in a disturbingly broad culture-wide replication of that dangerously fabricated version of female experience and 'women's time': 'My faith in directness was undermined.'

Amid its many provisionalities, 'The Language Murderer' exposes the generative way in which Lewis's richly conflicted sense of cultural identity leads her to question even as she savours the powers of language. Like all the poems in this sequence, 'Home Cooking' and 'A Poet's Confession' implicitly acknowledge in female silence an ironically powerful creative and controlling force. In 'Aphasia' the mismatch of words and meaning transforms linguistic expression into a disconcerting but somehow liberatingly distorted mirror image of itself: 'my mind's a junk shop of where I've been. / I'll never know now what I really mean' (*CA*, p. 155). Like the vernacular hybrid 'ling-di-long' of 'Home Cooking', the very phrase 'keeping mum' reiterates language's uncanny ability both to register and trope human experience. The closing lines of 'A Poet's Confession' are retrieved in *Keeping Mum*'s title sequence. This overarching literally 'intertextual' sequentiality both links and separates 'The Language Murderer' and 'Keeping Mum' in a replay of their own serially fragmented interior structures. Thus the two longer poems themselves both combine in and complicate a larger fragmented poetic narrative of Lewis's ever-extending problematising of her sense of cultural identity.

In keeping with this narrative trajectory, the eponymous second section of *Keeping Mum* (subtitled 'Memoirs of a Psychiatrist') picks up on the theme of language as simultaneously abused and abusive, which both 'Welsh Espionage' and 'The Language Murderer' explore. This extension of that theme represents, as Lewis's preface warns, 'a more radical recasting of the original detective story and a meditation on mental illness and language'. She goes on: 'Therapy's based on the premise that an accurate description of a situation releases the patient from being neurotically bound to it' (*CA*, p. 144). In this sense, then, a sequence that is almost double the length of the preceding one, and this time features just two voices, becomes at once an account – a poetically reconfigured textual representation – of an analytical treatment (via the notes and tapes which constitute the medical 'narrative' of the treatment process), and the analytical process itself. In another echo of Sexton's reflexively self-analytical poetics, as the preface promises, one of the poem's voices is that of an anonymised but apparently male doctor-analyst, 'a psychiatrist in a mental hospital, investigating how abuses of language had led to his patients' illnesses' (ibid.). The other belongs to his apparently Welsh female patient, most of whose lyrics are labelled 'Case Tapes' in a discreet superscript. (The register of her voice alters, aptly, when the tag changes: 'Finding the Bodies' is labelled 'Dream Work' while 'A Question' is tagged 'Case Notes', *CA*, pp. 163, 171).

One effect of the poem's radically narrowed palette is to intensify the connections between the two central characters (who mostly take it in turns to speak) and their self-transforming author; however, it also helps to underline the distance between all three. As self-investigating author, Lewis herself both is and is not the psychiatrist whose professional and emotional maturation arcs through the sequence. Having herself undergone psychiatric analysis and therapy she has a similarly uncertain relationship with the surely Dora-like patient 'Miss D', whose eventual death either coincides with, or follows, her doctor's retirement. (Lewis's married name is Davies.) Finally, then, in the quasi-narrative of the twenty lyrics making up the sequential process of the encounters through which we are obliquely invited to read and/or investigate her (and Wales's) own problematically dual cultural situation, Lewis emerges as both analysand and analyst, both subjectively bound into and yet freed by her professional objectivity from the abused and abusive nature of language in mediating cultural identity. Thus Lewis discreetly seems both to participate in and yet firmly distances, even absents, herself from the sequential conversation between the text's two (apparently conventional) central lyric voices. Overall, the whole sequence constructs a kind of four-way dialogue, implicating poet and reader alongside the principal characters, in which the convergent, overlapping themes of self-expression or self-representation and silence, truth and lies are simultaneously encoded and interrogated.

Figured in common as perpetrators, victims and investigators of the 'abuses' at issue, both of the (textual) speakers in this sequence savour and fear the ironically expressive potential of silence in equal measure. Early on, the physician confides in complacent-seeming couplets, 'my main job is to translate / pain into tales they can tolerate / / in another language' (*CA*, p. 160). In one of the poems, 'A Teenage Craze', Miss D recounts how a game with a new 'Englie' schoolfriend suddenly 'turned into strangling me / / for treason' (*CA*, p. 165). Recalling this event, the apparently guileless 'Welshie' almost triumphantly reports how, with the unfortunate victim in extremis unexpectedly her English torturer's 'nerve failed her. I was nearly dead. / But I was the one with the rush to the head'. For the consummately professional speaker of 'Psychiatrist

Twitcher', meanwhile, silence is excitingly powerful for altogether different reasons:

> You have to be patient, because speech is shy,
> won't come if you're noisy,
> or keep asking why.
>
> I use my silence as a khaki hide.

On the other hand the analyst is disconcerted to find his power reversed when he suddenly senses a hidden stalker:

> the glint of an eye
> . . .
> in here, with me.
>
> What is this presence that dares give chase
> and me, a doctor? My most dangerous case. (*CA*, p. 170)

Just as his adopting of silence in a professional context confirms and endorses his skill and sense of responsibility as a medical practitioner, so in disguise (the punning on 'hide' must surely be deliberate) the physician is ruthlessly disclosed in all his own vulnerably fragmented subjectivity.

In the overturning of the delicate power relations mutually constructing and thus binding together doctor and patient that 'Keeping Mum' effects, the process of analysis (as 'a technique for producing truth') is made to seem inherently but also generatively unreliable. The two figures/voices begin to seem to converge and merge. The duplicate processes of self-representation in which each is profoundly involved (through the therapeutic treatment itself) are revealed as inherently unreliable, mixing truth and fiction, genuine and fabricated. Similarly, the speakers' apparently distinct hermeneutic roles – nominally, as truth seeker and truth teller – are exposed as mutually insecure, and converge and collapse, again productively, into one another.

Arguably both 'The Language Murderer' and 'Keeping Mum' are suffused by and refract Lewis's personal, often very intimate history, even as they 'fictionalise' and 'objectify' it. That is to say, in their very different ways, each text discreetly depicts the author looking back in at a (perhaps composite) version of her culturally located 'self', a presence still somehow haunting a room she has just vacated. In this way, in the wake of 'Welsh Espionage', the two later sequences together end up retailing – or demonstrate, much as Sexton's poetry does, 'a technique for producing' – an overarching set of cultural truths, mediated as readily through silence as utterance and in which the knowable and the unknowable exist alongside each other in endless productive tension, in a kind of aptly unreliable narrative about the provisional and shifting relationship between language and identity. Such truths seem, complexly, the more authentic for being fictionalised, rendered uncertain and unstable, and authored – authorised – as much by the reader as its elusive-seeming author. Hovering in this fruitful way between fact and fiction, between different lyric voices, and between narrative and lyric genres, all three sequences foreshadow and summon 'How to Knit a Poem', in suggestively adumbrating authentic/genuine and fabricated/forged in both the textual (poetic) construct and the reading experience. In interview Lewis 'confessed' to me, amusedly: 'You see it's all about performance. Poetry is a kind of authentic lie. It's a pretend but it's not a pretend.'[35] Elsewhere she has conceded: 'my prose has turned out to be very revealing of my personal life, which has rather blown my cover. I suppose it's all there in code in the poetry.'[36]

5

Traverses: Gillian Clarke, Christine Evans, Catherine Fisher and Ireland/Wales

'Story, however (re)defined and (re)constructed, is a precondition of agency.'[1]

Ireland's geographical proximity to Wales underpins a cultural closeness – John Kerrigan calls it 'interpenetration' – which has long been recognised by scholars of Celtic history, if rather less readily by literary critics.[2] In a public lecture hosted by the Wales-Ireland Research Network in Cardiff in May 2008, Gwyneth Lewis described 'the Irish tradition [as] close enough to the Welsh to give us a sense of familiarity with stimulating differences. It's a family kinship.' Interestingly – perhaps even controversially – Lewis's choice of term radically extends the localised and rural purview of Ruth Bidgood's sense of a social community forged amid and bound up with the particular cultural complexities of mid Wales. However, Lewis remains circumspect about 'the differences which mean that the cultural politics of the two countries are far wider apart than their apparent proximity might suggest'.[3] Although thinkers like Alwyn and Brinley Rees were savouring the kinds of 'innumerable shared cultural, religious, historical and social connections' and divergences which Lewis ponders between the ancient worlds of Ireland and Wales, some decades ago, as Claire Connolly and Katie Gramich note, the cross-currencies linking the two countries in the modern period are only now attracting concerted critical attention.[4]

In the good-humoured wake of H. V. Morton, the Welsh cultural geographer Estyn Evans was among the first to flag the cultural consonances between the two countries with any scholarly purpose, in his path-breaking *The Personality of Ireland*, and the more pamphlet-like *The Personality of Wales* (1973), produced as a lecture for the BBC. Both Evans and Morton eschew the explicitly comparative approach of Rees and Rees; however, some more recent works encompass the Wales–Ireland axis which Connolly, Gramich and Paul O'Leary have helped to make visible.[5] Appearing in the wake of J. G. A. Pocock's influential 'archipelagic' historiography, a number of works including Linda Colley's *Britons* (1992), John Kerrigan's *Archipelagic English* (2008) and Glenda Norquay and Gerry Smyth's *Across the Margins* (2002) have – alongside O'Leary's assiduous searching of Irish migration patterns and labour history in Wales – helped to begin the work of broadening and deepening an emergent field of interdisciplinary study.

The literary axes between Ireland and Wales, if apparently limited by comparison with Scottish–Irish literary studies, were arguably first recognised relatively early in the twentieth century, as Connolly and Gramich testify, by Cecile O'Rahilly in her 1924 volume *Ireland and Wales: Their Historical and Literary Relations*.[6] Amid interest in other generic literary forms in any, or any combination of, the several relevant languages, contemporary scholars examining the contextual, thematic and formal consonances between the wealth of English-language poetry produced on each side of the Irish Sea have not ignored the women who help write it. On more than one occasion Linden Peach has marshalled various Ireland- and Wales-identifying writers, including women, in the name of the cultural-political emphases (especially gender and nationhood) which interest him.[7] A more recent essay by Jo Furber revisits the same thematic terrain (gender and nation) with a different mix of Welsh and Irish women poets.[8] Both venture, perhaps unknowingly, onto a territory usefully tilled in Catherine Brennan's study of nineteenth-century women poets, all of them connected in different ways with Wales.[9]

Brennan's astute reading of Emily Jane Pfeiffer's epic, *Glân-Alarch: His Silence and Song* (1877) is worth pausing on here for its interest in the sense of cultural consonance and relation which seems almost always to have existed, at some profound level, between Wales and Ireland. Betrothed to the young lord Eurien, by whose family she has been adopted and brought to Wales, Pfeiffer's Irish protagonist Mona gives voice to 'the passionate nationalism . . . the prophetic voice which foretells the fall of Wales as a political, cultural and linguistic reality'.[10] Thus, Brennan finds the poem 'assert[ing] kinship between Mona's valiant Irish people and the Welsh, and at the same time claim[ing] an ancient ethical precedent for the legitimacy of Welsh cultural identity'.[11] Pfeiffer's example not only provides literary-historical context for the presence of Ireland, and aspects of its nominally 'Celtic' disposition, in the work of some of her more recent successors. *Glân-Alarch* also arguably endorses Furber's confidently gendered and generalising assertion – echoing the view of commentators like Vicki Bertram, Jo Gill, and Jane Dowson and myself, among others – that poetry itself can be understood itself '[as] a powerful and subversive force in the making and unmaking of female identities'.[12]

This chapter examines that quietly subversive power in the context of the contemporary Wales, in whose history Ireland has for so long played so singular a part, and in particular through the stories that some women use in poems to explore the relationship between the two countries. The American narrative theorist and, coincidentally, poet Rachel Blau DuPlessis (adapting the ideas of philosopher Louis Althusser) speculates that 'narrative may function on a small scale . . . as a "system of representations by which we imagine the world as it is"'.[13] Ireland's adjacence to, and haunting of, the bounds of Wales's own geopolitical and mytho-historical terrain seems to me both to reflect and reflect on the two countries' entangled oral, literary and cultural histories. By extension, the relationship between the two nations can be shown to complicate each of the poetics I read here, not least in the shared effort to enunciate a cultural, if not always reliably or self-consciously gendered, sense of selfhood and position.

Despite the circumspection which Lewis recommends to Wales-based writers tempted to think of 'Celtic' Ireland as a kind of common storehouse, and to look there for literary and especially poetic models, Gillian Clarke, Christine Evans and Catherine Fisher have in their markedly different ways all seemed to find in Ireland an energising and neighbourly presence on their creative as well as topological horizon. For me, the thematics which detain Furber and Peach are of less interest than these poets' choice of mode: storytelling. First, there is the issue of form: what is the attraction of, as well as the purpose behind, the effort to discipline the conventionally self-extending linearities of story within the more economic but also self-fracturing imaginary of the traditional lyric? What, moreover, might it suggest about the relevance and/or desuetude of either narrative or lyric mode in the contemporary moment? Why might a *woman* poet writing in Wales want to draw on the special materiality of the legendary and/or mythic story? What might doing so reveal about her sense of political, aesthetic and/or imaginary relationship with the practice(s) of storytelling? Above all, perhaps, what kind of Wales produces, and is in turn *produced by*, the stories women frame in the form of the (lyric) poem? Once again, as we have repeatedly seen in this study, the productively uncertain generic space of the lyric sequence proves a usefully flexible way for all three writers to address the kinds of issues which are raised by such questions.

Storytelling, poetry and gender

Significantly, Rees and Rees open their ground-breaking interdisciplinary study with J. H. Delargy's description of the Irish storytelling farmer-fisherman Seán Ó Conaill, 'his mind a storehouse of tradition of all kinds, pithy anecdotes, and intricate hero-tales, proverbs and rimes and riddles, and other features of the rich orally preserved lore common to all Ireland three hundred years ago. He was a conscious literary artist.'[14] The sociocultural influence adumbrated in Delargy's lively sketch is reprised a decade later by Estyn Evans, alighting on 'such marked Irish traits as an addiction to story-telling . . . a wealth of international folk tales and a host of legends, highly imaginative stories and strange beliefs touching every native plant and animal'. Reaching for Lord George Hill's controversial social portrait 'Facts from Gweedore', Evans amusedly colours his own (and Delargy's) vignette: 'They are great talkers; as firing is plentiful, they sit up half the night in winter talking and telling stories; they therefore dislike living in detached houses.'[15]

The cultural power of the traditional storytelling which Clodagh Brennan Harvey, like Evans, locates in the rhythms of Ireland's rural life primarily derives from the intimacy of the relationship between teller, tale(s) and audience: 'The storyteller takes what he tells from experience – his own or that reported by others. And he in turn makes it the experience of those who are listening to his tale.'[16] Walter J. Ong is more exact: 'Narrative originality lodges not in making up new stories but in managing a particular interaction with this audience at this time – at every telling the story has to be introduced uniquely into a unique situation.'[17] The interpersonal intimacy which is, as Walter Benjamin suggests, so crucial to the sociocultural reach of the practice, both testifies to the teller's individual craftsmanship – as an original contribution to a specific cultural-historical moment, not to say posterity – and embeds and shores up the same figure's social function. Rees and Rees write:

> In Welsh, the very word for 'meaning' (*ystyr*) comes from the Latin *historia* which has given the English language both 'story' and 'history' . . . The old Welsh word for 'story', *cyfarwyddyd*, means 'guidance', 'direction',

> 'instruction', 'knowledge', 'skill' . . . Its stem, *arwydd*, means 'sign', 'symbol' . . . and derives from a root meaning 'to see'. The story teller (*cyfarwydd*) was originally a seer and a teacher who guided the souls of his hearers through the world of mystery.[18]

As Ong explains, since 'in the total absence of any writing, there is nothing outside the thinker, no text, to enable him or her to produce the same line of thought again', there is only one way to recover it:

> Think memorable thoughts. In a primary oral culture . . . you have to do your thinking in mnemonic patterns, shaped for ready oral recurrence. Your thought must come into being in heavily rhythmic, balanced patterns, in repetitions or antitheses, in alliterations and assonances, in epithetic and other formulary expressions . . . Serious thought is intertwined with memory systems.[19]

No wonder the figure of the *cyfarwydd* elides so readily with that of the poet. As Rees and Rees note, 'Traditional tales . . . were once a fundamental part of the culture of the aristocracy of the Celtic lands, and in Irish and Welsh tales from medieval manuscripts there are references to the recitation of tales by poets of high rank'.[20] Evans's study of Ireland would seem to endorse them: 'the Annals were cast in poetic or at least mnemonic form, using rhythm, alliteration and picturesque exaggeration'.[21] Welsh literary historian Glyn Jones is more scrupulous: 'That Wales had its bards is a circumstance known to most . . . That oftentimes these bards were also story-tellers whose medium was prose or prose and verse is . . . less widely diffused.'[22] Poet or not, however, the tale-teller's cultural-historical significance is inscribed in the public function of the role: in Emyr Humphreys's words, to 'celebrate and sustain the social order'.[23] Ong affirms that, in oral cultures, 'Knowledge is hard to come by and precious, and society regards highly those wise old men and women who specialize in conserving it, who know and can tell the stories of the days of old'.[24]

The political implications of that public regard are hard to overlook. For Blau DuPlessis, 'narrative structures and subjects are like working apparatuses of ideology, factories for the "natural" and "fantastic" meanings by which we live'.[25] In other words, stories like poems and other cultural artefacts help us to 'produce' the worlds in which we live – Ireland and/or Wales, for example – partly in revealing how such space/places are inhabited and understood by their occupants. (As if to bear her out, Humphreys describes how the emergence of the *canu gwerin* [folk poetry] afforded 'an entire class of people . . . a voice of their own [enabling them to] demand a larger say in the management of their own destiny.')[26] Ong suggests, moreover, that in the eventual shift from oral to written literary expression, the sociocultural pertinence of narrative only deepens: 'By separating the knower from the known . . . writing makes possible increasingly articulate introspectivity, opening the psyche as never before not only to the external objective world . . . but also to the interior self against whom the objective world is set.'[27] Rooted in so rich a cultural loam, women's poetic storytelling in contemporary Wales reiterates the political import of their aesthetic choices.

The links between politics, storytelling and the bard are complicated by the redoubtable figure of Gwerful Mechain, whose presence in a crowded (textual) literary record seems to confirm that in Wales, as far back as the fifteenth century, bards could not be assumed to be male.[28] Mechain's example notwithstanding, however, Harvey confirms the difficulty of clarifying the historical extent of women's involvement in traditional tale-telling in the absence of documentary proof, although in Ireland they do not seem to have been wholly excluded from the practice. If, as Harvey is left speculating, 'women participated less in the storytelling tradition than men', it may have been because 'It was not considered proper for a woman to tell the stories of traditional heroes', still less the kinds of stories fetched out for more public settings, such as 'ceremonial occasions: during night vigils at holy wells, after "stations" and religious services held in private houses, and at wakes and christenings'.[29] Harvey's anecdotal evidence of storytelling in early twentieth-century Ireland reveals the association of women's tale-telling instead with the less formal of the two varieties of Irish tale, the '*seanchas*', defined as 'shorter more realistic forms (including local and family history, tales about encounters with various supernatural beings, and genealogical lore)'.[30]

As Susan Stanford Friedman observes, 'Writers rooted in cultures where the oral tradition remains vital are more likely to regard narrative as food for the hungry rather than as the tyrant to be resisted'.[31] Yet women's exclusion from the authorising public discourse into which the figure of the storyteller taps can hardly but problematise the representativeness of what Humphreys has vaunted as the bardic (thus essentially patriarchal) forging of 'a new society, a new Wales'.[32] Certainly the gender relationships patterning this history help to explain Friedman's complaint 'that the lives of women have been systematically erased or trivialized in the dominant historical discourses', and her own determinedly scholarly efforts to ensure that the women writers of her own socio-historical moment are themselves fully enabled to 'participate in the construction of history, so that women's stories, as well as women-as-storytellers, will not be lost and forgotten'.[33] As Friedman's own work suggests, women who choose to tell stories in the framework of the poem are among those who lend their shoulders to this belated enterprise.[34] Their will to do so suggests not only a common desire to escape, in their poetic story making and telling, the confines of an oppressively gendered sociocultural imaginary; it can hardly help but implicate them in the generative unsettling of the grip exerted on poetic expression by certain conventions of form and genre.

Traditional literary criticism assumes that the kinds of poem which tell stories – in their earliest form, classical epics; in another incarnation, ballads – can do so only by subverting the conventional self-sufficiency of the lyric: its economy, unifying subjectivity and temporal coherence. Unlike narrative, lyric poems rarely presume on their own linearity beyond – typically – the semantic orchestration of their (proportionately few) words. In the poem, even if common grammatical conventions are eschewed, the logic of lineation ensures that words arrive in a particular order. That said, the poetic line cannot itself dictate even if it might hint at the temporal or experiential circumstances behind the words it organises. As I have shown in earlier chapters, especially chapters 3 and 4, generically mixed forms like the long poem and the poetic sequence neatly unsettle both the compaction and coherence of the lyric utterance and the continuity of narrative at the same time. Such forms plainly subvert their aesthetic roots in their textual and imaginary compass; their very scope precisely admits their linear, or at least quasi-linear, disposition. On the other hand, the discrete elements, be they verse paragraphs or more conventional-looking short lyrics, by definition interrupt the larger linear trajectory they collectively comprise. Saliently, for a critic like Leigh Gilmore, of course, 'Interruption is a discursive effect of gender politics and self-representation [that] evidences the possibilities of and limitations on women's self-representation[;] internally it erodes the illusion of textual coherence [while] externally, rupture works against hegemonic discourses of identity, whether they are psychological or political'.[35]

Conceptually as well as materially, the kinds of poem that – in today's colourfully sceptical world – tell stories (which are not epic or ballad) must dilate by unsettling the formal and generic confines with which they converse. Accordingly, it is in and through their formalities as much as anything that Friedman and others discover them destabilising the socio-historical power relations associated with their parent modes. By way of example, Friedman paraphrases the eminent American critic Marjorie Perloff, for whom the 'fragmented, collage like narratives [of 'postmodern' poems knowingly and deliberately] deconstruct a modernist separation between the poetic and the everyday, between the timeless lyrical moment and the historical'.[36] Finally, the different literary history of Wales casts the kind of poem Perloff describes here, trading simultaneously on the fracturing effect produced by lyric expression in narrative materials, and conversely the suturing of lyric utterance into narrative cohesion, in a more ancient light.

Writing about Welsh poetic tradition, Gladys Mary Coles perhaps unexpectedly retraces the undecideable formal habits Perloff describes to the remote history of the sixth century and the narrative poetry of the earliest bards, the *Cynfeirdd.* This literary history, represented by the figures of Taliesin and Aneirin, features 'non-linear' narrative, the stanzas of which 'can be read in any order, the variation-repetition technique generating a mosaic account . . . leaving gaps for the reader's/listener's imagination to inhabit'.[37] Ong would undoubtedly link the formal discontinuities which Coles describes to the oral origins of Welsh poetry. In his view, linearity of thought and expression is made possible by – is the product of – textuality; its organising logic makes little sense amid the fluidity and impermanence which condition the oral imaginary, where 'redundancy, repetition of the just-said [is what] keeps both speaker and hearer surely on the track'.[38] However, for me, like Friedman, finally it is in their generic hybridity – the permissive aesthetic space the different varieties of form afford and are afforded by their refuting of poetic tradition(s) – that sequences and long poems testify to and help stage 'women's revisionist reconstitution of narrative[,] by setting in play a collaborative dialogue between narrative and lyric'.[39] In the light of Gilmore's words, I find myself wondering instead whether women writing in Wales find (as their male counterparts also might) in the gap-filled, disjunctive yet linear formalities ushered in by hybrid forms like the long poem and the lyric sequential poem an authorising aesthetic freedom: in tapping it their work both proposes and traverses a kind of creative space, not unrelated to Massey's 'simultaneity of stories-so-far', more or less defined by that 'transgressive . . . potential', in which they collectively delight.[40]

Thus the women explored in this chapter surreptitiously lay claim to an oral and patriarchal 'Celtic' imaginary which, the fairy-tale-cum-nursery-rhyme-like ending of 'Letter from a Far Country' indicates, has long been informally theirs:

> *If we go hunting along with the men*
> *Who will light the fires and bake bread then?*
> *Who'll catch the nightmares and ride them away*
> *If we put to sea and we sail away?*
>
> *Will the men grow tender and the children strong?*
> *Who will teach the* Mam iaith *and sing them songs?*
> *If we adventure more than a day*
> *Who will do the loving while we're away?* (11.476–84, *GCCP*, p. 56)

As these closing quatrains lightly signal, the sea – particularly the Irish sea – provides an ambivalent backdrop to a text poised equivocally between narrative and lyric modes. A persistent presence in Clarke's oeuvre, the sea offers perhaps the simplest way of dramatising the cultural relationship between Ireland and Wales, in its separating of, and yet also fluid mediation between, the two nations. Kerrigan, for example, admits its significance to a cultural-literary study far broader than mine: 'The seas which we view on maps as surrounding and dividing the islands drew them together, and opened them to continental and Atlantic worlds'; in turn, he notices the 'capacity of the archipelago to foster fusions and transformations'.[41]

As Dewi Roberts notes, proportionately speaking, Wales has a considerable coastline: 'According to the Ordnance Survey, [it] totals . . . 1680.31 miles – further than Cardiff to Athens or Moscow – if you include all the islands.'[42] Ambivalent non-territorial borderland, the sea frames each of the different literary-cultural encounters I explore here, in all their tensions as well as connections. As Kerrigan says, 'A border can polarize identities, yet it can also simultaneously create zones, levels, and modes of negotiation and mutual interest'.[43] In the works I cite, seascapes and littoral landscapes come both to stage and justify the stories in which Wales and Ireland, for all the intervening breadth of the Irish Sea often at once collide and intersect. The literary exchanges such stories articulate (in both meanings of the verb) charge Clarke's careful excavation of the shaping of an individual's cultural self; broaden the cultural compass of Christine Evans's Bardsey/Llŷn and complicate Catherine Fisher's sifting of her own hybrid cultural genealogy. In the emphasis each places – however inexplicitly – on narrative modes and structures, all three writers re-gender and thus take their poetics beyond the confines of traditional habits of 'Celtic' storytelling, and the kinds of cultural landscapes it delineates.

Gillian Clarke: sea, stories, self

> The radio on the ocean-facing windowsill at Fforest was a teller of wild tales that came straight off the Irish Sea, as did the rain and the wind and the refracted light of the setting sun.[44]

In childhood, Clarke recalls, 'My mother taught me, by endless repetition and song, all the English nursery rhymes. She left the tall tales to my father. Song and story . . . What child could want more?'[45] Thanks perhaps to these influences, Clarke avers: 'All my poems are true stories.'[46] Yet a poet whose own fluency in Welsh was acquired only in adulthood, despite two Welsh-speaking parents, has implied that her poetry is inscribed by a sense of language as 'loss for a Welsh poet writing in English. The secret language, mother tongue of all the stories, of all the centuries of speech and song'.[47] Since her father used Welsh 'everywhere except at home', for Clarke, 'Welsh took on the nature of a forbidden tongue, a language of secrets from which I at first felt merely excluded, and later learned to value as something stored away for my future by my father, against my mother's wishes'.[48] In some ways the 'story' of 'The King of Britain's Daughter' (1993) belatedly answers this sense of cultural betrayal.

Located in her paternal grandmother's coastal home, Fforest Farm, the twelve-part lyric sequence not only exemplifies the merging of 'truth' and story in Clarke's lyric voice, but implicates her radio engineer father in the same creative process. As her meditative essay 'Cordelia's "nothing"' explains:

> The Irish Sea breaks on the shores of my father's land of Dyfed, specifically a small stretch of north Pembrokeshire. We are walking the beach. My father is a great storyteller, and today he tells me the story of Branwen and the giant Bendigeidfran, the children of Llŷr, explaining to his young daughter, mythologically, historically and geologically, two features of the coast close to my grandmother's farm . . . One is a vast rocking stone, or logan stone, probably Neolithic, balanced on the cliff and visible from the farmhouse. It is the giant's apple, or sometimes his pebble, as the story is ever-changing. The other is the black rock-pool vaguely the shape of a footprint and as big as a bath, which fills with sea water at high tide. It is, my father tells me, a footprint burnt into the shore by the enraged Bendigeidfran, setting off to Ireland to rescue Branwen from her cruel life as the rejected wife of the Irish king.[49]

'The King of Britain's Daughter' circles this incident, and the father–daughter relationship at its heart, in what becomes a partly autobiographical reworking of Branwen's liberation, at the hands of her twin brother Brân or Bendigeidfran, from the incarceration to which her husband the Irish king Matholwch subjects her. The Irish Sea, Ireland and its Pembrokeshire-facing coast frame Clarke's elegaic reworking of the story which her father wove around and through the familiar landmarks of Fforest's local coastline.

The sequence itself originated in a writing workshop which Clarke joined during the 1990 Hay Books Festival. For the title of 'Border: Fatherland, Motherland', she found her materials typically close by: 'What I saw at once was that border country in the self where mother and father meet, an edge where there is tension and conflict. At the same time it was the border where the two languages of Wales define themselves and each other.'[50] The poem obliquely equates a much loved parent with the Celtic king Llŷr, cognate with the Irish sea-god Lir as well as being the chief source for Shakespeare's ancient Britonic monarch. Recalling childhood trips to see Shakespeare's plays, Clarke recalls: 'They seemed familiar dramas, these father and daughter plays set in a damp Atlantic Ocean past in which I felt I stood and walked and spoke, and had my own part to play.'[51] Kerrigan recovers something of these dramatic nuances (as he notes, a sequence which Tony Conran would himself call 'symphonic' was in fact originally written as a libretto). In a reading which finds the work hovering suggestively between mass and opera ('Its voices shift from discursive recitative to the shapeliness of aria, then grandly resound like a chorus') Kerrigan's favouring of those terms is useful for way he succeeds in bringing to the different kinds of musical utterance the structural part each plays in the effect of the whole on its audience.[52]

In the text's closing sections, a voice unself-consciously reminiscent of the poet herself comes to conflate and ventriloquise both Llŷr's formidable offspring and Lear's wronged daughter Cordelia. At different times childlike and grimly adult, this voice lovingly recovers 'my father' ('my face in his coat') as a kind of technical wizard. Yet the poem exposes an undertow of tension in the parent–child relationship it embeds in the techno-historical realities of the Second World War, and mixes with Brân/Branwen's revenge on their Irish abusers:

> But things get tight and close,
> words, music, languages,
> all breathing together under that old carthen,

Cardiff, Athlone, Paris,
all tongue-twisted up,
all crackle and interference,
your ears hearing shimmer

like trying to stare at stars.

The last of the three sonnet-stanzas of 'Llŷr' seems to prefigure the tensions hinted at in the longer text:

Night falls on Llŷn, on forefathers,
Old Celtic kings and the more recent dead,
Those we are still guilty about, flowers
Fade in jam jars on their graves; renewed
Refusals are heavy on our minds.
My head is full of sound, remembered speech,
Syllables, ideas just out of reach;
. . .
When I was ten a fool and a king sang
Rhymes about sorrow, and there I heard
That nothing is until it has a word. (*GCCP* 68–9)

It is Branwen, her voice entwined with her twin's in the embedded sequence which concludes the longer poem, whose words recall both these, and an earlier moment when she wakes 'to hear / in the perpetual sound of waves / an outcry and the growl of war'. The sounds are prelude to the conflict of which Branwen is reluctant cause; if her words adumbrate the modern-day war haunting the remainder of the poem, the conjunction of 'sound' and 'waves' also recalls the mystical-seeming powers of the Lear-like radio engineer depicted in the preceding section 'The Heaviside Layer'.

In the layered sequentialities (incorporating two embedded sequences) of what Coles calls its 'circuitous narrative', 'The King of Britain's Daughter' rests productively between the autobiographical mode to which Clarke is always inclined and the mythic stuffs which her father fostered in her developing imaginary.[53] Poised uncertainly, suggestively, between these two poles, the sequence neatly both affirms and resists both (narrative) approaches. The thematic yoking of truth to the culturally resonant fictions of myth is matched in the work's equivocating between story and song. Ireland frames Clarke's self-conscious appropriation of her father's stories, and the contesting of its ideological function which her guilty-seeming interventions on them surreptitiously represent. Accordingly, her elegaic reply agonistically honours and resists his patriarchal presence: as Branwen's intermediary, the starling, affords her voice and freedom, so Clarke's imaginative traversing of the gulf dividing Ireland from Wales might be argued to have helped free her into poetic articulacy. The poem's final stanzas implicitly weigh the quasi-tidal provisionalities of its own textualities ('the sea writes on sand / . . . . / It discards, draft after draft, / each high tide a deadline') against the suddenly vulnerable-seeming materialities (of footprint and rocking stone) – compacted in the analogous 'pebble of basalt' and poignantly 'empty headland' – on which her father's storytelling depended (*GCCP*, p. 183).

Kerrigan reads into this often elliptical-seeming sequence 'a compound geography in which one locale can be variously situated and places [can] thus be sites of transport'.[54] I am inclined to understand his words from the different perspective of the 'compound[ed] geography' of the sequence's interleaving textual structures. In its resolute traversing of the traditionally gendered social and aesthetic conventions of storytelling, 'The King of Britain's Daughter' pushes, like any other lyric sequence, at the cultural-historic parameters of formal expression and engagement. Clarke's melding and reframing of legend and life story, in and through the interlaced and interlacing accounts told by and about both father and daughter figures, is replayed in her work's manoeuvring between and movement *beyond* the literary, cultural and (history suggests) gendered ordinances of lyric and narrative expression. Thus, like the others I have treated in the course of this book, the sequence might be said to produce and position – make imaginary but also aesthetic space for – itself, as well as the poet, in a new kind of suggestively uncertain literary and cultural place. It helps in women's collective telling of a new kind of story about Wales, and the women (as well as men) who in living also (re-)imagine it.

Christine Evans: Ireland and Bardsey

Lying some 50 miles west of Bardsey's most westerly point, Ireland can often be glimpsed from both the island and its nearest mainland, Pen Llŷn. The proximity of the coastlines partly explains the sense of cultural connection with Ireland which has survived in this area (its name plainly linked, via the Brythonic monarch Llŷr, with both the Irish province of Leinster and the Irish sea-god Lir), always shadowed by the sea. Local historian Enid Roberts notes:

> Archaeologists speak of the western sea-routes from the Mediterranean . . . passing between the Pillars of Hercules (the Straits of Gibraltar), reaching the western peninsulas – Brittany, Cornwall, Pembroke, Llŷn, Anglesey and Ireland. The sea was a means of joining these places together, [as well as] separating them from one another.

Roberts later cites Giraldus Cambrensis: 'There lies beyond Llŷn a small island where very religiously strict monks live, called *Coelibes* (unmarried men) or *Colidei* (worshippers of God)'. Roberts explains these shadowy religious figures as 'the Culdees, members of an old monastic order found in Ireland . . . derived from the Irish *célé Dé*, meaning servant of God'.[55] For her part, recollecting her very first journey there, Christine Evans remembers how Bardsey 'seemed to be waiting . . . as though, at any moment, the island could let go of its moorings and drift over the horizon, like a giant sea-beast resuming its migration to deep ocean'.[56]

Always conscious of the sea's ambivalent impact on her sense of cultural place, like her predecessors R. S. Thomas and Brenda Chamberlain, Evans often looks towards Ireland from this remote community. As we have already seen in the short lyric study 'Llŷn', discussed in chapter 3, for this area as for the inhabitants of those other small nation-states Cernyw (Cornwall) and Llydaw (Brittany), the Ireland marked by the Wicklow hills, silhouetted on the skyline, is merely a 'creaking of sail away' (*IDH*, p. 71). The trope recalls the region's maritime trade, and perhaps Llŷn's importance as an ancient centre of shipbuilding. Ironically, of course, Llŷn's coastal location also made it vulnerable to attack, as the historians remind us: '[Some] evidence of sea travel between Llŷn and Ireland is less peaceful . . . Armed men from Dublin invaded Llŷn in the twelfth century, and ransacked the church at Clynnog Fawr.'[57] Only one text constructs Llŷn's nearness to the Irish mainland – inscribed in the geological links between the peninsula and the larger island – in politically dependent terms:

> These hills at the gates of Llŷn are lifting
> blind muzzles to the sea
> that once they stalked: waiting
> against all hope
> for their ancient Irish masters
> to come home. ('Another Season', *LI*, p. 49)

The omission of 'Another Season' from the *Selected Poems* (2003) hints at its distinctiveness: typically, Evans's poems construct Ireland as a more generative cultural influence in her locality, in particular for the part it can be read as having played in the emergence of the complex, even cosmopolitan, nature of Bardsey's culture today.

While Bardsey's early history remains notoriously unclear, it is commonly assumed that its first inhabitants were 'missionaries from Gaul and Ireland'; Evans's recent, richly illustrated study of the island observes:

> Bardsey was at the heart of the trade routes for thousands of years. Ptolemy, in first-century Alexandria, drew the first map of the Irish Sea and Llŷn, probably getting his information from Phoenician traders . . . By then the first of the huts (*cytiau Gwyddelod*, as they are called in Welsh, Irishmen's huts) would have been occupied.[58]

It is in and through the shadowy figures around which the stories of the island's origins and early history have grown up that Evans finds Bardsey's Irish horizons nourishing the cultural hybridity which she has always prized in the island. A project which seems to have begun with 'Sevens', a plangent account of the solitary life and death of the island's most famous hermit, Elgar, is extended and refined in the eight-part title sequence of *Island of Dark Horses* (pp. 73–95), on which I touched for different reasons in chapter 3. Both the shorter and longer work testifies to the place of Ireland in the myths and stories which have helped to shape the cultural life and history of the island. For obvious reasons, perhaps, the sea proves central to both:

> All islands are fragments made significant by the sea's indifferent shifting formlessness, and meaning seems to snag and gather round them, enlarging their outlines on the horizons of the mind. Myths about them are almost universal across cultures, often as versions of the earthly paradise, for they are the perfect shape to build a dream – or a nightmare. In stories and sagas they offer opportunities, sanctuary and danger.[59]

'Sevens: the death of Elgar' retells in twelve seven-lined stanzas the moving legend of the English-born Elgar, whose remains were exhumed with those of the earlier Saint Dyfrig, and translated from Bardsey to Llandaff Cathedral in 1120. Both saints' lives are rehearsed in *The Book of Llandaff*. Kidnapped from his Devon home as a child, Elgar endured years of enslavement and privation in Ireland before, in the poem's words, being 'forced to act as royal executioner', for an oppressor identified by Chitty as *Ruaidri na saide Buide*, or 'Rory King of Connacht' (1087–92). The poem captures both the ghastly brutality of Elgar's duties and the sensitivity of the reluctant executioner:

the jerking dance played to its end;
the way fear-sweat dried acid and
panic or courage both set blue-white
in staring eyes. The hardest to forget
were those who told him they forgave him. (*IDH*, pp. 36–7)

When the chance of escape presents itself, the poem finds Elgar fleeing south to the 'safe harbour' from which he 'took ship / for home', only to be shipwrecked (*IDH*, p. 37). This is how, as *The Book of Llandaff* recounts in a passage containing several of the epithets still used to characterise Bardsey today, the refugee finds unexpected sanctuary on the island

> which in the British way is called the Rome of Britain, because of its distance and the dangerous crossing at the extreme end of the kingdom, and because of the sanctity and purity of the place. Sanctity because twenty thousand saints lie there, the bodies of confessors as well as martyrs. Purity because it is surrounded on all sides by the sea, both the dominating headland of the eastern shore and also the level and fertile pasture of the western – damp with sweet flowing springs and the sea-shore full of dolphins.[60]

Like its source, the poem plays on the Edenic qualities – beauty, peace, fecundity – of a haven situated 'halfway between / the passion of the sea and the purity of the sky' (*IDH*, p. 37). In this spiritually sanctified place, the miseries of Elgar's former life in Ireland are resolved in the transfiguring death which seems to offer benediction to the island itself:

At the last, they felt a hush
as in a shell, listening for a sea far-off
and round him saw a growing light,
luminous, pale gold
. . .
He saw their faces changing, and rejoiced. (*IDH*, p. 38)

'Island of Dark Horses' compares with its shorter counterpart 'Sevens' for its richer and more extensive (re)construction of Enlli's elusive early history.[61] Almost 700 lines the longer and a more adventurous text, the later sequence braids the legendary events and figures of the island's past with its recent history. It opens on the arrival of the island's earliest visitors, again fleeing an oppressor linked to Ireland. The close of the first section, '*Insula Sanctorum*', prepares for the formality of six sections named after the 'Hours' ('Lauds', 'Prime', 'Terce', 'Sext', 'None', 'Compline') at which 'The Divine Office' is said daily; the traditional regulator of orthodox Christian devotion.

Thus a poem ostensibly portraying a patently late twentieth-century 'day in the life of' Bardsey firmly foregrounds the island's ancient spiritual history. Conscious that the island's natural life remains 'innocent of the names and offices we give them', that cultural heritage contextualises and illumines what the poem sees as both 'Fragment of land, and a whole place, peopled, / generous with truths between the tide's / twin ceremonies of dark and light' (*IDH*, pp. 74, 75). Again and again, Evans returns to Ireland as a kind of cultural catalyst, a horizon in which to retrieve the centuries-old stories out of which generations of islanders have made sense of their surroundings. Her own poetic retellings, likewise poised in the porous space between the proven and the imagined, seem to remain for the most part sharply aware of their instabilities: as the poet remarks of the collection which became *Island of Dark Horses* 'where I construed connections not supported by historical probability, I drew attention to it as "fictionalising"'.[62] For Friedman, the genre in which Evans sources her materials – the story – is what makes this self-consciousness possible; as far as the former is concerned, the fecund imaginative space which is inhabited, and also generated, by story in and of itself 'refuses the binary of history and myth to construct a fusion or intermingling of the real and the sacred'.[63] Evans's lovingly detailed treatment of her island home discovers the offshore, generative but also menacing, presence of Ireland, as both place and the stuff of story, in all four realms.

Catherine Fisher: Irish-Welsh Gwent

Writing out of Newport, the civic centre of the Gwent coastline where she has lived all her life, Catherine Fisher's poetry commands a smaller audience than that of either of her peers. She has won more acclaim for the fantasy novels she writes for young adults. To some extent Fisher's poetic oeuvre deploys the same materials as her novels: they translate Wales's history, myth and legend into the much contested border territories which the estuarine Usk bisects as it heads to the Bristol Channel. Charged by her professional interest in narrative, and a shrewd sense of how stories – as well as poems (see her genuflection to Dafydd ap Gwilym in 'Gwern-y-Cleppa': I wonder / how you'd recognize it, / all your green Wales' *TUO*, pp. 32–3) – are implicated in the evolution of cultural history, identity and aesthetic expression, Fisher's work sits suggestively alongside that of Evans and Clarke.

For all her tireless searching of the sequestered terrain of the Gwent levels for the materials, places, topography and images which resonate so powerfully across her oeuvre, Fisher is openly intrigued by the pelagic ('There is no other language but the sea's', *TUO*, p. 38): two of her three collections flag the sea in their titles; the third, *Altered States* (2003), concludes with the powerful 'Estuary Poems' sequence. Finally, Fisher is herself Catholic-Irish, descended (like many Newport-based families) from refugees from the Great Famine on both sides of her family, who settled in Pillgwenlly: 'they came ashore and they didn't move any further, they sort of encamped themselves . . . . Most of my ancestors worked on the docks.'[64] These family connections with Ireland render it an important imaginative context for Fisher's complex sense of Wales; she too returns to seascape and shoreline, often via the sea voyage, in probing that thematic complex.

Interestingly, Fisher's first collection is entitled *Immrama*, an explicit appropriation of the generic Irish *immram* or *imram* (meaning 'voyage', or 'voyage tale'): a storytelling tradition of heroic voyages, invariably to otherworldly islands.[65] In drawing so openly on this ancient narrative genre, Fisher signals her interest in and affinity with Irish-Celtic literary tradition. She also implicitly positions herself – as the brilliantly wide-ranging lectures given in 1998 by Paul Muldoon (subsequently collected as *To Ireland, I*) make clear – in a venerable line of Irish-born writers reaching from Muldoon himself, author of two short lyrics entitled 'Immrama' and more than one longer work drawing on the genre, as far back as Jonathan Swift.[66] The title poem of Fisher's collection borrows the voice of an unidentified, presumably male hero, constructed as the embattled victim ('As you go on it gets harder') of a seemingly inexhaustible compulsion:

> You get used to the voices, the clinging fingers;
> in every port the warning
> 'Beyond here there is nothing but the sea'. ('Immrama', *Immrama*, p. 36)

It is of course in the 'beyond' that the speaker of 'Immrama' will discover the spiritual rewards he seeks: 'They say the scent of apples / wafts on the water; there is honey, hum of bees'. At some level Fisher's own faith underpins her interest in a genre plainly suited to the expression of Christian theology; but she finds the voyage tale useful for other reasons too. Weighing Muldoon's 'Immram' and 'Immrama', Richard Kirkland finds the Irish poet 'moving away from the fixed, the stable and the given factors of place . . . the process of exile [becomes] a focus for exploration'.[67] The exegesis would apply equally well to 'The Unexplored Ocean', title-sequence of Fisher's second collection, charting the experiences of the explorer James Hartshill on Captain Cook's voyages through the South Pacific. The work's final poem confides, 'Somewhere I travelled into someone different, / grew new thoughts and scars . . . / We have explored, and everything has changed' (p. 63).

Fisher's quiet questioning of her cultural place inclines her to ventriloquism. She often slips out of her own time- and gender-bound contexts into an array of other lives and voices: the figures of myth and legend like Noah and Merlin in *Immrama*; the devout, saintly and historical figures of *The Unexplored Ocean*, several of which are Welsh in origin; and perhaps most colourfully, the various shape-shifters peopling *Altered States*, including the (only) female voice of 'Blodeuwedd' (p. 43). Such poems work in two ways. In the first place, they bring myth and story into productive relation. Of her fictional work, Fisher explains, revealingly: 'I find that the mythic framework gives the story a more universal feel than a strictly realistic treatment would . . . Rather than hiding behind the myth, the story relives it, reanimates it.'[68] Her words betray a sense of dissatisfaction with the here and now to which she happily admits: 'The contemporary you see all around you, every day . . . But I like to look for other things. Things that you see just out of the corner of your eye or . . . that you don't quite see.'[69]

For Fisher, then, the poet's role seems precisely to expose the unfamiliar in the familiar, freshen perspectives and sharpen attention: 'I think poets have to . . . take things and say, look at this again. Look at that again.'[70] A keen amateur archaeologist, this poet's sifting of the vestigial traces left by the past on a contemporary landscape might be seen as a kind of imaginative voyaging, a self-displacement at odds with her sense of cultural rootedness. Of Wales, certainly, she remarks: 'Specifically it's the local landscape for me: the actual hills and forests.' Yet the fascination of Gwent, 'the place I know best', has as much to do with its imaginative potential as its actualities: 'I like to see what stories a place suggests.'[71] 'Llanddewi Fach' rebukes modern-day Wales for losing touch with the stories which its 'web of names' utters: 'Cado and Cybi, Tegfedd, Teilo, slender Cenedlon; / those relentless walkers in the rain, / spinners of words',

> . . . their foundations
> stark as the ribs of a stranded ship,
> their names studding the woven speech of strangers.

> They left us a bedrock
> of bones and memories,
> the ploughed field and the word (*TUO*, p. 25)

The text recalls David Lloyd, considering the symbolic relationship between name and place in the work of (Irish) Seamus Heaney, a poet Fisher admires: '[N]aming performs a cultural reterritorialization . . . communicating between actual and ideal continua.'[72] Fisher herself seems to confirm Lloyd: 'I'll use the name . . . well, like a spell in a sense, an evocation . . . to summon up the place and also to summon up an idea of the place to someone who hasn't been there.'[73] Conditioned by an ever-present history and its littoral geo-cultural situation (amid the ebbing 'tide of that tongue') Fisher's Gwent resists over-determination, as the fourteen sonnets of the 'Estuary Poems' reiterate.

Concluding *Altered States*, 'Estuary Poems' explores the cultural history and legacy of the immigrant-Irish community which still exists in Newport today, framed by the equivocal contexts of the estuarine Usk and the Gwent levels. The most distinguished historian of Irish migration to Wales, Paul O'Leary has recorded the particular pressure on Newport during the Irish famines in the mid-nineteenth century: 'Monmouthshire and Glamorgan accounted for three-quarters of all Irish immigrants to Wales'; of this influx, '87 per cent of the Irish-born were to be found in two enumeration districts, those containing and surrounding the town of Newport'. An imbalance which was due partly to the constituency of Newport's religious community ('Catholicism was far more securely established there than elsewhere in Wales') went on to precipitate a period of social crisis in the town. As O'Leary confirms, the itinerant Irish migrant – in nineteenth-century Britain widely associated with vagrancy – was viewed with suspicion in Wales.[74] Newport's perhaps understandable antagonism towards the flood of famine refugees was all too probably complicated, David Arnold suggests, by the vicious moral circle in which in the very act of charity a 'benefactor and donor confer[red] upon the other the permanent and demeaning status of the begging-bowl'.[75] O'Leary confirms the antipathy polarising haves and have-nots: 'The Welsh natives could not understand the foreigners with their strange language and customs, and looked upon them all as enemies. The Irish, forced into a foreign land through English oppression, clung to each other with an intense clannish spirit.' And yet he speculates that the two communities may have had more in common than either realised: 'The growth of Irish friendly societies – particularly in Newport – would suggest that some of the Irish shared the same basic values of respectability and self-improvement as Welsh members of friendly societies.'[76]

'Estuary Poems' sets the history and legacy of these inter-cultural tensions against the restive and ambivalent context of the estuary which has always framed them. It opens on the kind of pitiful scene caused when formal attempts to curb migrant numbers simply increased 'illicit landings of larger numbers on mud flats below the entrance to the harbour as a means of avoiding legal constraints':[77]

> See them flounder, waist-deep, long skirts dragging,
> sick with bilge-stink and hunger;
> the river mocks them with its dangerous *croeso*,
> the sucking pools, the children handed up,
> lethal tidewash, wet caress,
> fingers clutched in the soil and stones,
> till the bank is firm and the land forms (*AS*, p. 49)

Any refuge that Wales might have seemed to offer these desperate voyagers is overwritten by the misery of their physical and cultural situation; the 'lethal . . . caress' of the tidal river and oxymoronically 'dangerous *croeso*' offer poignantly little sense of safety. In the unwelcoming muddy littoral half-world where they are stranded, the equivocal legacy of deracination is painfully evident. Sonnet III resentfully ('It shouldn't have been like this') retrieves the elusive other-worldly idyll to which the voyage tale ('the story') ought lead: 'no sorrow there, no sickness, / but music and the long sweet centuries / of sunlight' (*AS*, p. 51). In Sonnet V, tidal change figures the imperceptible process of cultural cross-fertilisation, as 'Out in the dark fresh water becomes salt; / two tides join . . . word by unknown word'. As if by osmosis, cultural ties and affiliations shift and give way

> Home known, home heard of,
> home receding into legend, and all the while
> unnoticed, this is home, and no one says it
> till the moment's gone. (*AS*, p. 53)

The emphasis on utterance acknowledges that language is simultaneously complicit in and vulnerable to the 'unnoticed' relocation of 'home'. In Sonnet 'XI', the fracturing 'Babel-like' din of competing languages is also permissive ('Going abroad / is never strange because of this'); likewise the mute, isolate 'father home from the war, / the words "Céad míle fáilte" on his cake' is sympathetically treated (*AS*, p. 59).

There are clear if tacit parallels between the anonymous 'I' of the sequence and Fisher herself, caught in the conflicted gap between her disenfranchised Irish ancestors and the Wales which has anchored her own more recent life history. In those echoes, the work confirms O'Leary, discovering that even in 'people separated from their immigrant forebears by numerous generations, an awareness of a distinctive cultural heritage has not been entirely extinguished by successful integration'.[78] In Fisher's case, a poem published more than a decade ahead of 'Estuary Poems' suggests that that awareness may have been hard won. 'Great-grandmother', an elegy for the nameless illiterate matriarch whose 'name tops the family tree', foreshadows the attention which the later work pays to the role of language and writing in the construction of cultural identity. The 'crooked X' which stands for her ancestor's signature has ensured its survival in the public records where the speaker can scrutinise it (*Immrama*, p. 23).

That detail alone constructs in this vague but formidable figure an emphatically gendered survivor of two life-rocking traumas: famine and cultural dislocation/relocation. As such it endorses the Irish famine scholar Margaret Kelleher, learning how 'twentieth-century retellings of famine [afford] the female victim [an] explicit collective function, figuring both the crisis of famine and society's survival'. However, the inarticulate signature-mark 'that promises, and denies' also ironically enunciates (wordlessly) its author's muting and marginalising in the public history to which she has a powerful claim. Fisher's portrait thus dodges the reductive female characterisations which Kelleher identifies in other treatments (namely 'famine mother', 'ministering angel', and/or 'sacrificial victim').[79] Fisher's speaker imagines her ancestor ('the begetter of history') in a way that is at once more ambivalent (both heroic and tragic seeming) and more personal than any of Kelleher's models: as a kind of originary point ('two snapped twigs' . . . 'the long-sought prey') to which the 'trail' of her own genealogy can be retraced.[80] The 'two thin lines crossing' in which the influence of this silent but still powerful figure is etched offer a focal point for the speaker's *immrama*-like journey into the reaches of her own selfhood, its goal ratified in language highly redolent of Friedman's modelling of identity as positionality: 'our blood's intersection, our crossroads / our moment of meeting'. In all these features, Fisher's poem delicately anticipates the emphases of Kelleher's argument: by (re)gendering the brutal trauma of the Irish famine, expressing the inexpressible, the patently matriarchal, self-authorising but also anonymising 'x' – a signature which eloquently and paradoxically is not – she finds a way of imaging womanhood which sidesteps the coercive gaze of posterity. This highly self-referential, acutely personal and yet also keenly political figuring of text/identity-as-sign, as expressively human as it might appear reductive, warns us against underestimating it, in its oddly non-linguistic articulacy. Like a number of other poems by Fisher, it would seem to confirm O'Leary's suspicion that 'many of the Welsh-born sons and daughters of immigrants perceived themselves as being Irish in a way which the language of nationality cannot easily accommodate'.[81]

In the emotional but also historical ambiguities which poems like 'Great-Grandmother' open up for examination, Fisher seems both to depict and subvert the urge of genealogical enquiry, conflating the inescapably human compulsion(s) to 'trac[e] the past through its manifestations in the present, and recogniz[e] ourselves in the events of history'.[82] Negotiating between the historical and the present, Fisher also negotiates between Ireland and Wales; between the spiritual, political and, of course, cultural worlds both nations encompass. Her situation recalls Rachel Blau DuPlessis's imputing to narrative (and by extension to the kind of poetry, replete with generic uncertainty, on which this chapter has concentrated) the ideological means in and through which, complexly, 'we imagine the world as it is'.[83] All three writers for all their abiding differences, perhaps coincidentally drawing on the ambiguous intersections and tensions between Ireland and Wales, in certain hybrid poems seem to bear out Friedman's forthright assertion that 'The insistence on story, on narratives that claim historical and mythic discourse as the right and necessity of women poets, permeates the interplay of lyric and narrative in women's contemporary . . . poems.'[84] Interestingly however, neither Blau DuPlessis nor Friedman fully acknowledge the ways in which the poetic narratives I have been exploring succeed in crossing – opening up and interrogating – spatial as well as temporal differences. Positioned against the fluid dividing yet connecting backdrop of the Irish Ocean, the stories all three poets tell serve to extend, broaden and most importantly enrich the territorial and – to that extent cultural – compass of the north-, west- and south-Walian landscapes in and out of which they live and write.

6

Wales and/or Thereabouts: Sheenagh Pugh, Wendy Mulford and Zoë Skoulding

'The line that limits is also the line that dares'[1]

Any place, like any community, is produced by and produces different kinds of exclusion. This dialectic is both registered and subverted in the 'ontology of mobility' which Nigel Thrift ascribes to the 'almost/not quite subjects; almost/not quite selves; almost/not quite spaces and almost/not quite times' of late twentieth-century culture.[2] Specifically, for Thrift 'an ontology of mobility forces us to think about borders, . . . margins and centres, convergences and overlaps'.[3] Jahan Ramazani might argue that Thrift's paradigm finds rich expression in the responsively mobile and accommodating frame of the poem: 'Since metaphor derives from the Greek "transfer" or carry across', it should come as little surprise that poetry's figurative language enacts geographic and other kinds of movement.'[4] That dynamism partly helps explain the centrality of the poetic construct in the cultural-critical discourses of exile, not least the modernist criticism which finds writing itself definitively capable of producing the very kinds of catalysing, exclusory limits which it is concerned to traverse. In Theodor Adorno's words, 'In [the] text the writer sets up house.'[5]

Many literary critics have used the idea of exile to focus and inflect the creative histories of the now devolved, once 'British', regions. Centuries of willed and/or involuntary traversings of Wales's shifting, synecdochic borders are, of course, etched on the literary history which Kathryn Gray projects into the contemporary: 'For many new Welsh writers and writers from Welsh publishing stables the future seems to lie in going elsewhere and staying there, a fact mirrored in their often self-imposed exile outside Wales – their role as the outsider looking in and on.'[6] She writes, I assume knowingly, in the wake of Tony Conran, who has argued that exile helped charge the development of Wales's English-language poetics: 'The writers of the Second Flowering were almost all exiles, incomers or *revenants.'*[7] And yet, as Wendy Mulford notes, 'the choices that led a mid-century generation of writers born and/or raised in Wales to get out, constitute exile only in the loosest sense'.[8]

Certainly Gray's use of 'exile' and 'outsider' today seems unsafe in a 'secular and contingent world [where] homes are always provisional', and where 'old loyalties of class or gender or race fragment, dislocate, rupture, disperse; new loyalties of class and gender and race interrupt, disrupt, recombine, fuse. No one is quite sure of the ground on which they stand'.[9] (As Anne Cluysenaar muses, 'can one be an exile if one has never belonged anywhere?')[10] Whatever the particular circumstances which might mesh in its backstory, however, the experience of exile in general can hardly but be conditioned by gender.[11] Susan Stanford Friedman's unapologetically gendered 'geography of movement', a dynamism she detects in networks and pathways alike, plays out in the creative imaginary of the woman writer interested in 'location and dislocation, specificities of place and abstractions of space, particularly as these relate to language, race and ethnicity.'[12]

Each of the three poets I read in this chapter has her own reasons for – and her own distinctive way of – interrogating her sense of cultural relationship with Wales in and through the figurative and imaginary places and spaces to which travel – as both trope and theme – admits her.[13] Sharing an interest in 'displacement, relocation, cultural translation and untranslatability . . . in formal and stylistic as well as in thematic terms', Sheenagh Pugh, Wendy Mulford and Zoë Skoulding all discover in the always provisional and proliferative, always spatialised and spatialising resources of poetry a means of (re)negotiating the issue of cultural identification.[14] Accordingly each finds, or produces, in the domain of the poem precisely the kind of renovated textual locus which Thrift expects

> to write movement in a whole host of ways [including] both remaking the observed, through problematising the temporal and problematising perspective/voice, and revealing the observer, through making the text's conceptual apparatus explicit . . . Each and every one of these devices involves the use of many sites, both literally and metaphorically.[15]

In particular, in and through 'the poetic act that is contingent upon yet moves them out of [the] material experiences of place', all three end up unsettling the boundaries marking the actual and psychological terrain of the nation.[16] Katie Gramich speculates that Wales's twentieth-century women writers explore 'the experience of dispossession ultimately in order to assert their sense of belonging to Wales'.[17] Yet Pugh, Mulford and Skoulding seem to feel dispossessed no more than they assume that they belong to Wales in any clear-cut way. Instead they confirm political theorist Michael Billig, protesting that '"this" country cannot be physically indicated: what is there to point to? . . . [T]he whole context . . . stretches beyond the individual locations of any speaker or listener.'[18] One way in which they do this is to trouble the association between an ethnographically fixed or stable 'here' with the cultural construct called 'Wales' which grounds them all.

Linguists call the prepositions which signal position, so as to orient an utterer, utterance and/or its audience, 'deictics'. As I have argued elsewhere, deictic markers of place like 'here' and 'there' can provide poets with a discreetly political means of exploring the question of cultural positioning.[19] It is possible to read each of the three poets featured in this account through their attitude, implied or explicit, to the fixities which might be assumed to condition such signifiers. In their more or less overtly anti-deterministic use of words like 'here' and 'there', Skoulding, Mulford and Pugh collectively engage in what we might call a *dehiscent* re-conceiving – in Jacques Derrida's carefully organic metaphor, a 'splitting open' – of Wales's geopolitical and creative compass.[20] That is, they find their own ways of eroding and/or unfixing conventional political, ethnic and/or geographical constructions of nation as place, and in doing so make it possible for 'new [cultural] coinages, new intergeographic spaces, even new compound identities to come into being'.[21] Under the pressure of their poetic attention, what we might understand as the seedcase, or housing, of Wales's cultural imaginary is ruptured, bursting open into new means and modes of creative life. In the process, they confirm bell hooks's claiming 'Home [as] that place . . . where one discovers new ways of seeing reality'.[22]

'Their eyes / fixed on distance': Pugh and Wales, abroad

Sheenagh Pugh, whose first poem appeared in *Poetry Wales* in the summer of 1973, has never seemed to want, still less seek, the kind of visibility enjoyed by Gillian Clarke; Pugh's habit has been instead to dodge the kinds of national and gender positioning which Clarke's readers like to attribute to Wales's latest national poet. Pugh's *Long*

Haul Travellers (2008) speaks as insistently as any of her preceding collections about the importance of mobility in a sometimes spikey but invariably compassionate idiom. The second of two poems about Anthony Gormley's Merseyside art installation 'Another Place' (permanently located on Crosby Beach, the work features a hundred life-size cast-iron figures positioned at different depths in the sand along 3 kilometres of the foreshore), the tightly controlled couplets of 'Fixed' meditate on place as position. The central seventh stanza is reproachfully direct: 'Words like *home* and *always* / ambush them, pin them down' ('Fixed', *LHT*, p. 60). These words ironise the moment of stasis, or at least equilibrium, on which this tensile text concludes, as it considers the 'fixed' sculptural figures, their 'eyes / fixed on distance'.

For most of her long writing career resident in Wales, although she now lives in Shetland, in some ways Pugh's poetic vision seems always to have been 'fixed on distance', partly in its outspoken hostility to the kinds of political agenda which haunt culturally freighted terms like 'migrant' or 'itinerant'. Pugh prefers to safeguard the mobility of the geographically and linguistically oriented subject, the creative imaginary, and the reading as well as writing mind. From early poems like 'Amy Flew Away' (*Crowded by Shadows*, p. 20), the cohering logic of *Earth Studies and Other Voyages* (1982), or particular poems like 'What if this Road' (*IH*, p. 7), Pugh's is a poetics habitually drawn to edges, vantage points and farther prospects ('Climbing Hermaness', *SFTT*, pp. 16–19; 'The Door to the Sea', *LHT*, pp. 53–4; 'Saxa Vord', *LHT*, pp. 38–40). On the occasions when Pugh focuses on Welsh spaces, not least the south Wales where she used to live, it is typically to extend or dilate them (as in 'Buffalo Bill in Pontcanna', for example, *IH*, pp. 23, 41).

Describing this idiom as exilic would reduce its escapologist spirit, and simplify Pugh's venturesome interest in ways over and out, and in passage(s) across, between and through. The influential anthropologist James Clifford defines travel as the 'more or less voluntary practice of leaving familiar ground in search of difference, wisdom, power, adventure and altered perspective'.[23] In its attraction to the individualised though rarely isolated excursor, Pugh's poetry seems less interested in travel per se than in its allure for, and effects upon, the experientially hungry traveller. The creative bounds of her thematic portfolio – much like that of her friend Catherine Fisher – are extended rather in the more morally ambiguous form of the explorer, particularly the indomitable men who navigated – and opened up for commercial traffic – the perilous seaways of the Arctic. 'The Arctic Chart' (*Stonelight*, pp. 9–17) betrays Pugh's fascination with the kind of daft but sensational-seeming public heroism on which a voracious Victorian/Edwardian imaginary so enjoyed feeding. The sequence performatively voyages through the six landforms whose names both chart and enshrine the romantic, (in)vulnerable subjects each conjures. In and between the poignancies of the stories she recovers, Pugh pays tender tribute to her pioneering subjects' shared desire for the knowledge both empirical and spiritual perhaps best captured in Arctic explorer William Parry's sensing of 'an immense mind, unexplored, / unbounded; you could never chart it, / though you knew its name'; a pragmatic sense of selfhood so resilient that (etched in the place-names the Europeans left on the maps they drew) it spans both time and space; and perhaps above all the humility which always conditions their hubris ('more humbled / by each new wonder', 'The Parry Islands', *LHT*, pp. 10).

Perhaps unsurprisingly, because Pugh is an outspoken anti-feminist, her poetic subjects are often male and her speakers frequently ungendered; the female voice and/or experience rarely obtrude(s). The eleven-text sequence 'Lady Franklin's Man' (*TBL*, pp. 35–50) begs attention, then, for the way in which gender ends up complicating the various kinds of travel – out of domestic, cultural, political, geographical, psychic and later temporal place – it explores. In Melanie Petch's words, 'the journey is at once a context and metaphor for in-betweenness'.[24] The multidimensional shifts deepening the 'in-betweenness' which suffuses the sequence are perhaps inscribed in the slippages of its title. This adeptly signals both the Muse-like centrality of Lady Franklin's absent 'man' and, more obliquely, how a devoted wife ends up translating herself into her husband's unsubstantiated story; indeed, comes to overwrite his increasingly shadowy figure. Certainly, and perhaps unsurprisingly in a collection also housing the manifesto-like 'Fanfic', Pugh's stalwart Lady Franklin travels – seeks to live – in more than one dimension. Her wistful reaching after the difficult, alien world which Franklin – and courageous would-be rescuers like Bellot, Kennedy, Kane, Ross and Inglefield – had known so intimately, travelling 'west until west / became east, until nameless channels / became safe passage', re-echoes in the mixed emotions with which she finds herself caught – like Franklin himself – between a familiar, enervating and confining *here*, and the threatening, enfranchising unknown of *there*, 'The nothing, the emptiness, you sailed into' ('Lady Franklin Begins To Be Concerned'; 'Lady Franklin at Muckle Flugga', *TBL*, pp. 36, 39).

Lady Franklin's dynamism subverts her self-authored epigraph: 'I can never be a happy person, because I live too much in others.' Her embracing of the privations of Muckle Flugga, the most northern site in the Shetland Isles, seems an action as political as it might be naïve. As Gramich notes of a host of twentieth-century Welsh women writers, 'Women themselves increasingly venture outside their traditionally allocated places and spaces. They often find themselves at sites of contestation, contingent and in flux – shifting sites of resistance as well as complicity.'[25] The remarks bear just as helpfully on Lady Franklin's untiring efforts to keep Franklin's British public 'in mind / of him. The legend, the traveller / / in hard places' ('Lady Franklin Refuses to Wear Mourning', *TBL*, p. 40). If her nerveless promoting of her husband ('Your name floats free of you') is undertaken in the cause of his safe return, her 'spell' seems as important to her own sense of selfhood, the need to nurture in herself a like degree of resourcefulness and resilience ('Lady Franklin Hears a Ballad in the Street', *TBL*, p. 43).

Lady Franklin's endless (re)creation(s) of Franklin, and herself-in-him – her actual and cerebral travelling between her own identity and his, and the spectrum of selfhoods between (in/dependent, married, un/knowingly widowed) – are illumined by the contortions Seidel describes:

> If the imaginative boundary separates and supplements, differentiates and replicates, it is worth speculating for a moment on what happens . . . if the imaginer, instead of peering across the border from the known territory to the unknown, finds himself in an opposite position on the unknown side of the border trying to sustain the image of distant familiarity . . . The imaginer remembers from where he used to project.[26]

Or, as Seidel also puts it, 'The imagined outland is a version of the inland; the possible a version of the previous'.[27] Finally, to the new knowledge of their relationship suggested by her dogged trailing of her husband, we can add the itinerance recorded in 'Lady Franklin Resumes Her Travels' (*TBL*, pp. 46–7).

In her apparently affectionate construction of her redoubtable subject – charged rather than drained by the marginal situation in which her lost 'Man' leaves her – Pugh's sequence recalls Isobel Armstrong's reading of Felicia Hemans, whose 'insistent figuring of movement across and between cultural boundaries, with its emphasis on travel, could be seen as a search for the exotic, and escape from restrictions into the "other"', constructing at the same time in such textual but also cultural-political 'flight[s] across the boundary' a reflexively emblematic figuring of 'woman as traveller through the imagination'.[28] It is tempting to interpret Pugh's remaking of Lady Franklin's story in similarly emblematic terms, partly in the light of bell hooks's claims for 'that space in the margin that is a site of creativity and power'. Arguably, Lady Franklin comes to mark not only that here-like 'inclusive space where we recover ourselves', but also (and for Pugh as well as her twenty-first-century readers) embeds a correspondingly there-like position marking and marked by the 'possibility of radical perspectives from which to see and create, to imagine alternatives, new worlds'.[29]

Pugh's interest in travel is powerfully consonant with the poetic translations which this expert linguist has included in almost all her collections. The parallels between linguistic and bodily translation also re-echo in the textual flexings of another again sequential text: 'Murat Reis', an inventive revivification (part ode, part elegy) of a respectable seventeenth-century Dutchman turned – in stark contrast with Fisher's nobler-seeming sea-faring adventurers – ruthless privateer (*LHT*, pp. 25–31). Pugh's Reis is a seductive if quixotic renegade in his extravagant self-recreations; his gap-filled, poem-like story ('he vanishes, as a coastline will / in sudden fog') charts his self-transforming journey into the shrewdly professional pirate of the legend. Thus the solid-sounding burgher of Haarlem's public record ('Janszoon, Jansen, Jansz, perhaps') dissolves in the fabled 'Morad, Morato, Murat Reis' and its English misprision 'Matthew Rice'. Travel and translation cross in this literally exorbitant (in the Derridean sense), self-translating figure: Reis is himself translated in and by the stories through which his reputation has hurdled the limits of body and time as well as space, coming to rest, however surprisingly, in the gendered, geopolitical and aesthetic context in which I summon it here.

Although Pugh's idiom typically takes few formal risks, Reis's itinerant daring seems refracted in the formal insouciance of the sequence, with its interchanging stanzaic and rhyming structures, shifting margins and sometimes unpredictable lineation. Arguably, the 'territorial shifts by line, trope, sound, or stanza'; the 'flickering movements and juxtapositions' and the rupturing of 'the spatiotemporal passage from one "zone" to another' recall Ramazani's definitions of the 'travelling poem'.[30] But Pugh dislikes the kinds of critical labels she suspects of serving to confine and/or reduce her work. Perhaps as a result, if Wales has from time to time featured in her oeuvre, it is rarely if ever treated as any explicitly significant geopolitical or ethnographic referent. Despite her partly Welsh parentage, as far as I can see this poet no more expects to centralize Wales as poetic theme or locus than she would herself expect or seek to be constructed by it, as the place in which she happened to be living when her writing began to win her public attention. Her poetry is much more interested in moving us, as well as itself, beyond the cultural confines of the nation. In this sternly earthed idiom, the construction of human experience in and through geographical and historical, as well as linguistic, translation, comes discreetly to dilate the cultural space in and out of which it has been produced.

'Hoping apart a substance': Mulford's 'BOTH . . . AND' home/land

In terms of her background, ideological beliefs, creative practices, writing style and themes, Wendy Mulford could hardly differ more from Sheenagh Pugh, though the two poets must be near-contemporaries. Mulford's poetry is inherently suspicious of certainty, and above all of the links which conventional language use assumes between the signifier and its referent(s). In this demanding poetics, words are habitually loosened from the signifying frames which hold them in place; her poetry recalibrates its linguistic materials in apparently arbitrary but always suggestive-seeming ways. Such are the avant-garde habits of the 'non-mainstream' poetry circles Mulford found her way into in Cambridge in the 1960s and was herself instrumental in publishing.[31] Although what is known as the 'Cambridge school' of poetry has never lacked the specialist readership it courts, it seems to confirm exilic constructions of literary modernism, compounded for a woman (as feminist critics of modernism might anticipate) in the neglecting of female-authored work which propelled Mulford's own influential publishing activities.[32] In the context of Wales – where this politically engaged writer grew up – experimental poetry can seem more alienated still: John Goodby and Andrew Duncan reproach critical neglect of what they expose as a robust and vibrant strand of writing in Wales's anglophone poetic history.[33] Certainly, scholars like Shari Benstock suggest that the voice of the woman in this environment is worth listening out for: 'The coming together of an internalized and a lived expatriation gave rise [among female modernists] to very special forms of writing . . . the mark of an internalized condition that expatriation allowed to be externalized *through writing.*'[34]

Benstock's words reiterate how cultural and/or geopolitical space conditions (or *produces*) and is in turn conditioned (*produced by* experience); they also confirm how writing itself can simultaneously trope and encode as well as adumbrate the interrelation she describes. Mulford's own oeuvre and idiom roundly endorse her. Evacuated from London to her maternal grandmother's house in Abergavenny aged three, in 1944, several months after her mother and elder sister, from the children's home where she had been undergoing medical treatment, Mulford's sense of cultural affiliation with Wales was likely to be complex from the outset. Her departure for Cambridge after leaving school could not have helped, even had she returned to Monmouthshire instead of settling in East Anglia where she came to establish herself as poet, critic and publisher. Now writing out of Suffolk, where she has lived since the 1990s, Mulford has said, drily: 'it feels as if I have been trying to return [to Wales] all my life'.[35] In the early work *ABC of Writing* (composed in 1978–9) she constructs her relationship with Wales 'from outside looking in' ('y.', *ASS*, p. 69), in a self-deflecting projection which, interestingly, we have already encountered in various forms and for different reasons in the work of Gwyneth Lewis, Christine Evans and Ruth Bidgood; the poet is nevertheless insistent thirty years later that 'the sense of connection remains constant'.[36] Wales, she goes on, 'was the place where I found the family. It was the place where I found *space*, and it was the place I found my mother.'[37]

Thus it is that Wales becomes the defining locus of Mulford's own, crucially elective, experience of displacement; an identifying cultural anchorage that underpins and is woven through her creative consciousness. At the same time and more complexly, Mulford's poetics constructs Wales as a site of displacement, in which one term (in this instance 'place') gives way to, is supplanted by, and/or serves to elicit, another ('space'). The process reveals Wales as enticingly proliferative; as hooks says, 'spaces can be real and imagined. Spaces can tell stories and unfold histories. Spaces can be interrupted, appropriated, and transformed through artistic and literary practice.'[38] The reflexive interest which Mulford's work takes in its own attitude to Wales is arguably what contrasts most sharply with Pugh's writing. The temporal and geographical distance which the latter deploys acquires a more ambivalent edge in Mulford's self-expatriating poetics, in its stance and subject matter plainly more in thrall to, despite being situated farther from, the Wales grounding both writers.

The term 'displacement' can be glossed in more than one way. Besides the sense of political and cultural alienation for which James

Clifford borrows it, there are the implications of Freudian theory, where the term is used to describe and explain the subject's self-protective diverting of significance from one object onto another. Its surreptitious yoking of geopolitical and psychological discourses is partly why 'displacement' seems such an apt descriptor for Mulford's paratactic idiom, elliptically figured in a significant moment in *ABC* as 'hoping apart a substance, these politics of impossible / convergence, into gaps, presenting absence' ('s.' *ASS*, p. 67). These few words adeptly figure the layering of self, circumstance and context in the uncertainly exclusive/expansive place/space of Mulford's Wales. As she takes care to warn,

> it's not really a geographical state of exile I'm exploring. Or only in so far as it's metonymic of the larger spiritual psychic condition . . . Exile isn't quite the right word for a separated 'both/and' condition. It's not estrangement. It's like being separated in life from people in your family, but you stay connected and you reconnect the minute you meet up again.[39]

Her family's part in Mulford's equivocally separate/connected Wales is significant. 'Yr Heniaith' ('The Old Tongue'), published in 2009, concludes by rereading a Mulford-like (although in fact unidentified) subject's (dis)connected sense of homeland back into the bewildering but in some ways doubly exilic, in some ways doubly restorative experience of evacuation from wartime London to Wales:

> the darkness reveals the light
>   in my double exile
> war becomes peace   children's home
>   the hill farmstead
>   one way story (*TLB*, p. 56)

With presumably deliberate irony, the 'one way story' on which this spare text closes is contradictory: on one hand, it seems an affirmative gesture of the power of Wales over Mulford's own creative imaginary. It might equally signal and explain the compound sense of exilic relation to Wales which suffuses this and other texts by the poet. Although her childhood in Wales was happy, Mulford has retraced her radical politics (she was for many years an active member of the Communist Party, and campaigned on feminist and trade unions issues), to the inequities of the upper-middle-class lifestyle her grandmother took for granted. Another of the poems in *ABC of Writing*, 'p.' is Joycean in its disapproval of the toxic effect of social snobbery. I quote the text in full:

> Wales again
> outside the house is not inside the house and people live inside the house
> they do they do not live outside the house which makes outside the house a
> very much nicer place to be. the child lived outside the house
> and grew up ignorantly. she grew up in dreams. later she learned to see. she
> saw where the workpeople lived who worked inside the house and on the
> land. she watched and listened and so she learned.
> later she read and began to see
> why her people would never understand
> that there over there they could not see
> nor their own part in shaping that reality
> but loved their portraits livestock roses
> and thought the people 'thieving' boozing churls
> and calmed themselves with tracing ancestral charts back to bastard Earls
> ('p.', *ASS*, p. 66)

This poem's deliberate movement from socio-economic context to emotional/psychic subjectivity, in the growing linguistic facility of the subject, is neatly inverted in the earlier '1.' Arcing tenderly but not uncritically from text to context, '1.' dismantles the causal relationship generally assumed to exist between experience and writing:

> is a writing of the self a writing of writing?
> and is a writing of writing a writing of the self?
> double u one.
> mark one.
> is it? is it? tell me it is? shall I believe you? shallow backwards flowers
> anything a bluebell patch then barbed-wire then foxy bracken space-time
> aged five and stumbling podgy legs. Then fifteen then rocks then lichen
> sheepmowed mountain-crest and all the air ours over valleys over valleys
> beyond who lived there and who cared? ('1.', *ASS*, p. 64)

Like 'p.', '1.' partly interests for its mobilising of the peculiar freedoms of the childish and adolescent minds it rehabilitates. The impulse of the tesserae-like fragments collated in 'ABC' – often mediated by memory – seems primarily 'backward'; the text's tracking back through different timeframes in order to disinter and probe their secrets seems motivated in particular by two linked sorts of loss: poignantly, of childhood innocence and, less regrettably, political naivety. In each case, the sifting of a memory's archive, paralleled in the spatio-linguistic choreography of the text, seems intended to prise open the 'impossible / convergence' of place and feeling in a personal history for the sake of a maturing creative mind. Hence the joyous construction of place as 'beyond' into which the final lines of my excerpt career.

Written for the festschrift for her friend and fellow poet Jeremy Hooker which appeared in 2009, 'The Question' inspects the same self-investigating ethics with perhaps still more forensic care:[40]

> About the shadow and the lip
>   there may be
> Scar tissue
>   never mind that
> Somewhere
>   the river runs down
> Where's home
>   the trees answer
>   *
> Such a poise can put the
>   whole life in
> question
>   hesitancy holds
> the clue (*TLB*, 54–5)

The text's gestures at the speculative ('there may be') and the conditional ('*Such* a poise *can* put'), its one-sided dialogue ('never mind that') threading through lines never quite divided by their porous central margin, constitute an astutely performative examination of how 'hesitancy holds a clue'. Literally poised 'in the clearing' between question and answer, the poem queries its own capacity to represent the non-verbal world it mediates. It does not ask so much 'where are we?', or even 'where's home', as: 'can such a question ever be asked in the expectation of a satisfactory answer?' Examining the literal and literary 'spaces' enshrined in the poetic construct, Ian Davidson hunts out the poets who pursue the actual and cognitive spaces 'within the gaps, between word and its referent, between the subject that is constructed by the poem and the subject that constructs the poem'.[41] Opening up an instrumentally visual/textual but also cognitive space between its central-seeming (non-) question ('where's home?') and the punctuating question mark on which its momentum depends, the central self-referential term of this text – its eponymous 'Question' – lies in exactly those gaps, openly asking 'questions about what we know of the world, how we know it and how we represent that knowing back to ourselves'.[42] Hence the clearing in which the poem positions the flexing image of the 'tall pine' equivocally 'bending', gracefully signalling how Mulford's Welsh connections continue to charge and sustain her poetics.

Arguably her most significant text of recent years, Mulford's so far uncollected 2007 sequence 'Alltud' (its title *Cymraeg* for 'exile'), appositely observes as it draws to its semi-elegiac close: 'in emptiness / is my source'.[43] As I have said, in this habitually displacing idiom, 'emptiness' (arguably what 'p.' casts as 'absence'; also simply 'space') seems prized most for its nourishing of cultural freedoms; its disputing, refusing and/or alleviating of social and/or domestic mores. But emptiness can also be initiating and enabling as 'The Question' makes clear: in its enfranchising space(s), psychic/cerebral and by extension creative replenishment become possible. In 'Alltud', those potentialities are explored and realised on more than one level. Formally, the text's spatial geography (which is also to say its architecture) is extended and destabilised by a number of embedded sequences, each one discreetly displacing without ever fully disrupting the formal or linear logic of its 'parent' section. The sense that the cognitive spaces of the text can dilate like this is sharpened by the poem's own similarly self-displacing compulsion 'to get back to a place before or beyond language'.[44] Part 5 warns:

> No trace
> of my provenance remains.
>
> If you search for me you may find a brief label
> Name – species attributed – date caught
> taken as far as wind dries, as far as rain wets,
> as far as sun runs, as far as sea stretches
> as far as earth extends. ('Alltud', 160)

The sequence's broadening of its own hermeneutic possibilities is equally staged in its awareness of the uncertain role of memory in the creative consciousness: its capacity to fix being also and definitively to supplant. The contemporaneous voice of the first section (sited 'In the valley of the Wye, at Erwood, Powys') is gradually displaced by a succession of ever more remote topoi: the familiar experiences and landscapes of childhood ('A plant / remembered / balm-leaved figwort / / A section of track / right through the kissing gate / the Gavenny valley / / Skirrid Fach, Skirrid Fawr . . .') recede before the ambiguous, palimpsestic remains – landmarks which are in their ruin both manifestly present and manifestly incomplete and partial – of those ancient public centres of Wales's socio-economic history and influence, the abbeys and priories (Talley, Ewenny, Neath) of the 'Clever Cistercians', today's tourist attractions ('Alltud', 156). These in turn yield to the layers of the landscape on which they were literally founded: the very geological strata in which is preserved, as I discuss in chapter 1, the sedimentary narrative of any place's emergence into physical and cultural identity, 'since the great glaciers of the Pleistocene / when the ice retreated . . .' ('Alltud', 159). Revealing that she suffered from epilepsy earlier in her life, Mulford has speculated that the unreliable memory with which the condition left her directly affected both her writing, and her sense of selfhood: 'the coming and going of memory, and its relationship to my sense of identity, has I think been intimately linked with my creativity and my way of relating to the world'.[45]

Perhaps partly for this very personal and yet also manifestly generative reason, the unidentified often highly lyrical voice of 'Alltud' strenuously denies itself and us the kind of emotional, political even linguistic anchorages which might index its exilic status. Pertinently, Jeremy Hooker reads other texts by Mulford according to a different set of similarly ambiguous terms: those, he explains, of the Christian feminism to which her passionate allegiance to the communist cause gradually gave way in her later years and, for him, the idea of the pilgrimage in particular. Interestingly, the words Hooker cites to justify this idea (drawn from the capacious and idiosyncratic study of women saints entitled *Virtuous Magic* which Mulford co-authored with Sara Maitland) resonate as suggestively with 'Alltud' as with any of Mulford's earlier works. 'Pilgrimage', *Virtuous Magic* remarks, 'is an opening up, a prising apart of closure, of familiarities and securities and easily acquired knowledge, in pursuit at one and the same time of the unknown and the known'.[46] Not least because Mulford has elsewhere said of poetry that 'it's only in the process of writing that you discover what and why you are writing', it is tempting to understand 'Alltud' as a kind of textual pilgrimage, a journeying towards, which is also an honouring of, the spiritual power which Wales – a locus always for her 'both/and', constituting 'the unknown and the known' – represents to an expatriate poetic imaginary. Reflecting in conversation on section 6 'The Return', and particularly the line 'I am gone from the places that knew me', Mulford (trained in Jungian analysis) herself links the excavating, even exhuming, linguistic and figurative activity of the poem with her own (dis)placed and (dis)placing sense of cultural place:

> The things that have made me are not the same as those that have made as it were the mystery of the lands of Wales. But they are analogous in the sense that they are mysterious, and buried. And you have to go back through . . . ; you know that when you've been working in analysis . . .[47]

In the same interview the poet confides: 'My mother was a very strong influence on me and we had a very close bond. It has sometimes seemed to me that everything I've been creatively is, in part, down to her. Not the academic side, but the poetic.'[48] More recently still, the poet has lamented the circumstances which led to her mother's musical artistry being consigned 'in wartime, with two children, by the departure of her husband "to the underworld"'.[49] This Eurydicean construction of her own mother, a construction explicitly connected with her own determined sense of creative identity, plays into and helps illumine the reversed chronology around which Mulford arranges 'Alltud', subtly dismantling the topographical/geological, historical/prehistorical, and religious/mythic complex of her Wales. Significantly too, given the poet's retracing of her creativity to maternal influence, the sequence's remorselessly 'backward' trajectory for me recalls the powerfully gender-inflected trope of the buried – for Benstock always 'expatriated' – '*matria*' which Elizabeth Barrett Browning prompts Sandra Gilbert to identify with

> that which is repressed, rejected, colonized, written over, subjected, erased, silenced. The woman writer must discover her by peeling back the layers of patriarchy. The desire for this mother country is compelling, its discovery renewing, life-giving, passionate, transforming, and integrative. *Matria*, as Gilbert describes it, is the underside of *patria*, that which requires . . . a rising again up from under.[50]

On these terms, it seems all too possible that it is 'Wales-as-matria' which is renewingly (re)conceived in the dreamlike yet realistically west-Walian landscape towards which the closing lines of the sequence incline, as uttered in 'Elennith', its final section:

> *here* on the ridge-height
> looking across at your birth-place
> you are safe borne along
> *between* sheep-walk and peatland
> gathering strength for the journey
> from impassable bog-moor to western sea
> *there* the barque waits that will bear you
> to the edge ('Alltud', 161, my emphases)

Poised both on and 'between' 'ridge-height' and 'birth-place', and just as ambiguously between those crucial place deictics 'here' and 'there', 'near' and 'far', in much the same way, the last unpunctuated words of this magnificent poem resonantly deny their own formal and syntactic terminality. Temporally speaking, we are asked to look both behind – to an age of fable-like voyages often resolved in the sort of funereal (but never definitively deathly) 'barque' framed 'there' – and, more obviously, ahead. In its adroitly double-facing progress through a Wales figured as 'both' unavoidably material (known) 'and' wholly unreachable unknown), 'Alltud' marks out a new aesthetic space which both is and yet demonstrably cannot be 'home'.

For Mulford, as Jenkins sees in the 'poetics of many women, "home" is a condition of "dwelling-in-displacement"'.[51] Mulford told me, bluntly, Wales is 'not my address, in either sense of the word'.[52] Grown in a distinctive literary and cultural habitat, no wonder her idiom takes such searching delight in the paradoxical hermeneutics of the textual place/space(s), the dialogic 'here' and 'there' which the (always self-displacing) poetic construct enshrines. To retrieve Adorno again, 'For a [wo]man who no longer has a homeland, writing becomes a place to live'.[53] Mulford's distance from her 'native' Wales is plainly instrumental in producing, as much as being produced by, her richly (un)situated poetic identity. Conditioned by the suggestive sensation of 'not quite being at home' on various levels, 'Alltud' in turn problematises the homely/exilic topology of a keystone-like Wales this poet cannot reduce: '[Wales] is protean for me; it keeps changing. It is partly Illyria, partly imaginary [as well as] the first place I knew.'[54] In the generative psychic and textual ground(s) produced in/by her writing, hermeneutic certainty is invariably deferred; place is displaced, space is (en) gendered. Thus a fiercely independent poetics comes both to construct and mine its own aesthetic space(s), in terms which hooks would approve: 'We are transformed, individually, collectively, as we make radical creative space which affirms and sustains our subjectivity, which gives us a new location from which to articulate our sense of the world.'[55] The transforming political and aesthetic logic which motivates Mulford's poetic (dis)placing of Wales seems to me to endorse Clifford's defining 'Practices of displacement . . . as *constitutive* of cultural meanings rather than as their simple transfer or extension'.[56]

'Between here and there': Zoë Skoulding, wandering Wales

In an article entitled 'Wandering where I am', Zoë Skoulding describes herself 'walking up a bare hill in the Preselis, carrying a map of Brussels. In the distance is the hunched outline of Mynydd Carningli: I know exactly where I am, which is why I'm carrying a map of somewhere else.'[57] This 'day of site-specific explorations' spent with a group of artists sharing an 'interest in walking and ecology' is revisited in the playfully disorienting 'Preselis with Brussels Street Map':

> Up Europalaan under blue
> reach of sky bare feet in spongy moss
> I need a map to tell me where I'm
> not along the avenue de Stalingrad
> squeal of a meadow pipit
>
> skimming
> over rue de l'Empereur
> tread softly on the streets the sheep trails
> between bird call and bleat echo
> a street folds across two languages here and there[58]

Poised between the cartographic bilingual 'there' of cosmopolitan Brussels and the apparently unmediated, more sensuously three-dimensional (and also bilingual) 'here' of upland west Wales, this poem both honours and sends up the notion of site-specificity. The delicate immediacies of 'spongy moss', 'meadow pipit' and 'sheep trails' are held in balance with the textual signifiers of map and poem in which they are embedded, alongside other binaries like man/nature; overhead/underfoot; named/nameless. At the same time, the poem's unprogrammatic passage through these simultaneities renders it powerfully mobile.

Opening up the gap between actual and signified which map makers and users tend to occlude, 'Preselis With Brussels Street Map' produces a suggestively (dis)located, (dis)locating view of the invariably undecideable relationship between self and place, looker and looked-at landscape, here and there. Revisiting the real-life walk, undertaken with visual artist Ben Stammers, out of which the poem itself emerged, Skoulding notes how Stammers's 'attention to the place around us collides with the non-place of the map and works to heighten our sense of what this place is as well as what it isn't'.[59] In interview, Skoulding remarks, 'looking is often connected with power. Once you look, and represent, you are exerting a kind of power.'[60] At the same time, Skoulding admits: 'I was just very interested in how far the text itself can be like walking, like moving through a space.'[61] Open-mindedly wandering what she calls the 'much-written about' landscape of Wales, this Bradford-born, Bangor-based, non-Welsh-speaking poet suggests new and politically adventurous ways of thinking about, *looking* at, the relationship between place and self in a post-millennial age.[62]

Positioning itself in the lengthy literary tradition of the walk poem – a genre self-consciously interested in the spatialised, spatialising effects of its own literary-ambulatory activity – 'Preselis' confirms French theorist Michel de Certeau's view of walking as an essentially undecideable 'space of enunciation', in which 'the walker constitutes, in relation to his position, both a near and a far, a *here* and a *there*'.[63] As Skoulding explains, for de Certeau – whom she much admires – 'Walking . . . is about everyday life, getting on and finding a way through'. Following his lead, she constructs walking as 'a way of questioning the connections through which I understand where I am', not least because 'in everyday experience locations are pulled into unexpected conjunctions and dislocations that the rational overhead view of the map can never reveal'.[64] As I have said elsewhere, Skoulding's politically considered unsettling of the kinds of deictic markers by which authors, speakers, texts and readers normally locate and orient themselves, and perhaps most suggestively the place deictics 'here' and 'there', refracts and illumines her own carefully indeterminate sense of cultural place, and of Wales as a whole.

Rebecca Solnit locates the cultural-political power of pedestrianism at the heart of a socio-economic imaginary which has 'both shaped and been shaped by the spaces it passes through on two feet. Walking has created paths, roads, traderoutes, generated local and cross-continental senses of place; shaped cities, parks; generated maps, guidebooks [and] a vast library of walking stories and poems'.[65] Yet a hefty secondary literature confirms that the practice of walking is, inevitably, also deeply ambiguous. After all, on the one hand, the very mobility of walking must by definition mean that, for all practical purposes as de Certeau says, 'To walk is to lack a place'.[66] Yet for Skoulding walking also means, more generally and more holistically, 'seeing how the body fits in a place, and . . . what's underfoot'.[67] The literary critic Jeffrey C. Robinson manages to respect both stances:

> The walk implies a mixture or an alternation of committed responses and disinterested reflection, . . . The walker observes things from a distance . . . by definition detaches himself . . . by walking on. Yet the walker is in experience, feels and thinks in his movement through time and space.[68]

What Robin Jarvis calls 'the fascinating congruence between bodily action and mental process' pathologises these ambiguities.[69] For Rousseau, for instance, walking is hopelessly entangled with thinking: 'when I stay in one place I can hardly think at all; my body has to be on the move to set my mind going'.[70] Solnit endorses him:

> The rhythm of walking generates a kind of rhythm of thinking, and the passage through a landscape echoes or stimulates the passage through a series of thoughts. This creates an odd consonance between internal and external passage, one that suggests that the mind is also a landscape of sorts and that walking is one way to traverse it.[71]

More relevantly for me, 'Wandering' repeats Skoulding's determination to remember and respect the writing process as being itself 'a physical process in a specific place'.[72] This conviction – which obtains in all kinds of ways in Skoulding's singular, intelligent and wonderfully plastic-seeming poetry – crucially bears, of course, on her reader, from whom her writing tirelessly calls attention to the topography, the self-conscious spatio-textual arrangement, the visual and sonic shape of its own expression, to its thinking-out of itself on the page. As Solnit says, condensing the logic of centuries of literary endeavour, 'To write is to carve a new path through the terrain of the imagination . . . To read is to travel through that terrain'.[73]

The poetic terrain of *Remains of A Future City* (2008) is charged as much by Elizabeth Grosz's assertion that bodies and cities are 'mutually defining', as by de Certeau's formula that 'the act of walking is to the urban system what the speech act is to language'; what Skoulding later glosses as 'an appropriation, and acting out, a way of creating relationships, so that walking is a kind of rhetoric'.[74] Partly thanks to the inherent ambivalence(s) of both paradigms, and as the materially and temporally unreliable urbs of its title warns, this complex collection makes a suggestively indeterminate 'home' for the (dis)embodied voice which presides over so much of its richly imagined cultural ecology:[75]

> Between the buildings
> trees reach down
> to languages
> of soil and worms,
> leaves gloss argots of glass and steel;
> woods lie down on floors
> to bounce back
> every word, every word
> you speak
> with the long
> echo of your footsteps down into the mud.
> ('Building Site', *Remains*, p. 10)

This poem's construction of its eponymous 'site' – not to mention the city for which it is metonym – as a fertile and ever-evolving organism simultaneously authoring and authored by the experiential self, meditates on de Certeau's suspicion that 'Beneath the discourses that ideologize the city, the ruses and combinations of powers that have no readable identity proliferate'.[76] Retracing those powers to the disparate, proliferating, unself-conscious and above all unregulated body of urban walkers in whose ceaselessly contingent movements he invests the production of the city space, de Certeau explains: 'Their story begins on ground level . . . Their swarming mass is an innumerable collection of singularities. Their intertwined paths give their shape to spaces. They weave places together. In that respect . . . they are not localised; it is rather they that spatialize'.[77] What he says chimes with Skoulding's pondering how to reach 'beneath the readable surface of the city, of evading the control imposed by others [while] also refusing to see with map-vision or kestrel-vision and the kinds of power they imply'.[78]

The labyrinthine urban-pastoral environments of *Remains* – with its 'Baths of Amnesia', 'Bureau for the Suspension of Control', and among others its 'Noble and Tragic' Quarters – also explicitly summon the metropolitan fantasies of the European situationists, as rehearsed in Ivan Chtcheglov's (aka Ivain Gilles) 1958 manifesto 'Formula for a New City'. Chtcheglov not only reimagines the city in the humanist terms that Skoulding lifts: its correlation with 'the whole spectrum of diverse feelings that one encounters by chance in everyday life' requires its inhabitation in a defamiliarisingly mobile way. In Christopher Gray's relaxed translation, Chtcheglov defines the activity he famously dubs the 'dérive' thus: 'The main thing people would do would be to drift around all the time. Changing landscapes from one hour to the next would end with complete removal from one's surroundings.'[79] However, as Skoulding is careful to warn, while 'the "dérive" depends on chance, it is anything but aimless. It is an embodied process of re-ordering the connections that shape everyday life; it draws on environmental and subconscious factors obscured by capitalism as a re-ordering of space from a revolutionary utopian perspective.'[80]

Skoulding's anachronising of Chtcheglov's title in *Remains* – positioning us beyond a 'future' which is counter-intuitively already exhausted and over – holds at bay a once-radical aesthetics she finds passé as well as provocative. However, it also obliquely honours the political and creative possibilities embedded in the languid practices of situationism. As Skoulding explains: 'A lot of what I do has to do with situatedness and looking[,] and interrogating ways in which we look at and experience things. But it's also necessary to keep imagining how things could be different.'[81] The subversive attraction of wandering perhaps lies above all in its evasive disposition; its dynamism; itinerance by definition must of course refuse any kind of locating fixity. This is just as true, in perhaps a less radical but arguably more political way, by rambling, a practice which – although it is now widely regarded as a leisure activity – as Solnit points out originated in political activism and is still inclined to focus not 'on the boundary lines of ownership that break the land into pieces but on the paths that function as a kind of circulatory system connecting the whole organism. Walking is, in this way, the antithesis of owning. It postulates a mobile, empty-handed, shareable experience of the land.'[82]

It is precisely this characteristic which prompts the critic Roger Gilbert to draw an interestingly explicit analogy between walking – arguably, wandering in particular – and poetry: 'poems can be seen as exploratory movements that remain uncommitted to any particular goal or outcome beyond movement itself'.[83] Yet the apparently neutral interest in 'movement itself' may be precisely what makes the walk poem so adroit a form of cultural commentary. An essay co-written by Skoulding and Davidson notes: 'Walking contains within it a contradictory relationship between chance and control. Wandering without intent becomes a process of play and of losing control, walking the same patch repeatedly also becomes a process of taking control.'[84] Using the same psycho-geographic technique as 'Preselis' – in which the map of one site is deployed in the defamiliarising navigation of another – 'Forests with A–Z of Cardiff' situates itself and us in another dislocated and dislocatingly indeterminate milieu, in which rural and urban endlessly intervene on each other: 'From the station I turn right and right / again into plantation woodland:

> I bring gridlock
> with me and the forest
> falls in line between
> nowhere and nowhere (*Remains*, p. 49)

Caught on a kind of experiential cusp between street map and forest, this text again loses us, disorientingly but generatively, amid the rich visual and verbal play of what de Certeau might cast as '*forests of gestures* . . . [or] "a wandering of the semantic"'.[85] In this poem's weird topology, we find ourselves like the speaker moving impossibly but enfranchisingly between 'nowhere and nowhere', as the implacable urbs graphed in the *A–Z* contends with the silent fecund world with which it is blended. Tellingly, it seems only in the 'dream / of my body / hovering above / its mapped co-ordinates', as 'cities come and go like forests' and (conversely) 'forests come and go / like cities [that] I can see where I should be' (*Remains*, p. 49). The poem's inscription of its simultaneously mapped-and-sensed world in the (dis)embodied figure of the dreamer confirms how 'the dreaming mind wanders like the idle pedestrian: connections happen by chance and there are abrupt shifts from one experience to another'.[86] Equally, a body both dreamed and dreaming helps script the movement of what Davidson and Skoulding dub the 'rural dérive', tuned to the special techno-cultural circumstances of their own contemporary moment: 'Given [the] intensity of modern communication and its ability to locate the subject simultaneously in a range of contemporary experiences, it's hard to say where the city ends and the countryside begins.'[87] As Skoulding remarks elsewhere:

> One way of looking at countryside is to see how it's the 'contra terra' or converse of the city: pastoral is an urban dream of rural freedom. But the countryside is locked into the same networks of power as everywhere else and it always has been: the tops of these hills are marked with the remnants of settlements from a thousand years ago; the whole landscape would have been crossed by lines of defensive vision in the way that it's now crossed by phone lines, power cables, traffic and the languages shimmering across it in communication networks.[88]

Ultimately, the searching interest which this poet takes in the complex socio-cultural ecology of her surroundings returns us to the cultural-political structures which produce and are produced by them. As 'Disobedience' reminds us: 'We see what we want to see and in the way we want to see it.'[89] Hence the attraction of the dérive, urban or rural, for a poet for whom walking offers 'a way of slowing down, of seeing . . . how an individual journey, or the everyday pattern of a life, might weave its way between and underneath the structures of global capitalism'.[90] Skoulding returns to the 'shimmering' networks which render place so suggestively undecideable, in the uncertain textual/experiential, manmade/natural environment of the final poem in which Wales is (dis)locatingly *not*: 'Llanddwyn Beach with directions for Copenhagen' (*Remains*, p. 51). Llanddwyn beach runs beneath and between the two bridges (Pont Britannia and Telford) connecting Anglesey to mainland Wales. In their linking and dividing function, those companion structures – spanning island and mainland territories

– constitute zones as liminal and culturally uncertain as the beach on which they have been superimposed. The poem reiterates Skoulding's persisting interest in why (dis)locatedness might be argued to occur, and the kinds of reasons why it should matter.

The poem emerged from an experiment, in which Skoulding posted a request on the internet for directions from anywhere to anywhere. She waited more than a year for the anonymous instructions, used verbatim, for navigating central Copenhagen, on which this perhaps most self-consciously experimental and conceptually (geographically) permissive of the texts I have been concentrating on. While the poem's conjoined littoral/metropolitan loci somehow come to *contain* each other, the dialogue between them also moves us from the already peculiar hermeneutics of map reading to the more subjective, disorienting and collaborative processes of direction giving and following. In this supremely contingent text, each fragmented verbal construction leads the reader in any of several directions at once, articulating with any of the words and/or phrases in its vicinity. We are invited to drift in our own way(s) through its self-doubting textual conjunctions and disjunctions, the ecologically and temporally provisional context of its almost/not quite site-specific beach/city, and the ever-altering web of overlapping and intersecting socio-economic and cultural connections radiating outwards from the (dis)locating ground of this almost/not quite 'centre'. In and of itself the poem presumes that 'at any point you're going to be in a network of connections stretching all over the world. But that doesn't make what's in front of you any less important.'[91]

'Preselis', 'Forests' and 'Llanddwyn' represent three starkly different locations in Wales: the metropolitan anglophone south, the cultural heartlands of rural west Wales and a self-conscious but highly networked north. Yet none constructs Wales in geopolitically, let alone culturally, monolithic or homogeneous terms. They inscribe instead Massey's influential understanding of space as the 'product of interrelations', 'predicated upon the existence of plurality' and 'always under construction'; a multidimensional, dynamic matrix produced by and producing the kinds of geopolitical, geo-cultural forces it inscribes; 'a simultaneity of stories-so-far'.[92] Skoulding's politically and aesthetically charged poetic effort, to register the 'there' to which the contemporary 'here' of her own cultural context always, undecideably, offers access and vice versa, is motivated as much as anything by personal reasons:

> Wales is where my writing took shape; I write in English in a bilingual country, and I know that this context makes me see English as a provisional

> circumstance rather than something to be taken for granted: my national identity as a writer is therefore a set of negotiations rather than a fixed point within clearly defined national boundaries. Complex relationships between languages and cultures define Wales as much as Cymraeg itself does, and they define Europe too.[93]

Skoulding's own writing reiterates her conviction that 'by deliberately refusing to mean in conventional ways you can open up new ways of thinking, which is the only way that anything can be changed'.[94] The cultural blurring exposed by this still maturing poet's attentive wandering of the densely packed networks of the 'almost/not quite', urban/rural, national/international, virtual/actual cultural ecology of twenty-first-century Wales deliberately problematises cultural affiliation in the early twenty-first century. Her reflexively aleatory poetics takes her and us 'beyond there being an essential Wales and who it belongs to and who's allowed to write about it', proffering 'a way [of] being deliberately in between, of moving through the contradictory space between here and there (or global and local, Welsh and English, human and nonhuman)'.[95] Her imaginative, grounded writing slips inventively between the spaces across which it migrates, unfurling itself from its own linguistically unstable textual sites to offer me a valuably earthed but open-minded, culturally undecideable place-as-space from which to conclude a study which was always conceived in similarly exploratory terms.

Afterword: Tiffany Atkinson and Samantha Wynne Rhydderch

'This is how she writes, as one throws a voice – forward, into the void.'[1]

Reaching its end, I am uncomfortably conscious of how much my tour of a populous terrain has skirted. Among the many deserving writers I have unwillingly neglected are established figures like the poet-archivist Sally Roberts Jones, and the chief female experimentalist of her generation, Alison Bielski, still publishing in the pared-down, unpunctuated forms which first made her name alongside Peter Finch some five decades ago.[2] To them I might add Glenda Beagan, author of *Vixen* (Honno, 1996) as well as the short stories for which she is best known; the reputed Welsh-language author and prolific translator Elin ap Hywel, who like Menna Elfyn publishes in both languages, or even Carol Rumens (less readily identified than many with the north Wales in which she lives and works), whose teaching and mentoring has silently done so much to nurture the literary scene I have been exploring. But in the spirit of the poets' own unsettling, subversion and/or circumnavigating of various kinds of cultural determinants, it seems right in conclusion to turn my own gaze outwards, towards newer voices and newer works.

Samantha Wynne Rhydderch and Tiffany Atkinson are established and distinctive names in a maturing generation including names like Kathryn Gray, Jasmine Donahaye, Alexandra Duce-Mills, Nerys Williams and Helen Lopez. In two relatively recent works, each casts a spirited poetics well beyond Wales's irreducibly complex territorial, socio-historical and linguistic borders. For those who like to read in the poetic construct a 'textual synecdoche' for its historic, political and ethnographic moment, 'Catulla' (in Atkinson's acclaimed collection *Catulla et al*, Bloodaxe, 2011) and 'Erratics' (in Wynne Rhydderch's *Banjo*, Picador, 2012) both contest the will – amid post-devolutionary interest in the languages of self and nationhood – to (over-)determine the textual self.[3] Susan Bordo wonders, with apparent exasperation, 'What sort of body is it that is free to change its shape and location at will, that can become anyone and travel everywhere?'[4] We might point to the suggestively fluid body/space of the lyric sequence, in which both writers reconceive the relationship between (what is for them of necessity the female) poet, embodied subject, text and place.

This book finds poets using poetic form to say things about the kind of cultural locations and contexts in and out of which they write.[5] It is perhaps predictable that it should come finally to rest on the hybridic, self-fracturing, disjunctive yet associative mode of the sequence, uniquely capable of signifying outside the more conventional-seeming 'logical and narrative and thematic links' on which other literary forms rely.[6] It seems no accident that 'Catulla' (uttered by the twenty-first-century female namesake of the Roman master-lyricist, from her home in Aberystwyth) and the polyvocal 'Erratics' (in which members of Antarctic explorations led by Scott and Shackleton reflect on their expeditionary experiences) are both explicitly framed by contexts which converse suggestively with their authors' own cultural situation(s).

Both sequences can be read in relation to earlier works, as is to be expected of poets who, though experienced writers, are still building their literary careers. That said, the disarming mixture of self-deprecation and ebullience which is Catulla's trademark manner, although redolent of poems like 'Birthday' and 'In This One', is afforded a vibrant consistency in the extended text-space of the sequence which renders her poetic realization near-virtuosic.[7] In the twenty-one poems of 'Erratics', meanwhile, Wynne Rhydderch's habitual shape-shifting and ventriloquy is tuned – in contrast – as much to the collective as to the individual, each of her six different personae being delicately laced into his uniquely alienated, uniquely co-dependent, geo-historical situation. In interview, Wynne Rhydderch (born, as she likes to put it, into a 'sea-faring family') explains how the sequence evolved partly from her fascinated sense of

> a ship as being its own little community . . . That [degree of interdependence] can be claustrophobic but not if the community is well-run and if people are forgiving. . . And I wanted to explore that: not just the mechanical way that the ship works but the generosity of spirit required to keep the wheels of the community running smoothly.[8]

The differences between the two sequences notwithstanding, in each the use of dramatic monologue serves to complicate the distinctive psychic sensibility ('Intimate, fragmented, self-analytical, open') associated with the lyric sequence's ability to 'go . . . many-sidedly into who and where we are subjectively'.[9] Thus does Catulla give sometimes brassily self-confident, sometimes agonised, voice to the twin cultural and temporal topoi – Rome and Aberystwyth – which are conjoined in her. The never wholly decorous, never wholly concupiscent patrician of 'If You Are Reading' and '99' ('Skin long starved / of touch can grow obscenely sensitive') blends with both the lusting cartoonist of ennui-ridden Aberystwyth ('Dear Kate'), and the fragile romantic which 'Catulla' ('May you never know / how slow unlovely women burn') makes transparent.[10] Likewise, sequentiality permits the layered architecture of 'Erratics', each of its speakers (preferred over their famous leaders) portrayed as persuasively by what they bring to our attention, as by the voice which speaks them.[11] Thus Third Officer Gerald Doorly, genial and sexually confident discoverer of the comedies of shipboard life; thus the self-disciplined artistic sensitivity of 'Birdie' Bowers, the game ingénue Apsley Cherry-Garrard, and seemingly nerveless, banjo-playing, musician-meterologist Leonard Hussey.

Both sequences are also caught up with the materialities of the body, and an emphatically embodied sensibility. Again, this is a theme of other works by both poets. There are traces of Catulla's acute body-consciousness (her mood ranging from impish dirty-mindedness – 'bumhole bawdy', Atkinson calls it – to agonisedly unrequited desire) in the prize-winning 'Tea', 'Quantum Theory for Beginners' and perhaps most explicitly the florid, whorling eroticism of 'Anthuriam' (*Kink and Particle*, pp. 7, 26, 53).[12] Likewise Wynne Rhydderch's scrutiny of human physiology ('First Aid Class', 'The X-Ray Room', *Rockclimbing in Silk*, pp. 12, 13; 'Decoupage', *Not in These Shoes*, p. 1) is revisited in 'Erratics'. The physical difficulties of surviving extreme cold are refracted, memorably, in poems about the challenges of making bread ('Blackout'), contriving onboard entertainment ('Three sweaters beneath petticoats / / and tails', 'The Minstrels at Minus Sixty'), and photography ('He lost the tip of his tongue / when it stuck to the camera / / at thirty below', 'Ponting') in the hostile emptiness of the polar ice-cap.[13] More surprising, and as striking, are the parallels which are made between the sensory human body and the resonant, movingly erotic materialities of, say, a travel-battered piano ('Each string quivered as we unshipped / the keyboard. She braced herself / / beneath the rigging, her hitch pins visible, / her struts jumpy', 'The Piano', *Banjo*, p. 35), or Hussey's beloved banjo, lissom co-survivor of Elephant Island:

> Back in London I hung her above the desk
> in my practice so I could treasure
> her stretch marks for ever, cherish
> those five strings that made me sing. ('In My Arms', *Banjo*, p.64)

Despite the drollery which characterises both, 'Erratics' and 'Catulla' gravely confirm that bodies never make straightforward signifiers. Invariably (paradoxically) both 'radically unfixed and historically contingent' at any time, bodies are also always – as Atkinson notes – mediated and haunted by the kinds of 'ideologies which fashion our understanding of the world and our place in it'. And yet, at the same time, as her own feisty but thin-skinned, licentious but inhibited Catulla dramatizes, the body is also always 'the very location of the thinker's here and now, a site of ongoing negotiation between subject and object, inside and outside, thought and sensation, personal and political, self and world'.[14] That meeting between epistemology and psyche, between context and immediacy, is only compounded, as Stephen Connor's fascinating study shows, in the entangling of body and voice which occurs in ventriloquy.

As Connor observes, voice is a key marker of individuality, partly because it makes for sociality: 'Nothing else about me defines me so intimately as my voice, precisely because there is no other feature of myself whose nature it is thus to move from me to the world, and to move me into the world.' Accordingly, any utterance involves the kind of liberating self-splitting ('I cannot speak without putting myself in the position of the one who hears my voice; without becoming, in principle at least, my own interlocutor . . . My voice is, literally, my way of taking leave of my senses') which underpins the self-doubling masquerade of theatrical performance, closely related to ventriloquy:

> As I speak, I seem to be situated in front of myself, leaving myself behind. But if my voice is out in front of me, this makes me feel that I am somewhere behind it . . . This can make my voice a persona, a mask, or sounding screen. At the same time, my voice is the advancement of a part of me, an uncovering by which I am exposed . . .[15]

The written text can be thought of as language spatialised; as the vehicle in/by which the evanescently aural is choreographed, or comes to utter itself as, physical/visual thus spatially mediated form. From that angle, Connor's remarks helpfully point out and unpack the hermeneutics of dramatic monologue, especially its ventriloquised projection of the (fictional) persona and the (actual) poet, simultaneously, both alongside *and* ahead/behind one another, in a kind of inexplicit textual paso doble. The metaphor is intended to underline the crucial spatialities of the effects which Connor ascribes to ventriloquy, for two reasons.

First, for writer and reader alike, the creative possibilities of dramatic monologue are frequently ventriloquised (for some commentators, always) bound up with its (usually explicit, usually fictional, or at least fictionalised) contexts. Conventionally, the power of dramatic monologue resides in the theatrically obvious (typically temporal and/or geographical) gap it opens between its author, its speaker and its various kinds of audience; much of the pleasure of 'Catulla' and 'Erratics' lies in our admiring sense of the distance(s) dividing each 'multiply situated, historically specific' poet from the 'multiply situated, historically specific' subject(s) to whom her sequence gives (textual) voice.[16] The kind of self-splitting which performance in general, and ventriloquism specifically, offers the woman poet has been identified by feminist literary critics for its liberating impact on gender-construction and gender-politics, in the 'complex matrix between poet, text and speech, which is mediated through culture, intention, expression, language and the often prescriptive ideas of the woman poet and her role'.[17]

Turning from gender-implications to the cultural-geographical emphases of this study, I am especially interested in the effect of a split self on the *locatedness*, or otherwise, of the two sequences I am discussing. Where 'Catulla' summons first-century BC Italy to a coastal university town in contemporary west Wales, 'Erratics' teleports us to the vast, freezing expanse of Antarctica in the last century. In their bi-locatedness, therefore, the self-doubling voices which Connor struggles to situate are thrown, by each poet, across the temporal, experiential and cultural spaces he goes on to depict:

> In moving from an interior to an exterior . . . a voice also announces and verifies the co-operation of bodies and the environments in which they have their being. The voice goes out into space, but also always, in its calling for a hearing, or for the necessity of being heard, opens a space for itself to go out into, resound in, and return from.[18]

Susan Stanford Friedman urges critics to investigate 'what kind of culture work [texts] perform as they are read and reread'.[19] It seems to me that 'Erratics' and 'Catulla' concertedly exploit the vocal/textual mobility that Connor locates in ventriloquism, if nothing else to unsettle and problematize the perilous fixities of cultural place-making. Since culture is articulated by, lodges and migrates in normally vocal bodies, as I and others have already suggested, there is political as well as imaginative power to be found in the 'syncretist, intermingling and hybrid interfusions of self and Other' which ventriloquy makes possible.[20] For Wynne Rhydderch, those 'interfusions' help undo the constraining effects of geography, history, and/or gender expectations on a proudly eclectic poetic imaginary: 'Part of what keeps me going is pretending to be somebody else through my poems . . . I do so enjoy moving in and out of different poetic selves.'[21]

Perhaps above all, Wynne Rhydderch's inhabiting of her Edwardian subjects' emphatically embodied sensibilities permits us access – via the creative imaginary in and through which culture also circulates – to a spectrum of alien sensations and unreal-seeming experiences. Crucially, however, her ventriloquised mining of those materials self-consciously destabilises the poet's own 'place' in the resulting poem; paradoxically, in the effort 'to write poems that will convince the reader: this or that event really happened to the speaker', Wynne Rhydderch explains, 'I put myself into each one. For that moment when the poem passes through me I am completely one with it and then it's gone from me, yet a part of me remains there in those lines.'[22] Atkinson echoes her: 'While I frequently deploy the informal qualities of spoken language [and] often use the first person to address an implied listener directly, . . . each poem is necessarily a new voice, a fresh standpoint.' She confesses to the intentional pursuit of a 'frisson of defamiliarisation . . . on a localised scale and within a more broadly accessible linguistic matrix, by placing discourses in playful, surreal and sometimes uncomfortable encounters'.[23]

Secondly, as Connor reminds us, in ventriloquy the poetic construct itself takes on a kind of bodiliness. Essentially freed of anything but its self-consciously fictionalised speaker, the dramatic monologue acquires its own powers of articulation; it offers itself less as map or terrain than a textual mouth. Wynne Rhydderch puts this facility to one kind of use: again and again her poems find arresting ways to make actual the convergence of psychological and practical in the situations they explore. In the context of peril and loss which shadows 'Erratics' as a whole, such poems are not always easy to read. Take the performative intertwining of cable-making, knitting wool and emotional relationships in the couplets of 'Cable-Knit' ('Meta-cabling comprises / three-cable plaits containing two-cable strands. / / In such cases the inner cables sometimes / go their separate ways. Like Lucy and I. / / I am still shocked by the electricity / of her hair through my hands', *Banjo*, p. 38). Those wrangling materialities translate, with ghastly poignancy, to the developing tanks of Scott's Terra Nova's darkroom, after the retrieval of the polar party's frozen remains, wherein

> we saw our companions
> swim towards us from the Pole, blink
> in its milky light, walk from the stiff
>
> chrysalis of film that had lain
> eight months beside their indigo skin ('My Year Out', *Banjo*, pp. 51–2)

As the thread of its distressing story is played out through successive lines, negative by negative as it were, the poem seems reflexively to utter the very filmic quality of a process it somehow manages to enact as well as describe.

As Friedman notes, all knowledge is situated in, produced out of and/or addresses specific locations.[24] In their inventive navigating of the different spatialities on which the ventriloquised lyric sequence opens, the two poets I have been discussing write themselves out of time, place and self, in order to conjure and converse with the reorienting cultural topology of their shared geopolitical hinterland. 'Erratics' and 'Catulla' articulate – in that useful word's hinging activity – the contingent relationship between body and selfhood each lifts from the tethers of biography, politics, and literature. Amid the political shifts and uncertainties of twenty-first-century Wales, both texts refuse to be conscripted into the cause of a fixed (cultural) identity neither poet recognises, still less seeks for herself.

This book has charted how poets use literary texts to reach towards a cultural-aesthetic 'beyond', an undecidable horizon which neither displaces, trivialises nor refutes women's claim on the geopolitical and ethnographic territory known as Wales. I was, therefore, very tempted to conclude an account which long enjoyed the working title of *In These Stones* on the bruising discovery of 'the quartz that had been Scott, Wilson // and Bowers [. . . // . . .] Erratics: rocks that differ / from those native to where they're found' ('Geology', *Banjo*, p. 54). After all, that poem 'sings' (from precisely the temporal and geo-cultural 'beyond' which makes its subjects 'erratic') of both the resonant 'glass' and 'stones' in Gwyneth Lewis's millennial poem. But Atkinson's vital, mouthy 'Catulla' points me towards a more obvious exit point, in returning me to the gendered literary-political history which she, Lewis, and indeed any woman who chooses to write poetry confronts. In her frank and full-hearted way, Catulla offers a powerfully unvarnished riposte both to the seductive (and probably amused) shade of her classical progenitor, never above lewdness himself, and to the faux-politesse of the poetic tradition he helped father. In this last, literary context Atkinson insistently constructs the lyric poem as a socially as well as culturally permissive place, into and/or out of which any woman might throw any kind of voice – libidinous, moody, tentative – she chooses. Catulla thus throws open to us her unashamedly gendered sense of literary as well as cultural place, in and through the licensing spaces of her poems' own textual imaginary. I am grateful to her for a door 'that is, as exits always are, also an entrance, is a passage or hatch[;] in French, as in many other languages . . . the door, the passage, through which one becomes another is marked feminine'.[25]

Notes

Preface

[1] Menna Elfyn, 'Stones in seventeen frames', in Damian Walford Davies (ed.), *Megalith: Eleven Journeys in Search of Stones* (Llandysul: Gomer, 2006), p. 88.

[2] Vicki Bertram (ed.), *Kicking Daffodils: Twentieth-century Women Poets* (Edinburgh: Edinburgh University Press, 1997), p. 7.

[3] Jahan Ramazani, *A Transnational Poetics* (Chicago: University of Chicago Press, 2009), p. 55.

[4] Angela Leighton, *On Form: Poetry Aestheticism and the Legacy of a Word* (Oxford: Oxford University Press, 2007), p. 3.

[5] Maggie Humm, *Border Traffic: Strategies of Contemporary Women Writers* (Manchester: Manchester University Press, 1991), p. 2.

[6] Gwyneth Lewis, interview with Alice Entwistle (unpublished, November 2006).

[7] Gwyneth Lewis, *Sunbathing in the Rain: A Cheerful Book on Depression* (London and Philadephia: Jessica Kingsley Publishers, 2007), p. 55.

[8] Leighton, *On Form*, pp. 2–3.

[9] Lewis/Entwistle interview, 2006.

[10] Hélène Cixous, 'Sorties: Out and out: attacks/ways out/forays', in Catherine Belsey and Jane Moore (eds), *The Feminist Reader* (Oxford: Wiley-Blackwell, 1989), pp. 101–16 (p. 116).

[11] Homi K. Bhabha (ed.), *Nation and Narration* (London and New York: Routledge, 1990), pp. 8, 11.

[12] Homi K. Bhabha, *The Location of Culture* (London and New York: Routledge, 1994), p. 38.

[13] Humm, *Border Traffic*, p. 9.

[14] Bhabha, *Location*, p. 7.

[15] Christian Jacob, *The Sovereign Map: Theoretical Approaches in Cartography Throughout History* (Chicago: University of Chicago Press, 2006), p. 185.

[16] Denis Wood, *The Power of Maps* (London and New York: The Guilford Press, 1992), p. 19.

[17] Ned Thomas, 'Parallels and paradigms', in M. Wynn Thomas (ed.), *Welsh Writing in English* (Cardiff: University of Wales Press, 2003), p. 313. Francesca Rhydderch, '"I know it and I want to feel it": reflections on identity and criticism', *Poetry Wales*, 34/1 (1998), 53.

[18] Rhydderch, 'Reflections', 52.

Introduction

[1] Robert Crawford, *Identifying Poets: Self and Territory in Twentieth Century Poetry* (Edinburgh: Edinburgh University Press, 1993), p. 13.

[2] Stephen Knight, 'Remember Us?', *Poetry Wales*, 33/3 (1998), 40.

[3] Henri Lefebvre, *The Production of Space*, trans. Donald Nicholson-Smith (Oxford: Blackwell Publishing, 1991), pp. 101–2.

[4] Doreen Massey, *For Space* (London: Sage Publications, 2005), p. 9.

[5] Edward Relph, *Place and Placelessness* (London: Pion Books, 1976), p. 16.

[6] Doreen Massey, *Space, Place and Gender* (Cambridge: Polity Press, 1994), p. 5.

[7] Charles Bernstein, 'Poetics of the Americas', quoted in James Acheson and Romana Huk (eds), *Contemporary British Poetry: Essays in Theory and Criticism* (New York: SUNY Press, 1996), p. 4.

[8] Jeremy Hooker, *Imagining Wales: A View of Modern Welsh Writing in English* (Cardiff: University of Wales Press, 2001), p. 2, emphasis mine.

[9] Michael Savage, Gaynor Bagnall and Brian Longhurst (eds.), *Globalization and Belonging* (London: Sage, 2005), p. 29. Thanks are due to Katie Gramich for alerting me to this helpful account.

[10] Joanne P. Sharp, 'Gendering nationhood: a feminist engagement with national identity', in Nancy Duncan (ed.), *Bodyspace: Destabilizing Geographies of Gender and Sexuality* (London: Routledge, 1996), p. 99.

[11] Benedict Anderson, *Imagined Communities: Reflections on the Origin and Spread of Nationalism* (London and New York: Verso, 1983; revd 1991), p. 145.

[12] See, for example, Angela John (ed.), *Our Mothers' Land: Chapters in Welsh Women's History, 1830–1939* (Cardiff University of Wales Press, 1991); Jane Aaron, Teresa Rees, Sandra Betts and Moira Vincentelli (eds), *Our Sisters' Land: The Changing Identities of Women in Wales* (Cardiff: University of Wales Press, 1994); Jane Aaron, *Nineteenth Century Women's Writing in Wales: Nation, Gender and Identity* (Cardiff: University of Wales Press, 2007); Katie Gramich, *Twentieth Century Women's Writing in Wales: Land, Gender, Belonging* (Cardiff: University of Wales Press, 2007).

[13] Liz Yorke, *Impertinent Voices: Subversive Strategies in Contemporary Women's Poetry* (London: Routledge, 1991), p. 4.

[14] Katie Gramich and Catherine Brennan (eds), *Welsh Women's Poetry 1460–2001: An Anthology* (Dinas Powys: Honno, 2003), p. xvii.

[15] Nancy Hartsock, 'Foucault on power: a theory for women', in L. J. Nicholson (ed.), *Feminism/Postmodernism* (London: Routledge, 1990), pp. 157–75; quoted in Linda McDowell, 'Spatializing feminisim: geographic perspectives', in Duncan (ed.), *Bodyspace*, p. 42.

[16] Gillian Rose, '"As if the mirrors had bled": masculine dwelling, masculinist theory and feminist masquerade', in Duncan (ed.), *BodySpace*, p. 57.

[17] Jahan Ramazani, *A Transnational Poetics* (Chicago: University of Chicago Press, 2009), p. 2.

[18] Bonnie Honig, 'Difference, dilemmas, and the politics of home', in Seyla Benhabib (ed.), *Democracy and Difference: Contesting the Boundaries of the Political* (Princeton: Princeton University Press, 1996), pp. 272–3.

[19] Hélène Cixous, 'Sorties: out and out: attacks/ways out/forays', in Catherine Belsey and Jane Moore (eds.), *The Feminist Reader* (Oxford: Wiley-Blackwell, 1989), p. 113, my emphasis.

[20] Relph, *Place and Placelessness*, p. 8.

[21] Jeremy Hooker, *The Poetry of Place: Essays and Reviews 1970–1981* (Manchester: Carcanet, 1982), p. 160.

[22] Gillian Clarke, 'Voice of the tribe', in *At The Source* (Manchester: Carcanet Press, 2008), p. 62, quoted by Hooker, in *Imagining Wales*, pp. 24–5.

[23] Matthew Jarvis, *Welsh Environments in Contemporary Poetry* (Cardiff: University of Wales Press, 2008), p. 141.

[24] Hooker, *Imagining Wales*, p. 25.

[25] Liz Bondi, 'Locating identity politics', in Michael Keith and Steve Pile (eds), *Place and the Politics of Identity* (London: Routledge, 1993), p. 98.

[26] Kirsti Bohata, 'Beyond authenticity? Hybridity and assimilation in Welsh writing in English', in Tony Brown and Russell Stephens (eds), *Nations and Relations: Writing across the British Isles* (Cardiff: New Welsh Review, 2000), p. 113.

[27] Jasmine Donahaye, 'Identification, rejection and cultural co-option in Welsh poetry in English', in Daniel G. Williams (ed.), *Slanderous Tongues: Essays on Welsh Poetry in English 1970–2005* (Bridgend: Seren 2010), p. 230.

[28] Susan Stanford Friedman, *Mappings: Feminism and the Cultural Geographies of Encounter* (Princeton: Princeton University Press, 1998), p. 19.

[29] Crawford, *Identifying Poets*, p. 11.

[30] Kenneth R. Smith, 'Praise of the past: the myth of eternal return in women writers', *Poetry Wales*, 24/4 (1989), 51.

[31] Gareth Alban Davies, 'The multi-screen cinema: poetry in Welsh 1950–1990', in Hans Werner Ludwig and Lothar Fietz (eds), *Poetry in the British Isles: Non-Metropolitan Perspectives* (Cardiff: University of Wales Press, 1995), pp. 120–1. Matthew Jarvis borrows this term for English-speaking Ruth Bidgood, writing out of traditionally Welsh-speaking old Brecknockshire (*Welsh Environments*, p. 69).

[32] Jane Aaron and M. Wynn Thomas, 'Pulling you through changes: Welsh writing in English before during and after two referenda', in M. Wynn Thomas (ed.), *Welsh Writing in English* (Cardiff: University of Wales Press, 2003), p. 279.
[33] Hooker, *Imagining Wales*, p. 7.
[34] Rhydderch, 'Reflections' 51.
[35] Richard Gwyn, *Pterodactyl's Wing* (Llandybie: Parthian, 2003), p. xxvii.
[36] Aaron and Thomas, 'Pulling', p. 300.
[37] Kirsti Bohata, 'Postcolonialism revisited', *New Welsh Review*, 69 (2005), 38.
[38] Matthew Jarvis, 'Repositioning Wales: poetry after the second flowering', in Daniel G. Williams (ed.), *Slanderous Tongues: Essays on Welsh Poetry in English 1970–2005* (Bridgend: Seren, 2010), pp. 49, 52.
[39] Leigh Gilmore, *Autobiographics: A Feminist Theory of Women's Self-representation* (Ithaca: Cornell University Press, 1994), pp. 4–5. Pertinently, Ned Thomas notes that 'over a quarter of today's Welsh population was born outside Wales', 'Parallels and paradigms', in M. Wynn Thomas (ed.), *Welsh Writing in English* (Cardiff: University of Wales Press, 2003), pp. 310–26.
[40] Frances Williams, 'The end in Bridgend', *Poetry Wales*, 37/2 (2001), 48.
[41] Donahaye, 'Identification, rejection and cultural co-option', p. 229.
[42] Thomas, 'Parallels and paradigms', p. 325.
[43] Bohata, 'Beyond authenticity', p. 115.
[44] Massey, *Space, Place and Gender*, p. 5.
[45] Bhabha, *Location*, pp. 1–2.
[46] Linden Peach, 'Family and Inheritance: Sally Roberts-Jones', *Poetry Wales*, 25/4 (1990), p. 46. See for example the work of Linden Peach, Jeremy Hooker, and Kenneth R. Smith.
[47] Lewis/Entwistle interview, 2006.
[48] Massey, *For Space*, p. 9.
[49] Kenneth Rexroth, *The New British Poets* (New York: New Directions, 1949), pp. xxviii–ix.
[50] Tony Conran, *Frontiers in Anglo-Welsh Poetry* (Cardiff: University of Wales Press, 1997), pp. 165–7.
[51] Margiad Evans, *Poems from Obscurity* (London: A. Dakers, 1949); *A Candle Ahead* (London: Chatto & Windus 1956). A treatment of Evans's poetry is among the essays collected in *Rediscovering Margiad Evans* (University of Wales Press, forthcoming).
[52] Patrick McGuinness, *Lynette Roberts: Collected Poems* (Manchester: Carcanet Press, 2005), p. 9; John Pikoulis, 'Lynette Roberts and Alun Lewis', *Poetry Wales*, 19/2 (1983), 25.
[53] Tony Conran, 'Lynette Roberts: the lyric pieces', *Poetry Wales*, 19/2 (1983), 131, 133.
[54] Denise Levertov, *Selected Poems*, (Newcastle upon Tyne: Bloodaxe Books, 1987) pp. 19, 28, 157.

[55] Randal Jenkins, 'The New Anglo Welsh poets', *Poetry Wales*, 8/2 (1972), 8.

[56] Menna Elfyn 'Three heads', *New Welsh Review*, 90 (2010), 40.

[57] Luce Irigaray, *Sexes and Genealogies*, trans. G. C. Gill (New York: Columbia University Press, 1993), p. 177, quoted in Rose, 'As if', in Duncan (ed.) *Bodyspace*, pp. 61–2.

[58] Lee M. Jenkins, 'Interculturalism: Imtiaz Dharker, Patience Agbabi, Jackie Kay and contemporary Irish poets', in Jane Dowson (ed.), *The Cambridge Companion to Twentieth-Century British and Irish Women's Poetry* (Cambridge: Cambridge University Press, 2011), p. 121.

[59] Angela Leighton, *On Form: Poetry Aestheticism and the Legacy of a Word* (Oxford: Oxford University Press, 2007), p. 1.

[60] Bhabha, *Location*, p. 219.

[61] Ibid., p. 4.

[62] Celeste M. Schenck astutely constructs genre 'not as pure . . . aesthetic category, but instead as a highly textured . . . site of political contention, . . . a function of gender and geography'; see Schenck, 'Exiled by genre: modernism, canonicity, and the politics of exclusion', in Mary Lynn Broe and Angela J. C. Ingram (eds), *Women Writing in Exile* (Chapel Hill and London: University of North Carolina Press, 1989), p. 173.

[63] Friedman, *Mappings*, p. 5.

[64] Neil Smith and Cindi Katz, 'Grounding metaphor: towards a spatialized politics', in Michael Keith and Steve Pile (eds), *Place and the Politics of Identity* (London: Routledge, 1993), p. 77.

[65] Ramazani, Jahan, *The Hybrid Muse: Postcolonial Poetry in English* (Chicago: University of Chicago Press, 2001), p. 6.

[66] Ramazani, *Transnational*, pp. 4, 6.

[67] For more on this, particularly the part played by eisteddfodau in Wales's Welsh-language poetic culture, see Donald Evans, 'Contemporary strict metre poetry', *Poetry Wales*, 28/4 (1993), 56.

[68] Bhabha, *Location*, p. 219.

[69] Kathleen M. Kirby, 'Re: mapping subjectivity: cartographic vision and the limits of politics', in Duncan (ed.), *Bodyspace*, p. 47.

[70] J. Hillis Miller, 'Derrida enisled', *Critical Inquiry*, 33/2, special issue: 'The late Derrida' (2007), 276. Thanks to Claire Connolly for pointing me to this source.

[71] Bhabha, *Location*, p. 52; Nigel Thrift, 'Inhuman geographies: landscapes of speed, light and power', in Paul Cloke, Marcus Doel, David Matless, Martin Phillips and Nigel Thrift (eds), *Writing the Rural: Five Cultural Geographies* (London: Paul Chapman, 1994), p. 222.

1: On the Border(s): The Interstitial Poetries of the Contact Zone

[1] Susan Stanford Friedman, *Mappings: Feminism and the Cultural Geographies of Encounter* (Princeton: Princeton University Press, 1998), p. 104.

[2] H. V. Morton, *In Search of Wales* (3rd edn, London: Methuen & Co., 1932), p. 18.

[3] Anne Stevenson, 'Poetry and place', in Lothar Fietz, Paul Hoffmann and Hans-Werner Ludwig (eds), *Regionalität, Nationalität und Internationalität in der zeitgenössischen lyrik* (Hamburg: Attempto, 1990), p. 208.

[4] Friedman, *Mappings*, p. 3.

[5] Ibid., p. 19.

[6] Homi K. Bhabha, *The Location of Culture* (London and New York: Routledge, 1994), p. 2.

[7] Maggie Humm, *Border Traffic: Strategies of Contemporary Women Writers* (Manchester: Manchester University Press, 1991), p. 16.

[8] See Deryn Rees-Jones, *Consorting with Angels: Essays on Modern Women Poets* (Tarset: Bloodaxe, 2005), p. 176.

[9] Francesca Rhydderch, '"A home where they had never lived": the learning of identity', *Poetry Wales*, 33/3 (1998), 53.

[10] Tony Conran, *Frontiers in Anglo-Welsh Poetry* (Cardiff: University of Wales Press, 1997), p. 259.

[11] Gillian Clarke, 'Gillian Clarke', in David Lloyd (ed.), *Writing on the Edge: Interviews with Writers and Editors of Wales* (Amsterdam: Rodopi BV, 1997), p. 9.

[12] Tristan Hughes, 'From Yoknapatawpha to Ynys Môn', *New Welsh Review*, 69 (2005), 23.

[13] Katie Gramich and Catherine Brennan (eds), *Welsh Women's Poetry 1460–2001: An Anthology* (Dinas Powys: Honno, 2003), p. xviii.

[14] Jo Gill, *Women's Poetry* (Edinburgh: Edinburgh University Press, 2007), pp. 168–9; Gillian Clarke, 'Beginning with Bendigeidfran', *At The Source* (Manchester: Carcanet Press, 2008), p. 9.

[15] Daniel Williams (ed.), *Who Speaks for Wales? Nation, Culture, Identity* (Cardiff: University of Wales Press, 2003), p. xxiv.

[16] Bhabha, *Location*, p. 6.

[17] Gwyneth Lewis, 'Six Poems on Nothing', *Parables & Faxes* (Tarset: Bloodaxe, 1998), p. 31.

[18] Jonathan Bate, *The Song of the Earth* (London: Picador, 2001), p. 65.

[19] D. F. Cosgrove, *Social Formation and Symbolic Landscape* (London: Croom Helm, 1984), pp. 1, 2.

[20] Simon Pugh (ed.), *Reading Landscape: Country, City, Capital* (Manchester: Manchester University Press, 1990), p. 2; Prys Gruffudd, 'Prospects of Wales: contested geographical imaginations', in Ralph Fevre and Andrew Thompson (eds), *Nation, Identity and Social Theory: Perspectives from*

Wales (Cardiff: University of Wales Press, 1999), pp. 149, 166. Jeremy Hooker, 'Poets, language and land: reflections on English-language Welsh poetry since the Second World War', *Welsh Writing in English*, 8 (2003), p. 141.

[21] Anne Stevenson, 'Poetry and place', *Between the Iceberg and the Ship: Selected Essays* (Ann Arbor: Michigan University Press, 1998), pp. 161, 175. Stevenson returns to the theme of Gwynedd and the topography and culture of her north Walian home in the ten lyrics loosely gathered up in 'Some Poems from Cwm Nantcol', the concluding section of *A Report from the Border* (Tarset: Bloodaxe, 2003), pp. 47–64.

[22] See Alice Entwistle, 'Post-pastoral perspectives on landscape and culture', Jane Dowson (ed.), *A Cambridge Companion to Twentieth Century British and Irish Women's Poetry* (Cambridge: Cambridge University Press, 2011), pp. 136–53.

[23] Stevenson, 'Poetry and Place', *Between the Iceberg and the Ship*, p. 161.

[24] Anne Cluysenaar, 'An interview' with Alice Entwistle, *Poetry Wales* 44/3 (2008–9), 30.

[25] Anne Cluysenaar, *Migrations* (Blaenau Ffestiniog: Cinnamon, 2011), pp. 27–47.

[26] Anne Cluysenaar, Graham Harthill and Hilary Llewellyn-Williams, 'Form and spirituality: connections and contrasts in poetic practice', *Scintilla*, 11 (2007), 65.

[27] Wendy Mulford, 'Alltud', *Scintilla*, 11 (2007), 153–61.

[28] Wendy Mulford, 'Finding space: Wendy Mulford interviewed', *Poetry Wales*, 46/1 (2010), 37.

[29] Kenneth R. Smith, 'Praise of the past: the myth of eternal return in women writers', *Poetry Wales*, 24/4 (1989), 51.

[30] Jeremy Hooker, '"Calling the female into presence": the poetry of Wendy Mulford', *The Swansea Review*, 22 (2003), 139.

[31] Wendy Mulford and Sara Maitland, *Virtuous Magic: Women Saints and their Meanings* (London: Mowbray, 1998), p. 369.

[32] Hooker, 'Calling the female into presence', 138–9.

[33] Unpublished letter to Anne Cluysenaar, quoted in Cluysenaar, Harthill, Llewellyn-Williams, 'Form and spirituality', 80–1.

[34] Hilary Llewellyn-Williams, 'The thread of poetry: Hilary Llewellyn-Williams interviewed by David Hart', *Planet*, 162 (2004), 32.

[35] Robert Minhinnick, 'An interview with Hilary Llewellyn-Williams', *Poetry Wales*, 33/2 (1997), 28.

[36] Jeremy Hooker, *Imagining Wales: A View of Modern Welsh Writing in English* (Cardiff: University of Wales Press, 2001), p. 160.

[37] Hilary Llewellyn-Williams, 'Maze Stone', *Animaculture* (Bridgend: Seren, 1997), pp. 35–6.

[38] Jo Shapcott, *Tender Taxes* (London: Faber, 2001), pp. 25–53.

[39] Janet Phillips, 'The shape-shifter: an interview with Jo Shapcott', *Poetry Review*, 91/1 (2001), 21.

[40] Shapcott, *Taxes*, p. xi.

[41] Ibid., p. x.

[42] Matthew Jarvis, 'Repositioning Wales: poetry after the second flowering', in Daniel G. Williams (ed.), *Slanderous Tongues: Essays on Welsh Poetry in English 1970–2005* (Bridgend: Seren, 2010), pp. 30, 35–6.

[43] Edward Soja, *Postmetropolis: Critical Studies of Cities and Regions* (Oxford: Blackwell, 2000), p. 6.

[44] Bhabha, *Location*, pp. 44–5.

[45] Leigh Gilmore, *Autobiographics: A Feminist Theory of Women's Self-Representation* (Ithaca: Cornell University Press, 1994), p. 29.

[46] Raymond Williams, *The Year 2000* [1983], quoted by Timothy Brennan in 'The national longing for form', in Homi K. Bhabha (ed.), *Nation and Narration* (London: Routledge, 1990), p. 63.

[47] Avril Horner and Angela Keane (eds), *Body Matters: Feminism, Textuality, Corporeality* (Manchester: Manchester University Press, 2000), p. 6.

[48] Tiffany Atkinson (ed.), *The Body* (Basingstoke and New York: Palgrave Macmillan, 2005), p. 2.

[49] Elizabeth Grosz, *Volatile Bodies: Towards a Corporeal Feminism* (Bloomington and Indianapolis: Indiana University Press, 1994), p. xi.

[50] Atkinson, *The Body*, pp. 4–5.

[51] Elizabeth Grosz, 'Bodies-Cities', in Gary Bridge and Sophie Watson (eds), *The Blackwell City Reader* (Oxford: Blackwell Publishing, 2002), p. 297.

[52] Maggie Humm, *Border Traffic: Strategies of Contemporary Women Writers* (Manchester: Manchester University Press, 1991), p. 125.

[53] Alicia Suskin Ostriker, *Stealing The Language: The Emergence of Women's Poetry in America* (London: The Women's Press, 1987), p. 92. One historical context (rather than catalyst) for this thematic might be the notorious 1847 Westminster Report on Welsh schools (known as the 'Blue Books Report'), which ascribed people's immoral behaviour – specifically female licentiousness – to the fact that they spoke Welsh rather than English. See Gwyneth Tyson Roberts, *The Language of the Blue Books: The Perfect Instrument of Empire* (Cardiff: University of Wales Press, 1998); Jane, *Nineteenth Century Women's Writing in Wales: Nation, Gender, Identity* (Cardiff: University of Wales Press, 2007), pp.74–7; and Harri Garrod Roberts, *Embodying Identity: Representations of the Body in Welsh Literature* (Cardiff: University of Wales Press, 2009).

[54] Eavan Boland, *Object Lessons: The Life of the Woman and the Poet in our Time* (London: Vintage, 1996), p. 232.

[55] For the only English-language treatment of this subject, see Jane Aaron, 'A review of the contribution of women to Welsh life and prospects for the future', *Transactions of the Honourable Society of Cymmrodorion*, new series 8 (2002), 188–204.

[56] Menna Elfyn and María do Cebreiro, 'In conversation', *Poetry Wales*, 44/2 (2008), 11.
[57] Menna Elfyn, 'Beyond the boundaries: a symposium on gender in poetry', *Planet*, 66 (1987–8), 55.
[58] Elfyn, 'In conversation', 13.
[59] Boland, *Object Lessons*, p. 219.
[60] Francesca Rhydderch, '"Between my tongue's borders": contemporary Welsh women's poetry', *Poetry Wales*, 33/4 (1998), 40.
[61] Elfyn, 'In conversation', 11.
[62] Thomas, M. Wynn, *Corresponding Cultures: The Two Literatures of Wales* (Cardiff: University of Wales Press, 1999), p. 204.
[63] '"[H]uman": an old Welsh word for tennis' (*Nodiadau*/Notes, *PN*, p. 291).
[64] Peter Stallybrass and Allon White, *The Politics and Poetics of Transgression* (New York: Cornell University Press, 1986), p. 192.
[65] See *PN*, *Nodiadau*/Notes, p. 293.
[66] Kathryn Gray, 'Wales and the next generation', *New Welsh Review*, 67 (2005), 7.
[67] Vicki Feaver, 'Body and Soul: The power of Sharon Olds', in Alison Mark and Deryn Rees-Jones (eds), *Contemporary Women's Poetry: Reading/ Writing/Practice* (Basingstoke: Macmillan, 2000), p. 144.
[68] Pascale Petit, 'Your definition of a desperado poet suits me: an interview with Lidia Vianu' (2006) [p. 2].
[69] Pascale Petit, 'Amazonia', *Poetry Wales*, 34/2 (1998), 52.
[70] Although I do not do so here, it is possible to read the poems of chapbook *The Wounded Deer* (2005), later collected and amplified in *What The Water Gave Me* (Bridgend: Seren, 2010), dealing with the trauma-filled biography of surrealist modernist Mexican painter Frida Kahlo, in much the same way. See Petit's 'First Hand', *New Welsh Review*, 88 (2010), 6–7.
[71] Pascale Petit, 'Private and public wars', *New Welsh Review*, 72 (2006), 10, 14.
[72] Pascale Petit, 'Confessing the Amazon and Frida Kahlo', *The Poetry Paper*, 6 (2009–10), 15.
[73] Pascale Petit, 'Interviewed by Oana-Teodora Ionescu' (2009) [p. 3].
[74] Petit/Vianu interview, 'Your definition' [2].
[75] Petit/Ionescu interview, 2009 [3].
[76] Petit/Vianu interview, 'Your definition' [2]; Petit/Ionescu interview, 2009 [5].
[77] Deryn Rees-Jones, interview with Zoe Brigley, unpublished typescript (n.d.).
[78] Gillian Clarke, 'The power of absence: Gillian Clarke in conversation with Deryn Rees-Jones', *Planet*, 144 (2001), 56.
[79] Rees-Jones/Brigley TS.
[80] Rees-Jones/Brigley TS.

[81] Deryn Rees-Jones, *Consorting with Angels: Essays on Modern Women Poets* (Tarset: Bloodaxe, 2005), p. 192.

[82] For a germane account of Lewis's bifurcated sense of cultural affiliation, grounded in a close-reading of 'the complexity by which th[is] poem positions relations between language, text and the female body', see Rees-Jones, *Consorting*, pp. 187–99 (p. 189).

[83] Gwyneth Lewis, 'The poet I might have been', *New Welsh Review*, 91 (2011), 9.

[84] Angela Leighton, *On Form: Poetry Aestheticism and the Legacy of a Word* (Oxford: Oxford University Press, 2007), pp. 1, 3.

[85] Gwyneth Lewis, interview with Alice Entwistle (unpublished, November 2006).

[86] Menna Elfyn and Janice Moore Fuller, 'Music, translation and poetry: an interview with Menna Elfyn', *Asheville Poetry Review*, 25 October 2002 [1].

[87] Menna Elfyn, interview with Alice Entwistle (unpublished, June 2010).

[88] Doris Sommer, *Bilingual Aesthetics: A New Sentimental Education* (Durham and London: Duke University Press, 2004), p. 190.

[89] Elfyn/Entwistle interview, 2010.

[90] Sommer, *Bilingual Aesthetics*, p. 191.

[91] Lisa Lewis, 'Between words and worlds: the performance of translation', in Katja Krebs and Christopher Meredith (eds), *Five Essays on Translation* (Pontypridd: University of Glamorgan, 2005), p. 34.

[92] Lisa Lewis 'Between words', p. 36.

[93] Elfyn/Entwistle interview, 2010.

[94] Menna Elfyn, 'Three heads', *New Welsh Review*, 90 (2010), 37, 38.

[95] Elfyn/Entwistle interview, 2010.

[96] Elfyn, 'In conversation', 11–12.

[97] Sommer, *Bilingual Aesthetics*, p. 68.

[98] Michael Cronin, 'Spaces between Irish worlds: travellers, translators and the new accelerators', in Tony Brown and Russell Stephens (eds), *Nations and Relations: Writing across the British Isles* (Cardiff: New Welsh Review, 2000), p. 47; Bhabha, *Location*, p. 224.

[99] Grahame Davies, 'Sleeping with the enemy: the tensions of literary translation', in Katja Krebs and Christopher Meredith (eds), *Five Essays on Translation* (Pontypridd: University of Glamorgan, 2005), pp. 16, 12.

[100] Tudur Hallam, 'When a *bardd* meets a poet: Menna Elfyn and the displacement of parallel facing texts', in Daniel G. Williams (ed.), *Slanderous Tongues: Essays on Welsh Poetry in English 19702.005* (Bridgend: Seren, 2010), pp. 91, 93.

[101] Hallam, 'When a *bardd* meets a poet', pp. 95, 105, 98–9. Jane Aaron private email to the author, September 2012.

[102] Sherry Simon, *Gender in Translation: Cultural Identity and the Politics of Transmission* (London: Routledge, 1996), p. 166, quoted in Hallam 'When a *Bardd* meets a poet', p. 97.

[103] Elfyn, 'Music, translation' [2].
[104] Elfyn/Entwistle interview, 2010.
[105] Elfyn, 'Music, translation' [4].
[106] Cronin, 'Spaces between Irish worlds', pp. 44, 51.
[107] Elfyn, 'In conversation', 11–12.
[108] Elfyn/Entwistle interview, 2010.
[109] Ibid.
[110] M. Wynn Thomas, *Corresponding Cultures*, p. 204.
[111] Elfyn, 'Music, translation' [2].
[112] Bhabha, *Location*, p. 50 (author's emphasis).
[113] M. Wynn Thomas, *Corresponding Cultures*, p. 205.
[114] Elfyn, 'In conversation', 13, 14.
[115] Ian Gregson, *Contemporary Poetry and Postmodernism: Dialogue and Estrangement* (New York: St Martin's Press, 1996), p. 7.
[116] Hallam, 'When a *bardd* meets a poet', p. 107.
[117] Elfyn, 'Three heads', 33, 38. Krog's words echo French gender theorist Hélène Cixous: 'Writing is the passageway, the entrance, the exit, the dwelling-place of the other in me.' Hélène Cixous, 'Sorties: out and out: attacks/ways out/forays', in Catherine Belsey and Jane Moore (eds), *The Feminist Reader* (Oxford: Wiley-Blackwell, 1989), p. 105.
[118] John Berger, *Keeping a Rendezvous* (London: Granta, 1993), p. 48, quoted in Elfyn, 'Writing is a bird in the hand', in Jane Aaron (ed.), *Our Sister's Land: The Changing Identities of Women in Wales* (Cardiff: University of Wales Press, 1994), p. 284.

2: 'Not without strangeness': Ruth Bidgood's Unhomely Mid Wales

[1] Julia Kristeva, *Strangers to Ourselves*, trans. Leon S. Roudiez (New York: Columbia University Press, 1991), p. 191.
[2] Ruth Bidgood, 'Strangeness', *New and Selected Poems* (Bridgend: Seren, 2004), p. 183.
[3] Sigmund Freud, 'The uncanny', *The Standard Edition of the Complete Psychological Works of Sigmund Freud, Volume XVII (1917–1919): An Infantile Neurosis and Other Works* (London: Vintage, 2001), p. 225.
[4] Jeremy Hooker, 'Ceridwen's daughters: Welsh women poets and the uses of tradition', *Welsh Writing in English: A Yearbook*, 1 (1995), p. 136.
[5] Viktor Schlovksy, 'Art as technique' (1917), quoted by Nicholas Royle, *The Uncanny* (Manchester: Manchester University Press, 2003), pp. 4–5.
[6] Royle, *The Uncanny*, p. 1.
[7] Donna Heiland, *Gothic and Gender: An Introduction* (Oxford: Blackwell, 2004), p. 130.
[8] Rosemary Marangoly George, *The Politics of Home: Postcolonial Relocations and Twentieth-Century Fiction* (Cambridge: Cambridge University Press, 1996), pp. 2, 9.

[9] Bonnie Honig, 'Difference, dilemmas, and the politics of home', in Seyla Benhabib (ed.), *Democracy and Difference: Contesting the Boundaries of the Political* (Princeton: Princeton University Press, 1996), p. 270.

[10] Homi K. Bhabha, *The Location of Culture* (London and New York: Routledge, 1994), p. 9.

[11] Kenneth R. Smith, 'The poetry of place: the haunted interiors', *Poetry Wales*, 24/2 (1988), 59.

[12] Ruth Bidgood, 'History is now and Wales: an interview with Jason Walford Davies', *Planet*, 137 (October–November 1999), 50.

[13] Ruth Bidgood, 'Heartland', *Poetry Wales*, 26/3 (1991), 9.

[14] Bhabha, *Location*, p. 1.

[15] Heiland, *Gothic and Gender*, p. 130.

[16] Jeremy Hooker, *Imagining Wales: A View of Modern Welsh Writing in English* (Cardiff: University of Wales Press, 2001), p. 19. In this her work would seem to endorse Jarvis's finding her appropriating the tradition of Welsh-language 'political landscape writing' which he understands to be for a critic like Bohata, for example, primarily masculine. See Matthew Jarvis, *Welsh Environments in Contemporary Poetry* (Cardiff: University of Wales Press, 2008), p. 58.

[17] Anthony Vidler, *The Architectural Uncanny: Essays in the Modern Unhomely* (London and Massachusetts: MIT Press, 1992), p. ix.

[18] Kristeva, *Strangers*, p. 187.

[19] Melanie van der Hoorn, 'Exorcising remains: architectural fragments as intermediaries between history and individual experience', *Journal of Material Culture*, 8/2 (2003), 189–90.

[20] Bidgood, 'History is now', 53.

[21] Kenneth R. Smith, 'The portrait poem: reproduction of mothering', *Poetry Wales*, 24/1 (1988), 54.

[22] Bidgood, 'Heartland', 8; the quotation is of course from Gerard Manley Hopkins's 'Binsey Poplars'.

[23] Ruth Bidgood, interview with Alice Entwistle (unpublished, July 2007).

[24] Ruth Bidgood, 'Interview with Angela Morton', *New Welsh Review*, 10 (1990), 39–40.

[25] Bidgood, 'History is now', 51–2.

[26] Christopher Woodward, *In Ruins* (London: Chatto & Windus, 2001), p. 3.

[27] Anne Janovitz, *England's Ruins: Poetic Purpose and the National Landscape* (Oxford: Blackwell, 1990), pp. 9–10.

[28] Bidgood, 'Heartland', 9.

[29] Ruth Bidgood, 'Writer's diary', *Books in Wales/Llais Lyfrau*, 2/96 (1996), 4.

[30] David Punter, 'Shape and shadow: on poetry and the uncanny', in David Punter (ed.), *A Companion to the Gothic* (Oxford: Blackwell, 2000), pp. 195, 201.

[31] Thomas McFarland, *Romanticism and the Forms of Ruin: Wordsworth, Coleridge and the Modalities of Fragmentation* (Princeton: Princeton University Press, 1981), p. 5.

[32] Janovitz, *England's Ruins*, p. 56.
[33] Guy Rotella, *Castings: Monuments and Monumentality in Elizabeth Bishop, Robert Lowell, James Merrill, Derek Walcott and Seamus Heaney* (Nashville: Vanderbilt University Press, 2004), p. 16.
[34] Bhabha, *Location*, p. 7 (author's emphases).
[35] Kristeva, *Strangers*, p. 192.
[36] Royle, *The Uncanny*, p. 2.
[37] Gwyn A. Williams, *When Was Wales? A History of the Welsh* (Harmondsworth: Penguin, 1985), p. 50–1.
[38] Alwyn D. Rees, *Life in a Welsh Countryside* (Cardiff: University of Wales Press, 1951), pp. 99–100.
[39] Bidgood,'Heartland', 9.
[40] Bidgood, 'History is now', 47; unpublished letter to the author (24 November 2010).
[41] Bidgood, 'Heartland', 8.
[42] Controversially, the Welsh Assembly's 1994 'Spatial Plan' redefined 'Central Area' incorporated Ceredigion, Powys, Carmarthenshire, Conwy, Denbighshire, Gwynedd, Brecon Beacons NPA and Snowdonia NPA: Welsh Assembly Government. Appendix 3: 'Existing Regional Boundaries & Groupings', in *People, Places, Futures: The Wales Spatial Plan* (November 2004) p. 66. For the most recent version of the plan, at the time of writing, see *http://wales.gov.uk/location/central_wales/spatial/diagram/?lang=en* (accessed December 2010). Musing on the fluidity of the term 'mid Wales' Bidgood warns 'Some people use it to include the western part (beyond present Powys) of the old Elenyold (Cambrian mountains); some stick to the present Powys (ie Montgomeryshire, Radnor & Brecon) in which the former N W Breconshire is the old Hundred of Builth (which is where my patch is)' (unpublished letter to the author, 24 November 2010).
[43] Bidgood, 'Heartland', 8.
[44] Bidgood, unpublished letter to the author (24 November 2010).
[45] Ruth Bidgood, 'Statement', for Welsh Academi (April 1984), unpublished typescript.
[46] Bidgood 'History is now', 50.
[47] In conversation (Bidgood/Entwistle interview, 2007), Bidgood cited Harri Webb as the source of this final image. Thanks go to Jane Aaron for locating it in: 'You did well to get out of / This hole in the middle of Wales, / Only there is nowhere else / Anywhere.' 'In Memory Harri Jones', *The Green Desert: Collected Poems 1950–1969* (Llandysul: Gwasg Gomer, 1969), p. 47. Professor Aaron points out the note by editor of *Harri Webb: Collected Poems* (Llandysul: Gomer, 1995), Meic Stephens: 'Originally entitled "Epynt" the poem was written in 1965 for T. H. Jones (1921–65) who emigrated from Builth to Australia in 1959, and drowned there' (p. 401).
[48] Bidgood, 'Writer's diary', 4.
[49] Jarvis, *Welsh Environments*, pp. 69, 71.

[50] Ruth Bidgood, 'Interview with Sally Roberts-Jones and Alexandra Trowbridge-Matthews', *Roundyhouse*, 7 (2001), 23.
[51] Smith, 'The poetry of place', 64.
[52] Ruth Bidgood, *Parishes of the Buzzard* (Port Talbot: Alun Books, 2001), p. 9.
[53] Bidgood, 'History is now', 49 (emphasis mine).
[54] Bidgood/Entwistle interview, 2007.
[55] Ibid.
[56] Bidgood 'Interview with Angela Morton', 38.
[57] The poem itself glosses *cyheuraeth* as 'death-lament'.
[58] Bidgood/Entwistle interview, 2007.
[59] Bidgood, 'Interview with Roberts-Jones and Trowbridge-Matthews', 5.
[60] Bidgood/Entwistle interview, 2007. *Dechreunos* seems to have been a highly localised custom: see also Glyn E. Jones. 'Hala dechreunos – a knitting assembly in Breconshire?', *Folk Life: A Journal of Ethnological Studies*, 23 (1984–5), 116–18.
[61] For a differently nuanced treatment of this poem, see Jarvis's reading in *Welsh Environments* (pp. 63–5).
[62] George, *The Politics of Home*, p. 9.
[63] Bhabha, *Location*, p. 9.
[64] Bidgood/Entwistle interview, 2007.
[65] Royle, *The Uncanny*, p. 16.
[66] Bhabha, *Location*, p. 11.
[67] Bidgood, 'Interview with Roberts-Jones and Trowbridge-Matthews' 6.
[68] Royle, *The Uncanny*, p. 16.
[69] Royle, *The Uncanny*, p. 1–2.
[70] Katie Gramich and Catherine Brennan (eds), *Welsh Women's Poetry 1460–2001: An Anthology* (Dinas Powys: Honno, 2003), p. xxxii–iii.
[71] Bidgood, 'Interview with Roberts-Jones and Trowbridge Matthews', 8.
[72] Bidgood, 'History is now', 54.
[73] Hooker, 'Ceridwen's daughters', 133.
[74] Bidgood/Entwistle interview, 2007.
[75] Janovitz, *England's Ruins*, p. 15.
[76] Ibid.
[77] Bidgood/Entwistle interview, 2007.
[78] Punter, 'Shape and shadow', p. 203.
[79] Hooker, 'Ceridwen's daughters', 136.

3: Frontier Country: Christine Evans

[1] Christine Evans, *Walking Through*, BBC, 2007.
[2] Homi K. Bhabha, *The Location of Culture* (London and New York: Routledge, 1994), p. 134.

[3] Doreen Massey, *Space, Place and Gender* (Cambridge: Polity Press, 1994) p. 1; Susan Stanford Friedman, *Mappings: Feminism and the Cultural Geographies of Encounter* (Princeton: Princeton University Press, 1998), p. 5.
[4] Bhabha, *Location*, p. 218.
[5] Massey, *Space, Place and Gender*, p. 5 (my emphasis).
[6] The blurb which identifies the island as 'the subject' of the collection seems to be confirmed by a note on the volume's dedication page announcing that 'Royalties from this book will be donated to the Bardsey Island Trust (*Ymddiriedolaeth Enlli*) for its work "to salvage what is left of the traditional way of life of this unique community".'
[7] Christine Evans, interview with Alice Entwistle (unpublished, 2007).
[8] Evans, *Walking Through*.
[9] Evans/Entwistle interview, 2007; Justin Wintle, *Furious Interiors: Wales, R. S. Thomas and God* (London: HarperCollins, 1996), p. 281.
[10] Mary Chitty, *The Monks on Enlli 1: c.500 AD to 1252 AD* (self-published, 1992), p. 8.
[11] Christine Evans and Wolf Marloh, *Bardsey* (Llandysul: Gomer, 2008).
[12] Evans/Entwistle interview, 2007. In 1968 Evans's in-laws, then one of Bardsey's remaining four farming families, were still running the Tŷ Pella farm. Evans explains, 'My father-in-law, Wil Tŷ Pella . . . came to farm here in 1929, following his father, who was the grandson of an old island family who'd left for the mainland 50 years earlier' (unpublished letter to the author, 21 September 2007).
[13] Gillian Beer, 'The island and the aeroplane: the case of Virginia Woolf', in Homi K. Bhabha (ed.), *Nation and Narration* (London and New York: Routledge, 1990), p. 271.
[14] Beer, 'The island and the aeroplane', p. 269.
[15] This is far from Evans's invention. Thomas Pennant's account of a visit to Enlli prompts Chitty to note: 'successive residents bear witness to the fertility of the soil of Bardsey. In fact the poet Celli implied that the whole island was a garden of Eden, visited by God' (*The Monks on Enlli 1*, p. 66).
[16] Matthew Jarvis, 'Christine Evans's Bardsey: Creating Sacred Space', *Welsh Writing in English: A Yearbook of Critical Essays*, 11 (2006–7), pp. 191–6; Beer, 'The island and the aeroplane', p. 265.
[17] Matthew Jarvis, *Welsh Environments in Contemporary Poetry* (Cardiff: University of Wales Press, 2008), p. 111.
[18] Hence her 'unease, what I feel as the precariousness, of travelling over that alien other world, its shifting tides and whirlpools, the grasping hands of seaweed' (*Walking Through*).
[19] Beer, 'The island and the aeroplane', p. 265.
[20] Details about the lighthouse are drawn from 'A Short History of Bardsey', information pack supplied with the holiday lets by Bardsey Island Trust (2007) and kindly loaned to the author by Christine Evans.

[21] Evans/Entwistle interview, 2007.

[22] Massey, *Space, Place and Gender*, p. 120.

[23] Christine Evans, *On the Headland: Uwchmynydd* (illustrated by Kim Atkinson), Places/*Y Man a'r Lle 11* (Newtown: Gwasg Gregynog, n.d.), p. [iii].

[24] Evans and Marloh, *Bardsey*, p. 1.

[25] R. S. Thomas, 'A year in Llŷn', in *Autobiographies*, trans. Jason Walford Davies (London: Dent, 1997), pp. 113–14.

[26] Ibid., p. 123.

[27] Evans, *Walking Through*.

[28] Evans's father-in-law, Wil Evans, was for many years the Bardsey boatman, known locally as Wil Tŷ Pella; 'we called him Taid', Evans/Entwistle interview, 2007.

[29] Chitty, *The Monks on Enlli 1*, p. 8.

[30] Massey, *Space, Place and Gender*, p. 121.

[31] Katie Gramich, *Twentieth-Century Women's Writing in Wales: Land, Gender, Belonging* (Cardiff; University of Wales Press, 2007), p. 157.

[32] Massey, *Space, Place and Gender*, p. 5.

[33] Gramich, *Twentieth-Century Women's Writing*, p. 156.

[34] Edward Relph, *Place and Placelessness* (London: Pion Books, 1976). p. 122.

[35] R. S. Thomas, 'A year', p. 151.

[36] Christine Evans, 'Christine Evans', in Meic Stephens (ed.), *The Bright Field: An Anthology of Contemporary Poetry from Wales* (Manchester: Carcanet, 1991), p. 86.

[37] Massey, *Space, Place and Gender*, p. 81.

[38] Evans, 'Christine Evans', *The Bright Field*, p. 86.

[39] Evans/Entwistle interview, 2007.

[40] Beverly J. Stoeltje, '"A helpmate for man indeed": the image of the frontier woman', *Journal of American Folklore*, 88/347 (1975), 25.

[41] Chitty, *The Monks on Enlli 1*, p. 8.

[42] Unpublished email to the author, 2 June 2007.

[43] Evans/Entwistle interview, 2007.

[44] Ibid.

[45] Ibid.

[46] Ibid.

[47] Likewise in *On The Headland,* amid 'the lived-in untidiness of Uwchmynydd', and in a moment sharply reminiscent of the story of rural depopulation lamented in Ruth Bidgood's 'All Souls', Evans rehearses her own 'litany of houses gone dark or only intermittently illuminated – Pennant and Pant, Bryn Sander and Bwlch, Pencwm and Ystolhelyg – every winter more gaps in the chain of lights we look for at dusk. A quarter of places that were homes are used only in summer' ([iv]).

[48] Unpublished email to the author, 2 June 2007.

[49] Gramich, *Twentieth-Century Women's Writing*, p. 156; Evans, *Walking Through*.
[50] Evans/Entwistle interview, 2007.
[51] R. S. Thomas, 'Interview with Benedict Nightingale', *Guardian*, 4 March 1964.
[52] Evans/Entwistle interview, 2007.
[53] Ibid.
[54] Ibid.
[55] Evans, 'Christine Evans', in Sheenagh Pugh, Gloria Evans Davies, Christine Evans, Sally Roberts Jones and Val Warner, 'Is there a women's poetry?', *Poetry Wales*, 23/1 (1987), 44. See chapter 5 for more on the relationship between poetry and storytelling, instanced in that essay by Evans herself, Gillian Clarke and Catherine Fisher.
[56] Evans/Entwistle interview, 2007.
[57] Evans, 'Is there a women's poetry?', 44; Evans has been read as an explicitly female-centred writer by, for example, Linden Peach and Kenneth R. Smith.
[58] Evans/Entwistle interview, 2007.
[59] Evans, in 'Beyond the boundaries: a symposium on gender in poetry', *Planet*, 66 (1987–8), 44–5.
[60] Evans/Entwistle interview, 2007.
[61] Ibid.
[62] Evans, 'Is there a women's poetry?', 44–5.
[63] Evans, 'Beyond the boundaries', 44–5.
[64] Nigel Jenkins, 'Foreword' to *Burning the Candle* (Bridgend: Seren, 2006), p. 7.
[65] Ibid.
[66] Evans translates the phrase in the journal which follows the poem itself, in the entry recorded as 'Wednesday 21st May, last thing': 'I pick up my pocket Welsh Dictionary from where it has fallen off the shelf and idly flicking through it notice "*Canhwyllau llygaid*," the pupils of the eyes (literally, eye-candles)' (*BtC*, p. 89).
[67] Gramich, *Twentieth-Century Women's Writing*, p. 156.
[68] Evans/Entwistle interview, 2007.
[69] Harri Webb, Letter, *Poetry Wales* ['Special Issue on R. S. Thomas'] (1972), 123.
[70] Evans/Entwistle interview, 2007.

4: 'A kind of authentic lie': Gwyneth Lewis's English-Language Sequences

[1] This chapter originated in a paper given at the annual conference for the Association of Welsh Writing in English March 2007; another version appears in *Life Writing* (special issue on poetry and autobiography), 6/1 (2009), 27–4.

[2] Gwyneth Lewis, 'Negotiations: Gwyneth Lewis in conversation with Ian Gregson', *Planet*, 173 (2005), 55.
[3] Ibid., 56.
[4] Gwyneth Lewis, 'Whose coat is that jacket? Whose hat is that cap?', in W. N. Herbert and Matthew Hollis (eds), *Strong Words: Modern Poets on Modern Poetry* (Tarset: Bloodaxe, 2000), p. 269.
[5] Hélène Cixous, 'Sorties: out and out: attacks/ways out/forays', in Catherine Belsey and Jane Moore (eds), *The Feminist Reader* (Oxford: Wiley-Blackwell, 1989), pp. 104, 106.
[6] Ibid., pp. 116, 103.
[7] Gwyneth Lewis, *Sunbathing in the Rain: A Cheerful Book on Depression* (London and Philadephia: Jessica Kingsley Publishers, 2007), p. 149.
[8] Gwyneth Lewis, *Chaotic Angels: Poems in English.* (Tarset: Bloodaxe, 2005), p. 143.
[9] Gwyneth Lewis, interview with Alice Entwistle (unpublished, November 2006).
[10] Gwyneth Lewis, 'On writing poetry in two languages', *Modern Poetry in Translation*, 7 (1995), 80.
[11] Lewis, 'Negotiations', 52–3.
[12] Lewis, *Sunbathing in the Rain*, pp. 59, 194, 209, xvi–xvii.
[13] Jo Gill, 'Anne Sexton and confessional poetics', *The Review of English Studies*, 55/220 (2004), 427.
[14] Janet Phillips, 'The shape-shifter: an interview with Jo Shapcott', *Poetry Review*, 91/1 (2001), 21.
[15] Gill, 'Anne Sexton and confessional poetics', 427, 445.
[16] Leigh, *Autobiographics, A Feminist Theory of Women's Self-Representation* (Ithaca: Cornell University Press, 1994), pp. 226 (author's emphases), xv.
[17] 'The confession is a ritual of discourse in which the speaking subject is also the subject of the statement; it is also a ritual that unfolds within a power relationship, for one does not confess without the presence (or virtual presence) of a partner who is not simply the interlocutor but the authority who requires the confession, prescribes and appreciates it, and intervenes in order to judge, punish, forgive, console, and reconcile; a ritual in which the truth is corroborated by the obstacles and resistances it has had to surmount in order to be formulated; and finally, a ritual in which the expression alone, independently of its external consequences, produces intrinsic modifications in the person who articulates it: it exonerates, redeems, and purifies him. A technique . . . for producing truth' (Foucault, *The History of Sexuality*, vol. 1, pp. 61–2, quoted in Gill, 'Anne Sexton and confessional poetics', 432). I am indebted to Jo Gill for many of the ideas on which this treatment of Lewis draws.
[18] M. L. Rosenthal and Sally M. Gall, *The Modern Poetic Sequence: The Genius of Modern Poetry* (Oxford: Oxford University Press, 1983); Roland Greene, *Post-Petrarchism: Origins and Innovations of the Western Lyric Sequence* (Princeton: Princeton University Press, 1991), pp. 9–14.

[19] Lewis/Entwistle interview, 2006.
[20] Michael Thurston, '"Writing at the edge": Gillian Clarke's Cofiant', *Contemporary Literature*, 34/2 (2003), 285.
[21] Like the deservedly well-known 'Cofiant', many of Clarke's finest works to date have been lyric sequences, chief among them 'The King of Britain's Daughter' (1993).
[22] Lewis, 'Negotiations', 53.
[23] Lewis/Entwistle interview, 2006. Gratifyingly, Lewis was named as the winner of the Crown (*Y Goron*) at the National Eisteddfod in August 2012 for a sequence of poems on the subject of '*Ynys*' or 'The Island'.
[24] Gladys Mary Coles, 'The narrative tradition in contemporary Welsh poetry in English', *Poetry Wales*, 31/3 (1996), 20.
[25] The poem has caused consternation in its construction of the relationship between father and child, to Lewis's amused chagrin: 'When that poem . . . first came out, I remember, people always said: oh that poor girl, she's been abused. NO! No! I mean *CULTURALLY*! And I always think, oh dear, my poor father . . .' (Lewis/Entwistle interview, 2006).
[26] For a lively account of the story see the feature published in the 'First Person' series, *Guardian*, 18 November 2006.
[27] Lewis/Entwistle interview, 2006.
[28] Lewis, 'Negotiations', 53–4.
[29] Lewis/Entwistle interview, 2006.
[30] Lewis, 'Negotiations', 54.
[31] Gwyneth Lewis, 'Out of the blue', *MsLexia*, 26 (2005), 23.
[32] Lewis, 'Negotiations', 55.
[33] Ruth McElroy, 'The rhyming detective', *Planet*, 141 (2000), 22.
[34] Lewis/Entwistle, interview, 2006.
[35] Lewis/Entwistle interview, 2006.
[36] Lewis, 'Negotiations', 55.

5: Traverses: Gillian Clarke, Christine Evans, Catherine Fisher and Ireland/Wales

[1] Susan Stanford Friedman, *Mappings: Feminism and the Cultural Geographies of Encounter* (Princeton: Princeton University Press, 1998), p. 242.
[2] John Kerrigan, 'Divided kingdoms and the local epic: *Mercian Hymns* to *The King of Britain's Daughter*', *Yale Journal of Criticism*, 13/1 (2000), 14. Jim Shanahan, for example, discovers four Irish novels (published in the wake of French attacks on the west coasts of both Wales and Ireland in the eighteenth and nineteenth centuries) which use Wales as an implicitly critical means of cultural 'triangulation'. Interestingly, three of his chosen texts are anonymous, but attributed to women: Jim Shananan, '"The fostering aid

of a sister country"; Wales in Irish novels, 1796–1810', in Damian Walford Davies and Lynda Pratt (eds), *Wales and the Romantic Imagination* (Cardiff: University of Wales Press, 2007), p. 126. See also the accounts of the connections between R. S. Thomas and Irish literature by Damian Walford Davies (*Almanac*, 13 [2008–9], 1–26) and Sam Perry (*Almanac*, 13 [2008–9], 126–61), for example. Gramich finds Margiad Evans enjoying the differences and similarities between the two countries in her 'Journal in Ireland' (*New Welsh Review*, 89), while the Honno Classics edition of Menna Gallie's *You're Welcome to Ulster!* (ed. Angela John and Claire Connolly, 2010) savours the novel's witty reprising of Northern Irish and Welsh socio-historical cross-currencies in the 1960s.

3 Gwyneth Lewis, 'Criss-crossings; literary adventures on Irish and Welsh shores', *www.poetrysociety.org.uk/lib*, pp. 1, 3.

4 Claire Connolly and Katie Gramich, 'Introduction', *Irish Studies Review*, 17/1 (2009), 1.

5 More recent initiatives include the 2008 Academi-sponsored arts initiative 'Belfast meets Wales'; and the AHRC-funded Wales–Ireland interdisciplinary research network. Founded in 2007 and sponsored by the governments of both countries, through a series of symposia, conferences, seminars and public lectures, this important cultural initiative has been nurturing a robust new discourse with its own catalysing effects.

6 Cecile O'Rahilly, *Ireland and Wales: Their Historical and Literary Relations* (London: Longman, 1924).

7 See Linden Peach, *Ancestral Lines: Culture and Identity in the Work of Six Contemporary Poets* (Bridgend: Seren, 1992), pp. 15–29; 'Paper margins: the "outside" in poetry in the 1980s and 1990s', in Glenda Norquay and Gerry Smith (eds), *Across the Margins: Cultural Identity and Change in the Atlantic Archipelago* (Manchester: Manchester University Press, 2002), pp. 101–16.

8 Jo Furber, '"Wonderful what will come out of darkness": gender and nationhood in the work of Welsh and Irish women poets', in Daniel G. Williams (ed.), *Slanderous Tongues: Essays on Welsh poetry in English 1970–2005* (Bridgend: Seren, 2010), pp. 137–62.

9 Catherine Brennan, *Angers, Fantasies and Ghostly Fears: Nineteenth-Century Women from Wales and English-Language Poetry* (Cardiff: University of Wales Press, 2003).

10 As my colleague Kevin Mills has pointed out, her name echoes the Welsh name for Anglesey, Ynys Môn, also known as Mother of Wales.

11 Brennan, *Angers, Fantasies and Ghostly Fears*, p. 163–4.

12 Furber, 'Wonderful what will come', p. 159.

13 Louis Althusser, quoted by Rachel Blau DuPlessis, *Writing Beyond the Ending: Narrative Strategies of Twentieth-Century Women Writers* (Bloomington: Indiana University Press, 1985), p. 3.

[14] J. H. Delargy, 'The Gaelic story-teller'; quoted by Alwyn D. Rees and Brinley Rees, *Celtic Heritage: Ancient Tradition in Ireland and Wales* (London: Thames and Hudson, 1961), p. 13.

[15] Estyn Evans, *The Personality of Ireland: Habitat, Heritage and History* (Cambridge: Cambridge University Press, 1973), pp. 69, 96.

[16] Clodagh Brennan Harvey, *Contemporary Irish Traditional Narrative: The English Language Tradition* (Berkeley: University of California Press, 1992); Walter Benjamin, *Illuminations*, trans. Harry Zoorn (London: Pimlico, 1999), p. 87.

[17] Walter J. Ong, *Orality and Literacy: The Technologizing of the Word* (London and New York: Methuen, 1982), pp. 41–2.

[18] Rees and Rees, *Celtic Heritage*, p. 212.

[19] Ong, *Orality and Literacy*, p. 34.

[20] Rees and Rees, *Celtic Heritage*, pp. 15–16.

[21] Evans, *The Personality of Ireland*, p. 77.

[22] Glyn Jones, *The Dragon Has Two Tongues: Essays on Anglo-Welsh Writers and Writing*, ed. Tony Brown (Cardiff: University of Wales Press, 2001), p. xi.

[23] Emyr Humphreys, *The Taliesin Tradition: A Quest for the Welsh Identity* (Bridgend: Seren, 2000), p. 6.

[24] Ong, *Orality and Literacy*, p. 41.

[25] Blau DuPlessis, *Writing Beyond the Ending*, p. 3.

[26] Humphreys, *The Taliesin Tradition*, p. 61.

[27] Ong, *Orality and Literacy*, p. 105.

[28] Katie Gramich and Catherine Brennan (eds), *Welsh Women's Poetry 1460–2001: An Anthology* (Dinas Powys: Honno, 2003), pp. xvii–xxii.

[29] Harvey, *Contemporary Irish Traditional Narrative*, p. 12; Rees and Rees, *Celtic Heritage*, p. 14.

[30] Harvey, *Contemporary Irish Traditional Narrative*, p. 5.

[31] Friedman, *Mappings*, p. 229.

[32] Humphreys, *The Taliesin Tradition*, p. 60. It should not be forgotten how much Humphreys has done, ironically, to put women at the centre of that history in his own fiction, particularly the seven novels comprising the *Land of the Living* sequence. Thanks to Katie Gramich for pointing this out.

[33] Friedman, *Mappings*, p. 236.

[34] See especially 'Craving stories: narrative and lyric in feminist theory and poetic practice' (chapter 9) in *Mappings*, pp. 228–42, as well as Susan Stanford Friedman, 'When a "long" poem is a "big" poem: self-authorising strategies in women's twentieth-century "long poems"', in Robyn R. Warhol and Diane Price Herndl (eds), *Feminisms: An Anthology of Literary Theory and Criticism* (Basingstoke: Macmillan, 1997), pp. 721–38.

[35] Leigh Gilmore, *Autobiographics: A Feminist Theory of Women's Self-Representation* (Ithaca: Cornell University Press, 1994), p. 49.

[36] Friedman, *Mappings*, p. 229.

[37] Gladys Mary Coles, 'The narrative tradition in contemporary Welsh poetry in English', *Poetry Wales*, 31/3 (1996), 20.
[38] Ong, *Orality and Literacy*, p. 40.
[39] Friedman, *Mappings*, p. 234.
[40] Ibid. p. 242.
[41] John Kerrigan, *Archipelagic English: Literature, History and Politics 1603–1707* (Oxford: Oxford University Press, 2008), pp. 48, 88.
[42] Dewi Roberts (ed.), *Coastline: An Anthology of the Welsh Coast* (Llanwrst: Gwasg Carreg Gwalch, 2005), p.11.
[43] John Kerrigan, *Archipelagic English*, p. 34.
[44] Gillian Clarke, 'Cordelia's "nothing"', *At The Source* (Manchester: Carcanet Press, 2008), p. 32.
[45] Clarke, 'Beginning with Bendigeidfran', *At The Source* (Manchester: Carcanet Press, 2008), p. 10.
[46] Judith Kinsman (ed.), *Six Women Poets* (Oxford: Oxford University Press, 1992), p. 2.
[47] Gillian Clarke, 'The power of absence: Gillian Clarke in conversation with Deryn Rees-Jones', *Planet*, 144 (2001), 56.
[48] Clarke, 'Beginning with Bendigeidfran', p. 11.
[49] Clarke, 'Cordelia's "nothing"', p. 31.
[50] Gillian Clarke, 'The King of Britain's Daughter', in Tony Curtis (ed.), *How Poets Work* (Bridgend: Seren, 1996), p. 122.
[51] Clarke, 'Cordelia's "nothing"', p. 32.
[52] John Kerrigan, 'Divided kingdoms and the local epic: *Mercian Hymns* to *The King of Britain's Daughter*', *Yale Journal of Criticism*, 13/1 (2000), 17.
[53] Coles, 'The narrative tradition', 22.
[54] Kerrigan, 'Divided kingdoms', 19.
[55] Enid Roberts, *Bardsey Bound: Pilgrim Routes to Wales' Holy Island* (Talybont: Y Lolfa Cyf, 2008), pp. 22, 32.
[56] Christine Evans and Wolf Marloh, *Bardsey* (Llandysul: Gomer, 2008), p. 11.
[57] Elfed Gruffydd, *Llŷn*, trans. Gwyneth Owen (Llanrwst: Gwasg Carreg Gwalch, 2003), p. 34.
[58] Evans and Marloh, *Bardsey*, pp. 73, 72.
[59] Evans and Marloh, *Bardsey*, p. 135.
[60] Quoted by Mary Chitty, in what is presumably a translation from the original Latin, in *The Monks on Enlli 1: c.500 AD to 1252 AD* (self-published, 1992), p. 28.
[61] A note in the appendix which freely admits to having imagined the details of this section identifies Benlli as 'King of Powys, possibly Irish . . . [and] defeated in an uprising led by Cadell in 474'. There is some evidence to suggest that Bardsey may have been occupied at some point in the fifth or sixth centuries (see Chitty *The Monkson Enlli 1*, pp. 8, 12); commentators suspect that the island was inhabited earlier but no evidence has yet been found in support of this theory.
[62] Evans, *Bardsey*, p. 135.

[63] Friedman, *Mappings*, p. 237.
[64] Catherine Fisher, interview with Alice Entwistle (unpublished, 2007).
[65] Rees and Rees, *Celtic Heritage*, pp. 314–25.
[66] Paul Muldoon, *To Ireland, I: An Abecedary of Irish Literature* (London: Faber, 2000).
[67] Richard Kirkland, 'Paul Muldoon's "Immram" and "Immrama": writing for a sense of displacement', *Essays in Poetics*, 17/1 (1992), 38.
[68] Catherine Fisher, 'Myth and history', *New Welsh Review*, 89 (2011), 43.
[69] Fisher/Entwistle interview, 2007.
[70] Ibid..
[71] Ibid.
[72] David Lloyd, *Anomalous States: Irish Writing and the Post-Colonial Moment* (Dublin: Lilliput Press, 1993), p. 24.
[73] Fisher/Entwistle interview, 2007.
[74] Paul O'Leary, *Immigration and Integration: The Irish in Wales 1798–1922* (Cardiff: University of Wales Press, 2000), pp. 45, 218, 11. Both Anne O'Dowd (*Spalpeens and Tattie-Hokers: History and Folklore of the Irish Migratory Agricultural Worker in Ireland and Britain* (Dublin: Irish Academic Press, 1991)) and Janet Nolan (*Ourselves Alone: Women's Emigration from Ireland 1885–1920* (Lexington: University Press of Kentucky, 1989)) overlook migrant experiences in Wales. Ruth-Ann Harris (*The Nearest Place That Wasn't Ireland: Early Nineteenth-Century Irish Labor Migration* (Iowa State University Press, 1994)) cites her grandmother's stories 'about the Irish whom she remembered while she was growing up in Penarth, walking barefoot through Wales on their yearly search for work' but scarcely mentions Wales thereafter (p. xvii). O'Leary notes that 'evidence on the Irish in Wales is elusive and partial, suggesting avenues of enquiry but rarely enlightening fully' (p. 11).
[75] David Arnold, *Famine, Social Crisis and Historical Change* (New York and Oxford: Blackwell, 1988), quoted by Margaret Kelleher, *The Feminization of Famine: Expressions of the Inexpressible?* (Cork: Cork University Press, 1997), p. 227.
[76] O'Leary, *Immigration and Integration*, pp. 301, 65.
[77] Cecil Woodham-Smith, *The Great Hunger* (London: Hamish Hamilton, 1962), p. 280; O'Leary, *Immigration and Integration*, p. 87.
[78] O'Leary, *Immigration and Integration*, p. 313.
[79] Kelleher, *The Feminization of Famine*, pp. 8, 111.
[80] For a complementary reading of this poem, see the treatment in Katie Gramich's *Twentieth-Century Women's Writing in Wales: Land, Gender, Belonging* (Cardiff; University of Wales Press, 2007), pp. 158–9.
[81] O'Leary, *Immigration and Integration*, p. 6–7.
[82] Kelleher, *The Feminization of Famine*, p. 111.
[83] Blau DuPlessis, *Writing Beyond The Ending*, p. 3.
[84] Friedman, *Mappings*, p. 242.

6: Wales and/or Thereabouts: Sheenagh Pugh, Wendy Mulford and Zoë Skoulding

[1] Michael Seidel, *Exile and the Narrative Imagination* (New York: Yale University Press, 1986), p. 3.

[2] Nigel Thrift, 'Inhuman geographies: landscapes of speed, light and power', in Paul Cloke, Marcus Doel, David Matless, Martin Phillips and Nigel Thrift (eds), *Writing the Rural: Five Cultural Geographies* (London: Paul Chapman, 1994), p. 192.

[3] Ibid., p. 227.

[4] Jahan Ramazani, *A Transnational Poetics* (Chicago: University of Chicago Press, 2009), p. 56–7. For Ramazani, to notice poetry's making of 'complex intercultural relationships across boundaries of nation and ethnicity, without erasing those boundaries or the earlier hybridizations they contain, is to begin to explain how poetry helps newness enter the world' (p. 47).

[5] Quoted by Edward R. Said, *Reflections on Exile and Other Essays* (New York: Harvard University Press, 2000), p. 568.

[6] Kathryn Gray, 'Wales and the next generation', *New Welsh Review*, 67 (2005), 7.

[7] Tony Conran, 'Poetry Wales and the Second Flowering', in M. Wynn Thomas (ed.), *Welsh Writing in English* (Cardiff: University of Wales Press, 2003), p. 253, author's emphasis.

[8] Wendy Mulford, 'A city boy at heart: John James and the industrial south Welsh heartland', *Poetry Wales*, 44/1 (2008), 21.

[9] Said, *Reflections on Exile*, p. 185; Michael Keith and Steve Pile, 'Introduction part 1: the politics of place', in Michael Keith and Steve Pile (eds), *Place and the Politics of Identity* (London and New York: Routledge, 1993), p. 3.

[10] Anne Cluysenaar, unpublished email to the author, 25 August 2008.

[11] Said, *Reflections on Exile*, p. 186.

[12] Jo Gill, *Women's Poetry* (Edinburgh: Edinburgh University Press, 2007), p. 169.

[13] Susan Stanford Friedman, *Mappings: Feminism and the Cultural Geographies of Encounter* (Princeton: Princeton University Press, 1998), p. 68.

[14] Lee M. Jenkins, 'Interculturalism: Imtiaz Dharker, Patience Agbabi, Jackie Kay and contemporary Irish poets', in Jane Dowson (ed.), *The Cambridge Companion to Twentieth-Century British and Irish Women's Poetry* (Cambridge: Cambridge University Press, 2011), p. 121.

[15] Thrift, 'Inhuman geographies', p. 228.

[16] Melanie Petch, 'The mid-Atlantic imagination: Mina Loy, Ruth Fainlight, Anne Stevenson, Anne Rouse and Eva Salzman', in Jane Dowson (ed.), *The Cambridge Companion to Twentieth-Century British and Irish Women's Poetry* (Cambridge: Cambridge University Press, 2011), p. 82.

[17] Katie Gramich, *Twentieth-Century Women's Writing in Wales: Land, Gender, Belonging* (Cardiff; University of Wales Press, 2007), p. 191.

[18] Michael Billig, *Banal Nationalism* (London: Sage Publications, 1995), p. 107.

[19] See Alice Entwistle, 'Taking place', in Zoë Skoulding and Ian Davidson (eds), *Poetry and Place* (Amsterdam: Rodopi, 2013), pp. 69–92; 'Women poets and cultural positioning', in Peter Robinson (ed.), *The Oxford Handbook of Contemporary British and Irish Poetry* (Oxford: Oxford University Press, 2013).

[20] Jacques Derrida, 'White Mythology: Metaphor in the Text of Philosophy', quoted by Paul Cobley (ed.), *Routledge Companion to Semiotics and Linguistics* (London and New York: Routledge, 2001), p. 179.

[21] Ramazani, *Transnational Poetics*, p. 60.

[22] bell hooks, 'Choosing the margin as a space of radical openness', *Gender, Space, Architecture*, 1/5 (1999), 205.

[23] James Clifford, *Routes: Travel and Translation in the Late Twentieth Century* (Cambridge, MA: Harvard, 1997), pp. 90–1.

[24] Petch, 'The mid-Atlantic imagination', p. 87.

[25] Gramich, *Twentieth-Century Women Writers*, p. 201.

[26] Seidel, *Exile and the Narrative Imagination*, p. 4.

[27] Ibid., p. 3.

[28] Isobel Armstrong, *Victorian Poetry, Poetics, Politics* (New York: Routledge, 1993), p. 325.

[29] bell hooks, *Yearning: Race, Gender and Cultural Politics* (Boston, MA: South End Press, 1990), p. 52.

[30] Ramazani, *Transnational Poetics*, p. 53.

[31] See Jane Dowson and Alice Entwistle, *A History of Twentieth Century British Women's Poetry* (Cambridge: Cambridge University Press, 2005), pp. 160–3.

[32] 'Cambridge was influential and enabling for me. Very. But it was also a struggle . . . It wasn't until I discovered Denise [Riley] in the 1970s . . . that I began to have a sense of what could be, if the politics of the whole poetry scene in the mid to late 60s had been different' ('Finding space: Wendy Mulford interviewed', *Poetry Wales*, 46/1 (2010), 33).

[33] See *Angel Exhaust* ['The Welsh Underground'] 21 (2010), 5 and especially 101–14. Co-edited by John Goodby and Andrew Duncan, and devoted to 'modernist' writing in Wales, this lively and provocative issue of the journal sadly reproduces hardly any female-authored work and actively critiques still less.

[34] Shari Benstock, 'Expatriate modernism: writing on the cultural rim', in Celia Broe and Angela J. C. Ingram (eds), *Women's Writing in Exile* (Chapel Hill and London: University of North Carolina Press, 1989), p. 142.

[35] Mulford, 'A city boy' 22.

[36] Mulford, 'Finding space', 32.

[37] Ibid., 34 (my emphasis).
[38] hooks, 'Choosing the margin', 209.
[39] Mulford, 'Finding space', 36, 37.
[40] Christopher Meredith (ed.), *Moment of Earth: Poems and Essays in Honour of Jeremy Hooker* (Oakville, CT and Aberystwyth: Celtic Studies, 2007).
[41] Ian Davidson, *Ideas of Space in Contemporary Poetry* (London: Palgrave, 2007), p. 22.
[42] Ibid., p. 27.
[43] Mulford, 'Alltud', *Scintilla*, 11 (2007), 161.
[44] Peter Middleton, 'Breaking the perspex: recent poetry by Wendy Mulford', *Many Review*, 1 (1983), 3.
[45] Mulford, 'Finding space', 32.
[46] Wendy Mulford and Sara Maitland, *Virtuous Magic: Women Saints and their Meanings* (London: Mowbray, 1998), p. 3; quoted by Jeremy Hooker, '"Calling the female into presence": the poetry of Wendy Mulford', *The Swansea Review*, 22 (2003), 138.
[47] Mulford, 'Finding space', 36, 37.
[48] Ibid., 34.
[49] Wendy Mulford, 'Utterance', *Poetry Wales*, 47/1 (2011), 35.
[50] Benstock, 'Expatriate modernism', p. 143.
[51] Clifford, *Routes*, p. 254, quoted by Jenkins, 'Interculturalism', p. 119.
[52] Mulford, unpublished letter to the author, 2009.
[53] Quoted by Said, *Reflections on Exile*, p. 568.
[54] Mulford, 'Finding space', 34.
[55] hooks, 'Choosing the margin', 209.
[56] Clifford, *Routes*, p. 3 (author's emphasis).
[57] Zoë Skoulding, 'Wandering Where I Am', *Poetry Wales,* 42/3 (2007), 23.
[58] Zoë Skoulding, *Remains of a Future City* (Bridgend: Seren, 2008), p. 50.
[59] Skoulding, 'Wandering', 24.
[60] Zoë Skoulding, '"A city of words": Zoë Skoulding interviewed by Fiona Owen', *Planet*, 166 (2004), 59.
[61] Zoë Skoulding, interview with Alice Entwistle (unpublished, 2008).
[62] Skoulding, 'A city of words', 60.
[63] Michel De Certeau, *The Practice of Everyday Life*, trans. Steven Rendall (Berkeley: University of California Press, 1984), p. 99 (author's emphases).
[64] Skoulding, 'Wandering', 25, 24, 23.
[65] Rebecca Solnit, *Wanderlust: A History of Walking* (London: Verso, 2001), pp. 13–14.
[66] De Certeau, *The Practice*, p. 103.
[67] Skoulding, 'Wandering', 23, 24.
[68] Jeffrey C. Robinson, *The Walk: Notes on a Romantic Image* (Norman and London: University of Oklahoma Press, 1989), p. 4.
[69] Robin Jarvis, *Romantic Writing and Pedestrian Travel* (New York: Palgrave, 1997), p. 32.

[70] Solnit, *Wanderlust*, p. 19.
[71] Ibid., pp. 5–6.
[72] Skoulding, 'Wandering', 24.
[73] Solnit, *Wanderlust*, p. 72.
[74] de Certeau, *The Practice* p. 97; Skoulding, 'Wandering', 25.
[75] As Jonathan Bate and others have pointed out, the Greek root of 'ecology' is *oikos,* meaning 'home'. See *The Song of the Earth* (London: Picador, 2001).
[76] de Certeau, *The Practice*, p. 95.
[77] Ibid., p. 97.
[78] Skoulding, 'Wandering', 25.
[79] Ivain Gilles [Ivan Chtcheglov], "Formula for a new city", *Leaving the 20th Century: The Incomplete Work of the Situationist International*, trans. and ed. Christopher Gray (London: Rebel Press, 1998), pp. 16, 17.
[80] Zoë Skoulding, 'Geographies of the self', Ph.D. thesis, Bangor University, 2005.
[81] Skoulding, 'A city of words', 62.
[82] Solnit, *Wanderlust*, p. 162.
[83] Roger Gilbert, *Walks in the World: Representation and Experience in Modern American Poetry* (Princeton: Princeton University Press, 1991), p. 3.
[84] Ian Davidson and Zoë Skoulding, 'Disobedience: collaborative writing and the walk poem', in David Kennedy (ed.), *Necessary Steps: Poetry, Elegy, Walking, Wpirit* (Exeter: Shearsman Press, 2007), pp. 28–9.
[85] de Certeau, *The Practice*, p. 102.
[86] Skoulding, 'Wandering', 25.
[87] Davidson and Skoulding, 'Disobedience', p. 2.
[88] Skoulding, 'Wandering', 24.
[89] Davidson and Skoulding, 'Disobedience', p. 5.
[90] Skoulding, 'Wandering', 23.
[91] Skoulding, 'A city of words', 61.
[92] Doreen Massey, *For Space* (London: Sage Publications, 2005) p. 9.
[93] Skoulding, 'Border Lines', 15.
[94] Skoulding, 'A city of words', 62.
[95] Skoulding, 'A city of words', 61; 'Wandering', 24.

Afterword: Tiffany Atkinson and Samantha Wynne Rhydderch

[1] Hélène Cixous, 'Sorties: out and out: attacks/ways out/forays', in Catherine Belsey and Jane Moore (eds), *The Feminist Reader* (Oxford: Wiley-Blackwell, 1989), p. 112.
[2] A founder member of the English-language section of *Yr Academi Gymreig* (the Welsh Academy) in 1968, and its chair for much of the 1990s, Roberts Jones has published three significant collections: *Turning Away: Collected*

Poems 1952–1968 (Gwasg Gomer, 1969), *The Forgotten Country* (Gwasg Gomer, 1977) and *Relative Values* (Poetry Wales Press, 1985) and has been associated with Swansea University's Centre for Welsh Writing in English (CREW) from its earliest days. Alison Bielski started publishing in 1970; since then she has produced a steady stream of works often treating the legends and landscapes of her native south Wales, most recently *One Of Our Skylarks* (Cinnamon, 2012).

[3] Jahan Ramazani, *The Hybrid Muse: Postcolonial Poetry in English* (Chicago: University of Chicago Press, 2001), p. 4.

[4] Susan Bordo, 'Feminism, postmodernism, and gender scepticism', in Linda J. Nicholson (ed.), *Feminism/Postmodernism* (New York and London: Routledge, 1990), p. 145.

[5] Paula Burnett, 'Epic, a woman's place: a study of Derek Walcott's *Omeros* and Jean Binta Breeze's "A River Called Wise"', in Vicki Bertram (ed.), *Kicking Daffodils: Twentieth-Century Women Poets* (Edinburgh: Edinburgh University Press, 1997), p. 140

[6] M. L. Rosenthal, and Sally M. Gall, *The Modern Poetic Sequence: The Genius of Modern Poetry* (New York and Oxford: Oxford University Press, 1983), p. 7.

[7] Tiffany Atkinson, *Kink and Particle* (Bridgend: Seren, 2006), pp. 27, 47.

[8] Samantha Wynne Rhydderch, 'Samantha Wynne Rhydderch in conversation', with Alice Entwistle, *Poetry Wales*, 48/2 (2012), 54. *Rockclimbing in Silk* (Bridgend: Seren, 2001) and *Not in These Shoes* (London: Picador, 2006).

[9] Rosenthal and Gall, *The Modern Poetic Sequence,* pp. 9, 3.

[10] Tiffany Atkinson, *Catulla Et Al* (Tarset: Bloodaxe, 2011), pp. 11, 18, 26, 23, 12.

[11] Wynne Rhydderch explains that she selected her speakers 'because they're not heard. They're crucial to the story and yet you hardly ever hear them mentioned.' See 'in conversation' with Alice Entwistle, 54.

[12] Tiffany Atkinson, 'When did this happen?', *Poetry Wales*, 44/1 (2008), 48.

[13] Samantha Wynne Rhydderch, *Banjo* (London : Picador, 2012), pp. 45, 43–4, 46–7.

[14] Tiffany Atkinson, 'Introduction,' in Tiffany Atkinson (ed.), *The Body* (Basingstoke: Palgrave, 2005), pp. 1–11; pp. 2; 4–5 (author's emphases).

[15] Stephen Connor, *Dumbstruck: A Cultural History of Ventriloquism* (Oxford: Oxford University Press, 2000), pp. 5–7.

[16] Alan Sinfield, *Dramatic Monologue* (Critical Idiom ser.) (London: Methuen: 1977); Susan Stanford Friedman, *Mappings: Feminism and the Cultural Geographies of Encounter* (Princeton: Princeton University Press, 1998), p. 27.

[17] Deryn Rees-Jones *Consorting With Angels: Essays on Modern Women Poets* (Tarset: Bloodaxe, 2005), quoted in Jo Gill, *Women's Poetry*

(Edinburgh: Edinburgh University Press, 2007), p. 56; Gill's is a commendably terse and useful analysis of a rich and sprawling discourse.

[18] Connor, *Dumbstruck*, p. 6.

[19] Friedman, *Mappings*, p. 29.

[20] Ibid., p. 19.

[21] Wynne Rhydderch, 'In conversation' with Alice Entwistle, 53, 58.

[22] Samantha Wynne Rhydderch, 'Interviewed by Katherine Stansfield', *New Welsh Review*, 96, *www.newwelshreview.com/article.php?id=209*, 1. Wynne Rhydderch, 'In conversation' with Alice Entwistle, 56.

[23] Atkinson, 'When did this happen?', 48.

[24] Friedman, *Mappings*, p. 32.

[25] Jennifer Bloomer, 'D'Or', in Beatriz Colomina (ed.), *Sexuality and Space* (Princeton: Princeton Architectural Press, 1992), pp. 164–5.

Bibliography

Aaron, Jane. 'Echoing the (m)other tongue: cynghanedd and the English language poet', in Belinda Humfrey (ed.), *Fire Green as Grass: Studies of the Creative Impulse in Anglo-Welsh Poetry and Short Stories of the Twentieth Century* (Llandysul: Gomer, 1995), pp. 1–23.

——, 'A review of the contribution of women to Welsh life and prospects for the future', *Transactions of the Honourable Society of Cymmrodorion*, new series, 8 (2002), 188–204.

——, *Nineteenth Century Women's Writing in Wales: Nation, Gender and Identity* (Cardiff: University of Wales Press, 2007).

—— and M. Wynn Thomas, 'Pulling you through changes: Welsh writing in English before during and after two referenda', in M. Wynn Thomas (ed.), *Welsh Writing in English* (Cardiff: University of Wales Press, 2003), pp. 278–309.

——, Teresa Rees, Sandra Betts and Moira Vincentelli (eds), *Our Sisters' Land: The Changing Identities of Women in Wales* (Cardiff: University of Wales Press, 1994).

—— and Chris Williams (eds), *Postcolonial Wales* (Cardiff: University of Wales Press, 2005).

Acheson, James and Romana Huk (eds), *Contemporary British Poetry: Essays in Theory and Criticism* (New York: State University of New York Press, 1996).

Anderson, Benedict, *Imagined Communities: Reflections on the Origin and Spread of Nationalism* (London and New York: Verso, 1983; revd 1991).

Armstrong, Isobel, *Victorian Poetry, Poetics, Politics* (New York: Routledge, 1993).

Arnold, David, *Famine, Social Crisis and Historical Change* (New York and Oxford: Blackwell, 1988).

Atkinson, Tiffany, *Kink and Particle* (Bridgend: Seren, 2006).

——, 'When did this happen? Some thoughts on poetry and practice', *Poetry Wales*, 44/1 (2008), 45–50.

——, 'Black and white and re(a)d all over: the poetics of embarrassment', in Richard Marggraf Turley (ed.), *The Writer in the Academy: Creative Interfrictions* (Cambridge: D. S. Brewer, 2011), pp. 113–31.

——, *Catulla Et Al* (Tarset: Bloodaxe, 2011).

—— (ed.), *The Body* (Basingstoke and New York: Palgrave Macmillan, 2005).

Atwood, Margaret, *Survival: A Thematic Guide to Canadian Literature* (Toronto: McClelland and Stewart, 2004).

Bahktin, Mikhail, *Problems of Dostoevky's Poetics*, ed. and trans. Caryl Emerson (Minneapolis: University of Minnesota Press, 1984).

Bate, Jonathan, *The Song of the Earth* (London: Picador, 2001).

Beddoe, Deirdre, 'Munitionettes, maids and mams: women in Wales 1914–1939', in Jane Aaron (ed.), *Our Mothers' Land: Chapters in Welsh Women's History 1830–1939* (Cardiff: University of Wales Press, 1991), pp. 189–209.

—— (ed.), *Changing Times: Welsh Women Writing on the 1950s and 1960s* (Dinas Powys: Honno, 2003).

Beer, Gillian, 'The island and the aeroplane: the case of Virginia Woolf', in Homi K. Bhabha (ed.), *Nation and Narration* (London and New York: Routledge, 1990), pp. 265–90.

Benjamin, Walter, *Illuminations*, trans. Harry Zoorn (London: Pimlico, 1999).

Benstock, Shari, 'Expatriate modernism: writing on the cultural rim', in Celia Broe and Angela J. C. Ingram (eds), *Women's Writing in Exile* (Chapel Hill and London: University of North Carolina Press, 1989), pp. 19–40.

Berger, John, *Keeping a Rendezvous* (London: Granta, 1993).

Bertram, Vicki (ed.), *Kicking Daffodils: Twentieth-century Women Poets* (Edinburgh: Edinburgh University Press, 1997).

——, *Gendering Poetry: Contemporary Women and Men Poets* (London: Pandora Press, 2005).

Bhabha, Homi K., *The Location of Culture* (London and New York: Routledge, 1994).

—— (ed.), *Nation and Narration* (London and New York: Routledge, 1990).

Bianchi, Tony, 'Maps and travellers', *Planet*, 160 (2003), 66–74.

Bidgood, Ruth, *The Green Desert: Collected Poems 1950–1969* (Llandysul: Gwasg Gomer, 1969).

——, *The Given Time* (Swansea: Christopher Davies, 1972).

——, 'Statement', for Welsh Academi (April 1984), unpublished TS.

——, *Kindred* (Bridgend: Poetry Wales Press, 1986).

——, 'Interview with Angela Morton', *New Welsh Review*, 10 (1990), 38–42.

——, 'Heartland', *Poetry Wales*, 26/3 (1991), 7–12.

——, *Selected Poems* (Bridgend: Seren, 1995).

——, 'Writer's diary', *Books in Wales/Llais Lyfrau*, 2/96 (1996), 4.

——, 'History is now and Wales: an interview with Jason Walford Davies', *Planet*, 137 (October/November 1999), 47–54.

——, *Parishes of the Buzzard* (Port Talbot: Alun Books, 2001).

——, 'Interview with Sally Roberts-Jones and Alexandra Trowbridge-Matthews', *Roundyhouse*, 7 (2001), 21–25.

——, *New and Selected Poems* (Bridgend: Seren 2004).

——, Interview with Alice Entwistle (unpublished, July 2007).

——, *Hearing Voices* (Blaenau Ffestiniog, Gwynedd: Cinnamon Press, 2008).

——, *Time Being* (Bridgend: Seren, 2009).

Bielski, Alison, *One Of Our Skylarks* (Tanygrisiau: Cinnamon, 2012).
Billig, Michael, *Banal Nationalism* (London: Sage Publications, 1995).
Blau DuPlessis, Rachel, *Writing Beyond the Ending: Narrative Strategies of Twentieth-Century Women Writers* (Bloomington: Indiana University Press, 1985).
Bloomer, Jennifer, 'D'Or', in Beatriz Colomina (ed.), *Sexuality and Space* (Princeton: Princeton Architectural Press, 1992), pp. 163–82.
Bohata, Kirsti, 'Beyond authenticity? Hybridity and assimilation in Welsh writing in English', in Tony Brown and Russell Stephens (eds), *Nations and Relations: Writing across the British Isles* (Cardiff: New Welsh Review, 2000), pp. 89–121.
——, *Postcolonialism Revisited: Writing Wales in English* (Cardiff: University of Wales Press, 2004).
——, 'Postcolonialism revisited', *New Welsh Review*, 69 (2005), 31–39.
Boland, Eavan, *Object Lessons: The Life of the Woman and the Poet in our Time* (London: Vintage, 1996).
Bondi, Liz, 'Locating identity politics', in Michael Keith and Steve Pile (eds), *Place and the Politics of Identity* (London: Routledge, 1993), pp. 84–101.
Bordo, Susan, 'Feminism, postmodernism, and gender scepticism', in Linda J. Nicholson (ed.), *Feminism/Postmodernism* (New York and London: Routledge, 1990), pp. 133–56
Brennan, Catherine, *Angers, Fantasies and Ghostly Fears: Nineteenth-century Women from Wales and English-Language Poetry* (Cardiff: University of Wales Press, 2003).
Brennan, Timothy, 'The national longing for form', in Homi K. Bhabha (ed.), *Nation and Narration* (London: Routledge, 1990), pp. 44–71.
Brigley, Jude (ed.), *Exchanges: Poems by Women in Wales* (Dinas Powys: Honno Poetry, 1990).
Burnett, Paula, 'Epic, a woman's place: a study of Derek Walcott's *Omeros* and Jean Binta Breeze's "A River Called Wise"', in Vicki Bertram (ed.), *Kicking Daffodils: Twentieth-Century Women Poets* (Edinburgh: Edinburgh University Press, 1997), pp. 140–52.
Campbell, Duncan, 'Walking the line', *New Welsh Review*, 69 (2005), 13–18.
Carter, Erica, James Donald and Judith Squires (eds), *Space and Place: Theories of Identity and Location* (London: Lawrence & Wishart, 1993).
Chamberlain, Brenda, *Tide-Race* (Bridgend: Seren, 2007[1962]).
Charles-Edwards, Thomas, *Early Irish and Welsh Kinship* (Oxford: Oxford University Press, 1993).
Chitty, Mary, *The Monks on Enlli 1: c.500 AD to 1252 AD* (self-published, 1992).
——, *The Monks on Enlli 2: c.1252 AD* (self-published n.d.).
Cixous, Hélène, 'Sorties: out and out: attacks/ways out/forays', in Catherine Belsey and Jane Moore (eds), *The Feminist Reader* (Oxford: Wiley-Blackwell, 1989), pp. 101–16.

Clarke, Gillian, 'Interview with Gillian Clarke', in Susan Butler (ed.), *Common Ground: Poets in a Welsh Landscape* (Bridgend: Poetry Wales Press, 1985), pp. 194–98.
——, *Letting In the Rumour* (Manchester: Carcanet Press, 1989).
——, 'Letting in the rumour: a letter from a far country', *PBS Bulletin*, 141 (1989), 14.
——, 'The King of Britain's Daughter', in Tony Curtis (ed.), *How Poets Work* (Bridgend: Seren, 1996), pp. 122–36.
——, *Collected Poems* (Manchester: Carcanet Press, 1997).
——, 'The power of absence: Gillian Clarke in conversation with Deryn Rees-Jones', *Planet*, 144 (2001), 55–60.
——, 'Beginning with Bendigeidfran', *At the Source* (Manchester: Carcanet Press, 2008), pp. 8–15.
——, 'Cordelia's "nothing"', *At the Source* (Manchester: Carcanet Press, 2008), pp. 30–46.
——, 'Voice of the Tribe', *At the Source* (Manchester: Carcanet Press, 2008), pp. 55–63.
Clifford, James, *Routes: Travel and Translation in the Late Twentieth Century* (Cambridge, MA: Harvard University Press, 1997).
Cluysenaar, Anne, *Timeslips: New and Selected Poems* (Manchester: Carcanet Press, 1997).
——, 'An interview' with Alice Entwistle, *Poetry Wales*, 44/3 (2008–9), 27–30.
——, *Migrations* (Blaenau Ffestiniog: Cinnamon, 2011).
——, Graham Harthill and Hilary Llewellyn-Williams, 'Form and spirituality: connections and contrasts in poetic practice', *Scintilla*, 11 (2007), 63–82.
Cobley, Paul (ed.), *Routledge Companion to Semiotics and Linguistics* (London and New York: Routledge, 2001).
Coles, Gladys Mary, 'The narrative tradition in contemporary Welsh poetry in English', *Poetry Wales*, 31/3 (1996), 20–5.
Colley, Linda, *Britons: Forging the Nation 1707–1837* (New Haven, CT: Yale University Press, 1992).
Connolly, Claire and Katie Gramich, 'Introduction', *Irish Studies Review*, 17/1 (2009), 1–4.
Connor, Stephen, *Dumbstruck: A Cultural History of Ventriloquism* (Oxford: Oxford University Press, 2000).
Conran, Tony, *The Cost of Strangeness: Essays on the English Poets of Wales* (Llandysul: Gomer, 1982).
——, 'Lynette Roberts: the lyric pieces', *Poetry Wales*, 19/2 (1983), 125–33.
——, 'Review of Gillian Clarke's King of Britain', *New Welsh Review*, 6/3 (1993–4), 67–8.
——, *Frontiers in Anglo-Welsh Poetry* (Cardiff: University of Wales Press, 1997).
——, 'Poetry Wales and the second flowering', in M. Wynn Thomas (ed.), *Welsh Writing in English* (Cardiff: University of Wales Press, 2003), pp. 222–54.
—— (ed.), *Welsh Verse 1967* (Bridgend: Seren, 1986).
Corbett, Sarah, *The Red Wardrobe* (Bridgend: Seren, 1998).

——, *The Witch Bag* (Bridgend: Seren, 2002).
——, *Other Beasts* (Bridgend: Seren, 2008).
Cosgrove, D. F., *Social Formation and Symbolic Landscape* (London: Croom Helm, 1984).
Crawford, E. Margaret (ed.), *The Hungry Stream: Essays on Emigration and Famine* (Belfast: The Institute of Irish Studies, 1997).
Crawford, Robert, *Devolving English Literature* (Oxford: Clarendon, 1992).
——, *Identifying Poets: Self and Territory in Twentieth Century Poetry* (Edinburgh: Edinburgh University Press, 1993).
Cronin, Michael, 'Spaces between Irish worlds: travellers, translators and the new accelerators', in Tony Brown and Russell Stephens (eds), *Nations and Relations: Writing across the British Isles* (Cardiff: New Welsh Review, 2000), pp. 42–55.
Curtis, Tony (ed.), *Wales: The Imagined Nation: Essays in Cultural and National Identity* (Bridgend: Seren, 1986).
Darby, Wendy Joy, *Landscape and Identity: Geographies of Nation and Class in England* (Oxford and New York: Berg Publishers, 2000).
Davenport-Hines, Richard, *Gothic: Four Hundred Years of Excess, Horror, Evil and Ruins* (London: Fourth Estate, 1998).
Davidson, Ian, *Ideas of Space in Contemporary Poetry* (London: Palgrave, 2007).
—— and Zoë Skoulding, 'Mind melding', *New Welsh Review*, 67 (2005), 37–47.
—— and Zoë Skoulding, 'Disobedience: collaborative writing and the walk poem', in David Kennedy (ed.), *Necessary Steps: Poetry, Elegy, Walking, Spirit* (Exeter: Shearsman Press, 2007), pp. 28–35.
Davies, Gareth Alban, 'The multi-screen cinema: poetry in Welsh 1950–1990', in Hans Werner Ludwig and Lothar Fietz (eds), *Poetry in the British Isles: Non-Metropolitan Perspectives* (Cardiff: University of Wales Press, 1995), pp. 116–33.
Davies, Grahame, 'Sleeping with the enemy: The tensions of literary translation', in Katja Krebs and Christopher Meredith (eds), *Five Essays on Translation* (Pontypridd: University of Glamorgan, 2005), pp. 10–21.
Day, Graham and Gareth Rees (eds), *Regions, Nations and European Integration: Remaking the Celtic Periphery* (Cardiff: University of Wales Press, 1991).
de Certeau, Michel, *The Practice of Everyday Life*, trans. Steven Rendall (Berkeley, CA: University of California Press, 1984).
Derrida, Jacques, 'White mythology: metaphor in the text of philosophy', trans. Alan Bass, in *Margins of Philosophy* (Chicago: University of Chicago Press, 1982).
Donahaye, Jasmine, 'Identification, rejection and cultural co-option in Welsh poetry in English', in Daniel G. Williams (ed.), *Slanderous Tongues: Essays on Welsh poetry in English 1970–2005* (Bridgend: Seren 2010), pp. 226–46.
Dowson, Jane and Alice Entwistle, *A History of Twentieth Century British Women's Poetry* (Cambridge: Cambridge University Press, 2005).
Duff, David (ed.), *Modern Genre Theory* (Harlow, Essex: Longman/Pearson Educational, 2000).

Duncan, Andrew, 'Editorial: in search of a Welsh avant-garde', *Angel Exhaust*, 21 (2010), 5–6.
Earle, Jean, *The Sun In the West* (Bridgend: Seren, 1995).
Elfyn, Menna, 'Beyond the boundaries: A symposium on gender in poetry', *Planet*, 66 (1987/88), 54–5.
——, 'Writing is a bird in the hand', in Jane Aaron, Teresa Rees, Sandra Betts and Moira Vincentelli (eds), *Our Sisters' Land: The Changing Identities of Women in Wales* (Cardiff: University of Wales Press, 1994), pp. 280–6.
——, *Eucalyptus: Detholiad o Gerddi 1978–1994 / Selected Poems 1978–1994* (Llandysul: Gomer, 1995).
——, 'Stones in seventeen frames: Arthur's Stone / Maen Ceti Burial Chamber, Gower, Wales', in Damian Walford Davies (ed.), *Megalith: Eleven Journeys in Search of Stones* (Llandysul: Gomer, 2006), pp. 85–90.
——, *Perfect Blemish: New and Selected Poems 1995–2007 / Perffaith Nam: Dau Ddetholiad & Cherddi Newydd 1995–2007* (Tarset: Bloodaxe, 2007).
——, 'Three heads', *New Welsh Review*, 90 (2010), 33–41.
——, Interview with Alice Entwistle (unpublished, June 2010).
—— (ed.), *Trying the Line: A Volume of Tributes to Gillian Clarke* (Llandysul: Gomer, 1997).
—— and María do Cebreiro, 'In conversation', *Poetry Wales*, 44/2 (2008), 10–14.
—— and Janice Moore Fuller, 'Music, translation and poetry: an interview with Menna Elfyn', *Asheville Poetry Review*, 25 October 25 2002, no p., *www.ashevillepoetryreview.com/2002/issue-12/interview-with-menna-elfyn*, accessed 18 July 2012.
Entwistle, Alice, 'An interview with Anne Cluysenaar', *Poetry Wales*, 44/3 (2008–9), 27–30.
——, 'Finding space: Wendy Mulford interviewed', *Poetry Wales*, 46/1 (2010), 32–7.
Evans, Christine, *Looking Inland* (Bridgend: Poetry Wales Press, 1983).
——, 'Beyond the boundaries: a symposium on gender in poetry', *Planet*, 66 (1987–8): 44–5.
——, *Cometary Phases* (Bridgend: Seren, 1989).
——, 'Christine Evans', in Meic Stephens (ed.), *The Bright Field: An Anthology of Contemporary Poetry from Wales* (Manchester: Carcanet, 1991), pp. 86–96.
——, *Island of Dark Horses* (Bridgend: Seren, 1995).
——, *On the Headland: Uwchmynydd* (Illustrated by Kim Atkinson) Places / *Y Man a'r Lle 11* (Newtown: Gwasg Gregynog, 1999).
——, *Burning the Candle* (Llandysul: Gomer, 2006).
——, *Growth Rings* (Bridgend: Seren, 2006).
——, Interview with Alice Entwistle (unpublished, 2007).
——, *Walking Through*, BBC Film, 2007.
—— and Wolf Marloh, *Bardsey* (Llandysul: Gomer, 2008).
Evans, Donald, 'Contemporary strict metre poetry', *Poetry Wales*, 28/4 (1993), 56–8.

Evans, Estyn, *The Personality of Ireland: Habitat, Heritage and History* (Cambridge: Cambridge University Press, 1973).
——, *The Personality of Wales*, BBC, 1973.
Evans, Margiad, *Poems from Obscurity* (London: A. Dakers, 1949).
——, *A Candle Ahead* (London: Chatto & Windus, 1956).
Feaver, Vicki, 'Body and soul: the power of Sharon Olds', in Alison Mark and Deryn Rees-Jones (eds), *Contemporary Women's Poetry: Reading/Writing/ Practice* (Basingstoke: Macmillan, 2000), pp. 140–56.
Fisher, Catherine, *Immrama* (Bridgend: Seren, 1988).
——, *The Unexplored Ocean* (Bridgend: Seren, 1994).
——, *Altered States* (Bridgend: Seren, 1999).
——, Interview with Alice Entwistle (unpublished, 2007).
——, 'Myth and history', *New Welsh Review*, 89 (2011), 41–6.
Foster, Thomas, *Transformations of Domesticity in Modern Women's Writing: Homelessness at Home* (London: Palgrave MacMillan, 2002).
Foucault, Michel, *The History of Sexuality*, vol. 1: *An Introduction*, trans. Robert Hurley (Harmondsworth: Penguin, 1978).
Freud, Sigmund, 'The uncanny', *The Standard Edition of the Complete Psychological Works of Sigmund Freud, Volume XVII (1917–1919): An Infantile Neurosis and Other Works* (London: Vintage, 2001), pp. 217–56.
Friedman, Susan Stanford, 'When a "long" poem is a "big" poem: self-authorising strategies in women's twentieth-century "long poems"', in Robyn R. Warhol and Diane Price Herndl (eds), *Feminisms: An Anthology of Literary Theory and Criticism* (Basingstoke: Macmillan, 1997), pp. 721–38.
——, *Mappings: Feminism and the Cultural Geographies of Encounter* (Princeton: Princeton University Press, 1998).
Furber, Jo, '"Wonderful what will come out of darkness": gender and nationhood in the work of Welsh and Irish women poets', in Daniel G. Williams (ed.), *Slanderous Tongues: Essays on Welsh poetry in English 1970–2005* (Bridgend: Seren, 2010), pp. 137–62.
Gallie, Menna, *You're Welcome to Ulster!*, ed. Angela John and Claire Connolly (Dinas Powys: Honno, 2010).
Gantz, Jeffrey, *Early Irish Myths and Sagas*, trans. Jeffrey Gantz (London: Penguin, 1981).
Garlick, Raymond, *An Introduction to Anglo-Welsh Literature* (Cardiff: University of Wales Press, 1972).
—— and Roland Matthias, *Anglo-Welsh Poetry 1480–1980* (Bridgend: Seren, 1992).
Gee, Maggie and Lisa Appignanesi, 'The contemporary writer: gender and genre', in Judy Simons and Kate Fullbrook (eds), *Writing: A Woman's Business: Women, Writing and the Marketplace* (Manchester: Manchester University Press, 1998), pp. 172–82.
George, Rosemary Marangoly, *The Politics of Home: Postcolonial Relocations and Twentieth-Century Fiction* (Cambridge: Cambridge University Press, 1996).

Gilbert, Roger, *Walks in the World: Representation and Experience in Modern American Poetry* (Princeton: Princeton University Press, 1991).

Gill, Jo, 'Anne Sexton and confessional poetics', *The Review of English Studies*, 55/220 (2004), 426–45.

——, *Women's Poetry* (Edinburgh: Edinburgh University Press, 2007).

Gilles, Ivain [Ivan Chtcheglov], 'Formula for a new city', *Leaving the 20th Century: The Incomplete Work of the Situationist International*, trans. and ed. Christopher Gray (London: Rebel Press, 1998).

Gilmore, Leigh, *Autobiographics: A Feminist Theory of Women's Self-representation* (Ithaca: Cornell University Press, 1994).

Goodby, John, '"Undispellable lost dream": Welsh modernist and avant-garde poetry', *Angel Exhaust*, 21 (2010), 101–14.

Gramich, Katie, *Twentieth-Century Women's Writing in Wales: Land, Gender, Belonging* (Cardiff: University of Wales Press, 2007).

——, 'Margiad Evans's "Journal in Ireland"', *New Welsh Review*, 89 (2010), 61–70.

—— and Catherine Brennan (eds), *Welsh Women's Poetry 1460–2001: An Anthology* (Dinas Powys: Honno, 2003).

Gray, Kathryn, 'Wales and the next generation', *New Welsh Review*, 67 (2005), 4–10.

Greene, Roland, *Post-Petrarchism: Origins and Innovations of the Western Lyric Sequence* (Princeton: Princeton University Press, 1991).

Gregson, Ian, *Contemporary Poetry and Postmodernism: Dialogue and Estrangement* (New York: St Martin's Press, 1996).

——, *The New Poetry in Wales* (Cardiff: University of Wales Press, 2007).

Grosz, Elizabeth, *Volatile Bodies: Towards a Corporeal Feminism* (Bloomington and Indianapolis: Indiana University Press, 1994).

——, 'Bodies-cities', in Gary Bridge and Sophie Watson (eds), *The Blackwell City Reader* (Oxford: Blackwell Publishing, 2002), pp. 297–303.

Gruffudd, Prys, 'Prospects of Wales: contested geographical imaginations', in Ralph Fevre and Andrew Thompson (eds), *Nation, Identity and Social Theory: Perspectives from Wales* (Cardiff: University of Wales Press, 1999), pp. 149–67.

Gruffydd, Elfed, *Llŷn*, trans. Gwyneth Owen (Llanrwst: Gwasg Carreg Gwalch, 2003).

Gwyn, Richard (ed.), *Pterodactyl's Wing* (Llandybie: Parthian, 2003).

Hallam, Tudur, 'When a *bardd* meets a poet: Menna Elfyn and the displacement of parallel facing texts', in Daniel G. Williams (ed.), *Slanderous Tongues: Essays on Welsh Poetry in English 1970–2005* (Bridgend: Seren, 2010), pp. 89–111.

Harris, Ruth-Ann, *The Nearest Place That Wasn't Ireland: Early Nineteenth-Century Irish Labor Migration* (Illinois: Iowa State University Press, 1994).

Hart, David, 'The thread of poetry: Hilary Llewellyn-Williams interviewed', *Planet*, 162 (2004), 28–34.

Hartsock, Nancy, 'Foucault on power: a theory for women', in L. J. Nicholson (ed.), *Feminism/Postmodernism* (London: Routledge, 1990), pp. 157–75.

Harvey, Clodagh Brennan, *Contemporary Irish Traditional Narrative: The English Language Tradition* (Berkeley: University of California Press, 1992).

Heiland, Donna, *Gothic and Gender: An Introduction* (Oxford: Blackwell, 2004).

Herbert, Trevor and Gareth Elwyn Jones, *Post-War Wales* (Cardiff: University of Wales Press, 1995).

Hillis Miller, J., 'Derrida enisled', *Critical Inquiry*, 33/2, special issue: 'The Late Derrida' (2007), 248–76.

Honig, Bonnie, 'Difference, dilemmas, and the politics of home', in Seyla Benhabib (ed.), *Democracy and Difference: Contesting the Boundaries of the Political* (Princeton: Princeton University Press, 1996), pp. 257–77.

Hooker, Jeremy, *The Poetry of Place: Essays and reviews 1970–1981* (Manchester: Carcanet, 1982).

——, *The Presence of The Past: Essays on Modern British and American Poetry* (Bridgend: Poetry Wales Press, 1987).

——, 'Ceridwen's daughters: Welsh women poets and the uses of tradition', *Welsh Writing in English: A Yearbook*, 1 (1995), 128–44.

——, 'A new kind of nature poetry', *Poetry Wales*, 33/2 (1997), 29–31.

——, *Imagining Wales: A View of Modern Welsh Writing in English* (Cardiff: University of Wales Press, 2001).

——, '"Calling the female into presence": the poetry of Wendy Mulford', *The Swansea Review*, 22 (2003), 134–48.

——, 'Poets, language and land: reflections on English-language Welsh poetry since the Second World War', *Welsh Writing in English*, 8 (2003), 141–56.

hooks, bell, *Yearning: Race, Gender and Cultural Politics* (Boston, MA: South End Press, 1990).

—— 'Choosing the margin as a space of radical openness', *Gender, Space, Architecture*, 1/5 (1999), 203–9.

Horner, Avril and Angela Keane (eds), *Body Matters: Feminism, Textuality, Corporeality* (Manchester: Manchester University Press, 2000).

Hughes, Tristan, 'From Yoknapatawpha to Ynys Môn', *New Welsh Review*, 69 (2005), 20–4.

Huk, Romana (ed.), *Assembling Alternatives: Reading Postmodern Poetries Transnationally* (Connecticut: Wesleyan University Press, 2003).

Humfrey, Belinda (ed.), *Fire Green as Grass: Studies of The Creative Impulse in Anglo-Welsh Poetry and Short Stories of the 20th Century* (Llandysul: Gomer, 1995).

Humm, Maggie, *Border Traffic: Strategies of Contemporary Women Writers* (Manchester: Manchester University Press, 1991).

Humphreys, Emyr, *The Taliesin Tradition: A Quest for the Welsh Identity* (Bridgend: Seren, 2000).

Irigaray, Luce, 'The limits of transference', in Margaret Whitford (ed.), *The Irigaray Reader* (Oxford: Blackwell Publishing, 1991), pp. 105–17.

——, *Sexes and Genealogies*, trans G. C. Gill (New York: Columbia University Press, 1993).

Jacob, Christian, *The Sovereign Map: Theoretical Approaches in Cartography Throughout History* (Chicago: University of Chicago Press, 2006).

James, Angharad, 'A stage of their own: women and performance poetry', *Planet*, 135 (1999), 54–61.

Janowitz, Anne, *England's Ruins: Poetic Purpose and the National Landscape* (Oxford: Blackwell, 1990).

Jarvis, Matthew, 'Christine Evans's Bardsey: Creating Sacred Space', *Welsh Writing in English: A Yearbook of Critical Essays*, 11 (2006–7), 188–209.

——, *Welsh Environments in Contemporary Poetry* (Cardiff: University of Wales Press, 2008).

——, 'Repositioning Wales: poetry after the second flowering', in Daniel G. Williams (ed.), *Slanderous Tongues: Essays on Welsh Poetry in English 1970–2005* (Bridgend: Seren, 2010), pp. 21–59.

Jarvis, Robin, *Romantic Writing and Pedestrian Travel* (New York: Palgrave, 1997).

Jenkins, Lee M., 'Interculturalism: Imtiaz Dharker, Patience Agbabi, Jackie Kay and contemporary Irish poets', in Jane Dowson (ed.), *The Cambridge Companion to Twentieth-century British and Irish Women's Poetry* (Cambridge: Cambridge University Press, 2011), pp. 119–35.

Jenkins, Randal, 'The new Anglo Welsh poets', *Poetry Wales*, 8/2 (1972), 5–11.

John, Angela (ed.), *Our Mothers' Land: Chapters in Welsh Women's History, 1830–1939* (Cardiff: University of Wales Press, 1991).

Jones, Bobi, 'Demise of the Anglo-Welsh?', trans. Richard Poole, *Poetry Wales*, 28/3 (1993), 14–18.

Jones, Glyn E., 'Hala dechreunos – a knitting assembly in Breconshire?', *Folk Life: A Journal of Ethnological Studies*, 23 (1984–5), 116–18.

Jones, Glyn, *The Dragon Has Two Tongues: Essays on Anglo-Welsh Writers and Writing* (Cardiff: University of Wales Press, 2001).

Jones, Gwyn (ed.), *The Oxford Book of Welsh Verse in English* (Oxford: Oxford University Press, 1977).

Jones, Noragh, *Living in Rural Wales* (Llandysul: Gomer, 1993).

Jones, R. Gerallt (ed.), *Poetry of Wales 1930–1970* (Llandysul: Gomer, 1974).

Kaplan, Caren, *Questions of Travel: Postmodern Discourses of Displacement* (Durham, NC: Duke University Press, 1996).

Keith, Michael and Steve Pile, 'Introduction part 1: the politics of place', in Michael Keith and Steve Pile (eds), *Place and the Politics of Identity* (London and New York: Routledge, 1993).

Kelleher, Margaret, *The Feminization of Famine: Expressions of the Inexpressible?* (Cork: Cork University Press, 1997).

Kerrigan, John, 'Divided kingdoms and the local epic: *Mercian Hymns* to *The King of Britain's Daughter*', *Yale Journal of Criticism*, 13/1 (2000), 3–21.

——, *Archipelagic English: Literature, History and Politics 1603–1707* (Oxford: Oxford University Press, 2008).
Kinsella, John, *Disclosed Poetics: Beyond Landscape and Lyricism* (Manchester: Manchester University Press, 2007).
Kinsman, Judith (ed.), *Six Women Poets* (Oxford: Oxford University Press, 1992).
Kirby, Kathleen M., 'Re: Mapping subjectivity: Cartographic vision and the limits of politics', in Nancy Duncan (ed.), *Bodyspace: Destabilizing Geographies of Gender and Sexuality* (London: Routledge, 1996), pp. 45–55.
Kirkland, Richard, 'Paul Muldoon's "Immram" and "Immrama": writing for a sense of displacement', *Essays in Poetics*, 17/1 (1992), 35–43.
Knight, Stephen, 'Remember Us?', *Poetry Wales*, 33/3 (1998), 37–41.
Kristeva, Julia, *Strangers to Ourselves*, trans. Leon S. Roudiez (New York: Columbia University Press, 1991).
Lefebvre, Henri, *The Production of Space*, trans. Donald Nicholson-Smith (Oxford: Blackwell Publishing, 1991).
Leighton, Angela, *On Form: Poetry Aestheticism and the Legacy of a Word* (Oxford: Oxford University Press, 2007).
Levertov, Denise, *Selected Poems* (Newcastle Upon Tyne: Bloodaxe Books, 1987).
Lewis, Gwyneth, 'Interview with Richard Poole', *Poetry Wales*, 31/2 (1995), 24–32.
——, 'On writing poetry in two languages', *Modern Poetry in Translation*, 7 (1995), 80–3.
——, 'Interview with Richard Poole', *PN Review*, 23, 3 (1997), 24–9.
——, *Parables & Faxes* (Tarset: Bloodaxe, 1998).
——, 'Tenuous and precarious: the comic muse', *Poetry Review*, 88/3 (1998), 17–19.
——, 'Whose coat is that jacket? Whose hat is that cap?', in W. N. Herbert and Matthew Hollis (eds), *Strong Words: Modern Poets on Modern Poetry* (Tarset: Bloodaxe, 2000), pp. 265–9.
——, *Keeping Mum* (Tarset: Bloodaxe, 2003).
——, *Chaotic Angels: Poems in English* (Tarset: Bloodaxe, 2005).
——, 'Negotiations: Gwyneth Lewis in conversation with Ian Gregson', *Planet*, 173 (2005), 51–56.
——, 'Out of the blue', *MsLexia*, 26 (2005), 22–3.
——, 'Gwyneth Lewis in America: interview with Kathryn Gray', *New Welsh Review*, 70 (2005), 8–13.
——, 'I can never know if I did the right thing', *Guardian*, 17 December 2005.
——, Interview with Alice Entwistle (unpublished, November 2006).
——, *Sunbathing in the Rain: A Cheerful Book on Depression* (London and Philadelphia: Jessica Kingsley Publishers, 2007).
——, 'Criss-crossings: literary adventures on Irish and Welsh shores' (2008) *http://www.poetrysociety.org.uk/lib/tmp/cmsfiles/File/review/Volume%20 98/983lewis.pdf.*

——, *A Hospital Odyssey* (Tarset: Bloodaxe, 2010).
——, 'The Poet I Might Have Been', *New Welsh Review*, 91 (2011), 9–13.
——, *Sparrow Tree* (Tarset: Bloodaxe, 2011).
Lewis, Lisa, 'Between words and worlds: the performance of translation', in Katja Krebs and Christopher Meredith (eds), *Five Essays on Translation* (Pontypridd: University of Glamorgan, 2005), pp. 33–41.
Llewellyn-Williams, Hilary, 'Poet of the natural world', *Poetry Wales*, 26/1 (1990), 17–19.
——, *Hammadruz* (Bridgend: Seren, 1990).
——, *Animaculture* (Bridgend: Seren, 1997).
——, *Greenland* (Bridgend: Seren, 2003).
——, 'The thread of poetry: Hilary Llewellyn-Williams interviewed by David Hart', *Planet*, 162 (2004), 28–34.
Lloyd, David, *Anomalous States: Irish Writing and the Post-Colonial Moment* (Dublin: Lilliput Press, 1993).
Lloyd, David T., *The Urgency of Identity: Contemporary English-Language Poetry from Wales* (Evanston: Northwestern University Press, 1994).
——, *Writing on the Edge: Interviews with Writers and Editors of Wales* (Amsterdam: Rodopi BV, 1997).
Ludwig, Hans-Werner and Lothar Fietz (eds), *Poetry in the British Isles: Non-Metropolitan Perspectives* (Cardiff: University of Wales Press, 1995).
Mark, Alison and Deryn Rees-Jones, *Contemporary Women's Poetry: Reading/Writing/Practice* (Basingstoke: Macmillan, 2000).
Massey, Doreen, *Space, Place and Gender* (Cambridge: Polity Press, 1994).
——, *For Space* (London: Sage Publications, 2005).
Matthias, Roland. *A Ride Through the Wood: Essays on Anglo-Welsh Literature* (Bridgend: Poetry Wales Press, 1985).
Mazey, Mary Ellen and David R. Lee, *Her Space, Her Place: A Geography of Women* (Washington, DC: Association of American Geographers, 1983).
McDowell, Linda, 'Spatializing feminism: geographic perspectives', in Nancy Duncan (ed.), *Bodyspace: Destabilizing Geographies of Gender and Sexuality* (London: Routledge, 1996), pp. 28–44.
McElroy, Ruth, 'Cymraes oddi cartref? Welsh women writing home and migration', *Welsh Writing in English: A Yearbook*, 3 (1997), 134–56.
——, 'The rhyming detective', *Planet*, 141 (2000), 21–6.
——, '"For a mothertongue is a treasure but not a God": Gwyneth Lewis and the dynamics of language in contemporary Welsh poetry', *Journal for the Study of British Cultures*, 12/1 (2005), 39–53.
McFarland, Thomas, *Romanticism and the Forms of Ruin: Wordsworth, Coleridge and the Modalities of Fragmentation* (Princeton: Princeton University Press, 1981).
McGuinness, Patrick, 'The shape-shifter's kingdom: Gwyneth Lewis', *New Welsh Review*, 64 (2004), 4–14.

Meredith, Christopher (ed.), *Moment of Earth: Poems and Essays in Honour of Jeremy Hooker* (Oakville, CT and Aberystwyth: Celtic Studies, 2007).
Middleton, Peter, 'Breaking the perspex: recent poetry by Wendy Mulford', *Many Review*, 1 (1983), 3–9.
Minhinnick, Robert, 'An interview with Hilary Llewellyn-Williams', *Poetry Wales*, 33/2 (1997), 25–9.
Monash, Chris, *Writing The Irish Famine* (Oxford: Clarendon Press, 1995).
Morgan, Clare, 'Exile and the kingdom: Margiad Evans and the mythic landscape of Wales', *Welsh Writing in English*, 6 (2000), 89–118.
Morgan, Gerald (ed.), *This World of Wales: Anglo-Welsh poetry from the 17th–20th Century* (Cardiff: University of Wales Press, 1968).
Morley, David and Kevin Robins, 'No place like Heimat: images of home(land) in European culture', in Erica Carter, James Donald and Judith Squires (eds), *Space and Place: Theories of Identity and Location* (London: Lawrence and Wishart, 1993), pp. 3–31.
Morton, H. V., *In Search of Wales* (3rd edn, London: Methuen & Co, 1932).
——, *In Search of Ireland* (London: Methuen Publishing, 2000).
Muldoon, Paul, *To Ireland, I: An Abecedary of Irish Literature* (London: Faber, 2000).
Mulford, Wendy, *And Suddenly Supposing: Selected Poems* (Buckfastleigh: Etruscan Books, 2002).
——, 'Alltud', *Scintilla*, 11 (2007), 153–61.
——, 'A city boy at heart: John James and the industrial south Welsh heartland', *Poetry Wales*, 44/1 (2008), 20–4.
——, *The Land Between* (Hastings: Reality Street, 2009).
——, 'Finding space: Wendy Mulford interviewed', *Poetry Wales*, 46/1 (2010), 32–7.
——, 'Utterance', *Poetry Wales*, 47/1 (2011), 34–6.
—— and Sara Maitland, *Virtuous Magic: Women Saints and their Meanings* (London: Mowbray, 1998).
Nolan, Janet, *Ourselves Alone: Women's Emigration from Ireland 1885–1920* (Lexington: University of Kentucky Press, 1989).
Norquay, Glenda and Gerry Smyth (eds), *Across the Margins: Cultural Identity and Change in the Atlantic Archipelago* (Manchester: Manchester University Press, 2002).
O'Dowd, Anne, *Spalpeens and Tattie-Hokers: History and Folklore of the Irish Migratory Agricultural Worker in Ireland and Britain* (Dublin: Irish Academic Press, 1991).
O'Leary, Paul, *Immigration and Integration: The Irish in Wales 1798–1922* (Cardiff: University of Wales Press, 2000).
O'Rahilly, Cecile, *Ireland and Wales: Their Historical and Literary Relations* (London: Longman, 1924).
Ong, Walter J., *Orality and Literacy: The Technologizing of the Word* (London and New York: Methuen, 1982).

Ostriker, Alicia Suskin, *Stealing The Language: The Emergence of Women's Poetry in America* (London: The Women's Press, 1987).

Peach, Linden, 'Family and inheritance: Sally Roberts-Jones', *Poetry Wales*, 25/4 (1990), 45–8.

——, 'A decentred self? The long poems of Christine Evans', *Poetry Wales*, 27/1 (1991), 35–8.

——, *Ancestral Lines: Culture and Identity in the Work of Six Contemporary Poets* (Bridgend: Seren, 1992).

——, 'The imagination's caverns: identity and symbolism in the work of Gillian Clarke and Christine Evans', in Belinda Humfrey (ed.), *Fire Green as Grass: Studies of The Creative Impulse in Anglo-Welsh Poetry and Short Stories of the 20th Century* (Llandysul: Gomer, 1995), pp. 146–55.

——, 'Wales and the cultural politics of identity: Gillian Clarke, Robert Minhinnick and Jeremy Hooker', in James Acheson and Romana Huk (eds), *Contemporary British Poetry: Essays in Theory and Criticism* (New York: State University of New York Press, 1996) pp. 373–96.

——, 'Paper margins: The "outside" in poetry in the 1980s and 1990s', in Glenda Norquay and Gerry Smith (eds), *Across the Margins: Cultural Identity and Change in the Atlantic Archipelago* (Manchester: Manchester University Press, 2002), pp. 101–16.

Petch, Melanie, 'The mid-Atlantic imagination: Mina Loy, Ruth Fainlight, Anne Stevenson, Anne Rouse and Eva Salzman', in Jane Dowson (ed.), *The Cambridge Companion to Twentieth-Century British and Irish Women's Poetry* (Cambridge: Cambridge University Press, 2011), pp. 119–35.

Petit, Pascale, 'Amazonia', *Poetry Wales*, 34/2 (1998), 52–4.

——, *The Zoo Father* (Bridgend: Seren, 2001).

——, 'In the ruins of the Templo Mayor', *Poetry Wales*, 37/3 (2002), 21–4.

——, *The Huntress* (Bridgend: Seren, 2005).

——, 'Private and public wars', *New Welsh Review*, 72 (2006), 8–14.

——, 'Your definition of a desperado poet suits me: an interview with Lidia Vianu' (2006) [4pp], *http://lidiavianu.scriptmania.com/pascale_petit*, accessed 29 June 2010.

——, 'Interviewed by Oana-Teodora Ionescu', 2009 [10pp], *http://paascalepetit.blogspot.com/2009/06/interview-by-oana-teodora-ionescu* [3], accessed 29 June 2010.

——, 'Confessing the Amazon and Frida Kahlo', *The Poetry Paper*, 6 (2009–10), 15.

——, *What The Water Gave Me* (Bridgend: Seren, 2010).

——, 'First hand', *New Welsh Review*, 88 (2010), 6–7.

Phillips, Janet, 'The shape-shifter: an interview with Jo Shapcott', *Poetry Review*, 91/1 (2001), 18–21.

Pikoulis, John, 'Lynette Roberts and Alun Lewis', *Poetry Wales*, 19/2 (1983), 9–29.

Pittock, Murray G. H., *Celtic Identity and the British Image* (Manchester: Manchester University Press, 1999).

Pocock, J. G. A., 'British history: a plea for a new subject', *Journal of Modern History*, 47 (1975), 601–21.

Poole, Ross, *Nation and Identity* (London and New York: Routledge, 1999).

Price, Angharad, 'Travelling on the word-bus: Gwyneth Lewis's Welsh poetry', *PN Review*, 25/5 (1999), 49–51.

Pugh, Sheenagh, *Earth Studies and Other Poems* (Bridgend: Poetry Wales Press, 1982).

——, *Sing for the Taxman* (Bridgend: Seren, 1993).

——, *Id's Hospit* (Bridgend: Seren, 1997).

——, *Stonelight* (Bridgend: Seren, 1999).

——, *The Beautiful Lie* (Bridgend: Seren, 2002).

——, *Long-Haul Travellers (*Bridgend: Seren, 2008).

——, Gloria Evans Davies, Christine Evans, Sally Roberts Jones and Val Warner, 'Is there a women's poetry', *Poetry Wales*, 23/1 (1987), 30–56.

Pugh, Simon (ed.), *Reading Landscape: Country, City, Capital* (Manchester: Manchester University Press, 1990).

Punter, David, 'Shape and shadow: on poetry and the uncanny', in David Punter (ed.), *A Companion to the Gothic* (Oxford: Blackwell, 2000), pp. 193–206.

Ramazani, Jahan, *The Hybrid Muse: Postcolonial Poetry in English* (Chicago: University of Chicago Press, 2001).

——, A *Transnational Poetics* (Chicago: University of Chicago Press, 2009).

Rees, Alwyn D., *Life in a Welsh Countryside* (Cardiff: University of Wales Press, 1951).

—— and Brinley Rees, *Celtic Heritage: Ancient Tradition in Ireland and Wales* (London: Thames and Hudson, 1961).

Rees-Jones, Deryn, 'Facing the present: the emergence of female selves in the poetry of Ruth Bidgood', *Poetry Wales*, 26/3 (1991), 9–12.

——, *The Memory Tray* (Bridgend: Seren, 1994).

——, *Signs Around a Dead Body* (Bridgend: Seren, 1998).

——, *Quiver* (Bridgend: Seren, 2004).

——, *Consorting with Angels: Essays on Modern Women Poets* (Tarset: Bloodaxe, 2005).

Reicher, Steve and Nick Hopkins, *Self and Nation* (London: Sage Publications, 2001).

Relph, Edward, *Place and Placelessness* (London: Pion Books, 1976).

Rexroth, Kenneth, *The New British Poets* (New York: New Directions, 1949).

Rhydderch, Francesca, '"A home where they had never lived": the learning of identity', *Poetry Wales*, 33/3 (1998), 52–5.

——, '"Between my tongue's borders": contemporary Welsh women's poetry', *Poetry Wales*, 33/4 (1998), 39–45.

——, '"I know it and I want to feel it": reflections on identity and criticism', *Poetry Wales*, 34/1 (1998), 50–4.

Roberts, Dewi (ed.), *Coastline: An Anthology of the Welsh Coast* (Llanwrst: Gwasg Carreg Gwalch, 2005).
Roberts, Enid, *Bardsey Bound: Pilgrim Routes to Wales' Holy Island* (Talybont: Y Lolfa Cyf, 2008).
Roberts, Gwyneth Tyson, *The Language of the Blue Books: The Perfect Instrument of Empire* (Cardiff: University of Wales Press, 1998).
Roberts, Harri Garrod, *Embodying Identity: Representations of the Body in Welsh Literature* (Cardiff: University of Wales Press, 2009).
Roberts, Lynette, *Lynette Roberts: Collected Poems*, ed. Patrick McGuinness (Manchester: Carcanet Press, 2005).
Roberts Jones, Sally, *Turning Away: Collected Poems 1952–1968* (Llandysul: Gwasg Gomer, 1969).
——, *The Forgotten Country* (Llandysul: Gwasg Gomer, 1977).
——, *Relative Values* (Bridgend: Poetry Wales Press, 1985).
Robinson, Jeffrey C., *The Walk: Notes on a Romantic Image* (Norman and London: University of Oklahoma Press, 1989).
Rose, Gillian, '"As if the mirrors had bled": masculine dwelling, masculinist theory and feminist masquerade', in Nancy Duncan (ed.), *BodySpace: Destabilizing Geographies of Gender and Subjectivity* (London and New York: Routledge, 1996), pp. 56–74.
Rosenthal, M. L. and Sally M. Gall, *The Modern Poetic Sequence: The Genius of Modern Poetry* (Oxford: Oxford University Press, 1983).
Rotella, Guy, *Castings: Monuments and Monumentality in Elizabeth Bishop, Robert Lowell, James Merrill, Derek Walcott and Seamus Heaney* (Nashville: Vanderbilt University Press, 2004).
Royle, Nicholas, *The Uncanny* (Manchester: Manchester University Press, 2003).
Ryan, Patrick, 'Celticity and the storyteller identity: the use and misuse of ethnicity to develop a storyteller's sense of self', *Folklore*, 117/3 (2006), 313–28.
Said, Edward R., *Reflections on Exile and Other Essays* (New York: Harvard University Press, 2000).
Savage, Michael, Gaynor Bagnall and Brian Longhurst., *Globalization and Belonging* (London: Sage, 2005).
Schenck, Celeste M., 'Exiled by genre: modernism, canonicity, and the politics of exclusion', in Mary Lynn Broe and Angela J. C. Ingram (eds), *Women Writing in Exile* (Chapel Hill and London: University of North Carolina Press, 1989), pp. 225–50.
Schlovksy, Viktor, 'Art as technique' [1917], in Philip Rice and Patricia Waugh (eds), *Modern Literary Theory: A Reader* (3rd edn, London: Arnold, 1996), pp. 16–21.
Schwyzer, Philip and Simon Mealor, *Archipelagic Identities: Literature and Identity in the Atlantic Archipelago 1550–1800* (Aldershot: Ashgate, 2004).
Seidel, Michael, *Exile and the Narrative Imagination* (New York: Yale University Press, 1986).

Shananan, Jim. '"The fostering aid of a sister country": Wales in Irish novels, 1796–1810', in Damian Walford Davies and Lynda Pratt (eds), *Wales and the Romantic Imagination* (Cardiff: University of Wales Press, 2007), pp. 122–40.

Shapcott, Jo, *Tender Taxes: Versions of Rilke's French Poems* (London: Faber, 2001).

Sharp, Joanne P., 'Gendering nationhood: a feminist engagement with national identity', in Nancy Duncan (ed.), *Bodyspace: Destabilizing Geographies of Gender and Sexuality* (London: Routledge, 1996), pp. 97–108.

Shatskikh, Elena, 'An interview with Pascale Petit', *Contemporary British Poetry*, *http://eng.1september.ru/articlef.php?ID=200701409*, 1–6, accessed 29 June 2010.

Simon, Sherry, *Gender in Translation: Cultural Identity and the Politics of Transmission* (London: Routledge, 1996).

Sinfield, Alan, *Dramatic Monologue* (Critical Idiom ser.) (London: Methuen, 1977).

Skoulding, Zoë, '"A city of words": Zoë Skoulding interviewed by Fiona Owen', *Planet*, 166 (2004), 57–62.

——, *The Mirror Trade* (Bridgend: Seren, 2004).

——, 'Geographies of the self', Ph.D. thesis, Bangor University, 2005.

——, 'Border lines', *Poetry Wales*, 42/4 (2007), 15–17.

——, 'Wandering where I am', *Poetry Wales*, 42/3 (2007), 23–27.

——, Interview with Alice Entwistle (unpublished, 2008).

——, *Remains of a Future City* (Bridgend: Seren, 2008).

Smith, Kenneth R., 'A vision of the future?', *Poetry Wales*, 24/3 (1988), 46–52.

——, 'The poetry of place: the haunted interiors', *Poetry Wales*, 24/2 (1988), 59–65.

——, 'The portrait poem: reproduction of mothering', *Poetry Wales*, 24/1 (1988), 48–54.

——, 'Praise of the past: the myth of eternal return in women writers', *Poetry Wales*, 24/4 (1989), 50–8.

Smith, Neil and Cindi Katz, 'Grounding metaphor: towards a spatialized politics', in Michael Keith and Steve Pile (eds), *Place and the Politics of Identity* (London: Routledge, 1993), pp. 67–83.

Soja, Edward, *Postmetropolis: Critical Studies of Cities and Regions* (Oxford: Blackwell, 2000).

Solnit, Rebecca, *Wanderlust: A History of Walking* (London: Verso, 2001).

Sommer, Doris, *Bilingual Aesthetics: A New Sentimental Education* (Durham, NC and London: Duke University Press, 2004).

Stallybrass, Peter and Allon White, *The Politics and Poetics of Transgression* (New York: Cornell University Press, 1986).

Stephens, Meic (ed.), *The Bright Field: An Anthology of Contemporary Poetry from Wales* (Manchester: Carcanet, 1991).

—— and Peter Finch (eds), *Green Horse: An Anthology by Young Poets in Wales* (Swansea: Christopher Davies, 1978).

Stevenson, Anne, 'The compassionate sensibility of Christine Evans', *Poetry Wales*, 25/2 (1989), 13–15.
——, 'Poetry and place', in Lothar Fietz, Paul Hoffmann and Hans-Werner Ludwig (eds), *Regionalität, Nationalität und Internationalität in der zeitgenössischen lyrik* (Hamburg: Attempto, 1990), pp. 199–212.
——, 'Identity, language and Welsh poetry', *Poetry Wales*, 31/2 (1995), 38–43.
——, 'Poetry and place', *Between the Iceberg and the Ship: Selected Essays* (Ann Arbor: University of Michigan Press, 1998), pp. 112–19.
——, *The Collected Poems: 1955–1995* (Tarset: Bloodaxe, 2000).
——, *A Report from the Border* (Tarset: Bloodaxe, 2003).
Stoeltje, Beverly J., '"A helpmate for man indeed": the image of the frontier woman', *Journal of American Folklore*, 88/347 (1975), 25–41.
Stuart Williams, John and Meic Stephens (eds), *The Lilting House: An Anthology of Anglo-Welsh Poetry 1917–1967.* (London: Dent; Llandybie: Christopher Davies, 1969).
Thomas, M. Wynn, 'Prints of Wales: contemporary Welsh poetry in English', in Hans Ludwig and Lothar Fietz (eds), *Poetry of the British Isles: Non-Metropolitan Perspectives* (Cardiff: University of Wales Press, 1995), pp. 97–113.
——, *Corresponding Cultures: The Two Literatures of Wales* (Cardiff: University of Wales Press, 1999).
—— (ed.), *The Page's Drift: R. S. Thomas at Eighty* (Bridgend: Seren, 1993).
Thomas, Ned, 'Parallels and paradigms', in M. Wynn Thomas (ed.), *Welsh Writing in English* (Cardiff: University of Wales Press, 2003), pp. 310–26.
Thomas, R.S., 'Interview with Benedict Nightingale', *Guardian*, 4 March 1964.
——, 'The creative writer's suicide', *Planet*, 41 (1978), 30–3.
——, 'A year in Llŷn', in *Autobiographies*, trans. Jason Walford Davies (London: Dent, 1997), pp. 113–74.
Thoreau, Henry David, 'Walking' [1851], in Carl Bode (ed.), *The Portable Thoreau* (New York: Viking, 1964), pp. 592–630.
Thrift, Nigel, 'Inhuman geographies: landscapes of speed, light and power', in Paul Cloke, Marcus Doel, David Matless, Martin Phillips and Nigel Thrift (eds), *Writing the Rural: Five Cultural Geographies* (London: Paul Chapman, 1994) pp. 191–248.
Thurston, Michael, '"Writing at the edge": Gillian Clarke's Cofiant', *Contemporary Literature*, 34/2 (2003), 275–300.
Van der Hoorn, Mélanie, 'Exorcising remains: architectural fragments as intermediaries between history and individual experience', *Journal of Material Culture*, 8/2 (2003), 189–213.
Vianu, Lidia, 'An image of contemporary literature: desperado literature. An interview with Pascale Petit', *http://lidiavianu.scriptmania.com/pascale_petit.htm*, accessed 29 June 2010.
Vidler, Anthony, *The Architectural Uncanny: Essays in the Modern Unhomely* (London and Massachussetts: MIT Press, 1992).

Walford Davies, Damian and Lynda Pratt (eds), *Wales and the Romantic Imagination* (Cardiff: University of Wales Press, 2007).

Webb, Harri, Letter, *Poetry Wales*, 7/4 (special issue on R. S. Thomas) (1972), 122–3.

Welsh Assembly Government, *People, Places Futures: The Wales Spatial Plan* (Cardiff: Welsh Assembly Government, 2004).

Williams, Daniel (ed.), *Who Speaks for Wales? Nation, Culture, Identity* (Cardiff: University of Wales Press, 2003).

——, 'Introduction', in Daniel G. Williams (ed.), *Slanderous Tongues: Essays on Welsh poetry in English 1970–2005* (Bridgend: Seren 2010), p. 7–18.

Williams, Frances, 'The end in Bridgend', *Poetry Wales*, 37/2 (2001), 46–8.

Williams, Gwyn, *The Land Remembers: A View of Wales* (London: Faber, 1977).

Williams, Gwyn A., *When Was Wales? A History of the Welsh* (Harmondsworth: Penguin, 1985).

Williams, Merryn, 'The poetry of Ruth Bidgood', *Poetry Wales*, 28/3 (1993), 336–41.

Williams, Nerys, 'Gwyneth Lewis: taboo and blasphemy', *Poetry Wales*, 38/3 (2003), 23–8.

Williams, Raymond, *The Country and The City* (London: Chatto and Windus, 1973).

——, 'Welsh culture', in Daniel Williams (ed.), *Who Speaks for Wales? Nation, Culture, Identity* (Cardiff: University of Wales Press, 2003), pp. 5–11.

Wintle, Justin, *Furious Interiors: Wales, R. S. Thomas and God* (London: Harper Collins, 1996).

Wood, Denis, *The Power of Maps* (London and New York: The Guilford Press, 1992).

Woodham-Smith, Cecil, *The Great Hunger* (London: Hamish Hamilton, 1962).

Woodward, Christopher, *In Ruins* (London: Chatto & Windus, 2001).

Wynne Rhydderch, Samantha, *Rockclimbing in Silk* (Bridgend: Seren, 2001)

——, *Not in These Shoes* (London: Picador, 2006).

——, 'Samantha Wynne Rhydderch in conversation', Alice Entwistle, *Poetry Wales*, 48/2 (2012), 53–8.

——, *Banjo* (London: Picador, 2012).

——, 'Interviewed by Katherine Stansfield' *New Welsh Review*, 96, *www.newwelshreview.com/article.php?id=209*.

Yorke, Liz, *Impertinent Voices: Subversive Strategies in Contemporary Women's Poetry* (London: Routledge, 1991).

Index of Names

Aaron, Jane 3, 5, 30, 43, 168n, 170n, 174n, 176n, 177n, 179n, 196
Actaeon 37
Adorno, Theodor 135
Althusser, Louis 114, 186n
Anstey, Sandra 7
Aneirin 119
ap Gwilym, Dafydd 128
ap Hwyel, Elin 159
Armstrong, Isobel 140, 149, 191, 196
Arnold, David 131, 189n, 196
Artemis 37
Atkinson, Tiffany 7, 29, 159–66, 174n, 182n, 194n, 195n, 194, 196
  '99' 161
  'Anthuriam' 161
  'Birthday' 160
  'Catulla' 159–63, 165–6
  Catulla et al. 159, 194, 196
  'Dear Kate' 161
  'If You Are Reading' 161
  'In This One' 160
  Kink and Particle 161, 194n, 196
  'Quantum Theory for Beginners' 161
  'Tea' 161

Bacon, Francis 47
Barrett Browning, Elizabeth 149
Bate, Jonathan 20n, 172n, 193, 197
Beagan, Glenda 159
Beddoe, Deirdre 3, 197
Beer, Gillian 73, 74, 181n, 197
Bendigeidfran 121, 122, 172n, 188n, 199
Benjamin, Walter 115, 187n 197
Benstock, Shari 142, 149, 191n, 192n, 197
Berger, John 46, 177n 197
Bernstein, Charles 2, 168n
Bertram, Vicki xvi, 114, 167n, 194n, 197, 198
Bevan, Nye 39
Bhabha, Homi K. xviii, 2, 7, 11, 13, 15, 18, 19, 42, 45, 48, 49, 53, 55, 61, 63, 70, 167n, 170n, 171n, 172n, 174n, 176n, 177n, 178n, 179n, 180n, 181n, 195
  Third Space 2, 15, 70
Bidgood, Ruth 6, 13, 47–68, 70, 71, 92, 100, 112, 143, 169n, 177n, 178n, 179n, 180n, 182n, 197, 210, 214
  'All Souls' 60, 182
  'Carreg-y-Frân 52
  'Chancery: Opening Music' 67, 68
  'Green Man at Bwlch' 51
  'Grievance' 67
  'Grumbles to her Sister 67
  'Guerinou' 64–66
  Hearing Voices 66–7, 197
  'Heol y Mwyn (Mine Road)' 52
  'Incident in Vengeance Wood' 65
  'Journeys' 51
  'Kindred' 55–6, 57
  'McNamara's Mistress' 66
  'Meeting the Bus' 49–50
  'Neighbour' 55
  New and Selected Poems 51, 52, 53, 56, 60,

Parishes of the Buzzard 59, 180n, 197
'Patricio 2001 65
'Question' 53
Selected Poems 51, 52
'Shepherd's Cottage' 52, 53
'Slate Quarry, Penceulan' 52
'Sources' 68
'Strangeness' 47–8
'The Given Time' 53, 54
The Given Time 52
'The Hermitage' 65, 66
Time Being 49–50
'Tŷ'n-y-Llŵyn ' 65
'Valley-before-Nos' 60–4 passim, 67
'Viewpoint' 50
Bielski, Alison 6, 7, 9, 159, 194n, 198
Billig, Michael 137, 191n, 198
Blau DuPlessis, Rachel 114, 116, 134, 186n, 187n, 189n, 198
Bohata, Kirsti 4, 169n, 170n, 178n, 198,
Boland, Eavan 30, 174n, 175n 198
Bordo, Susan 160, 194n, 198
Bowcott, Howard 8
Bowers 'Birdie' 161
Brân 122
Branwen 121–4
Brennan, Catherine 19, 64, 113, 168n, 172n, 186n, 187n, 198, 203

Cambrensis, Giraldus 125
Chamberlain, Brenda 9, 10, 11, 125, 198
The Green Heart 10
Tide Race 10
Cherry-Garrard, Apsley 161
Chitty, Mary 71, 72, 78, 80, 126, 181n, 182n, 188n, 198
Chtcheglov, Ivain 154, 193, 203
Cixous, Hélène 4, 92, 167n, 169n, 177n, 184n, 193n, 198
Clare, John 10
Clarke, Gillian xvii, 4, 6–9, 11, 14, 19, 20, 36, 85, 86, 100, 112, 114, 115, 117, 120, 121–4, 128, 137, 169n, 172n, 175n, 183n, 185n, 188n, 199, 201, 209, 213
'Babysitting' 85
'Beginning with Bendigeidfran' 172n, 188n
'Cofiant' 9, 100
Collected Poems 8, 120, 123
'Cordelia's "Nothing"'
'Letter from a Far Country' 7, 8–9, 19, 86, 120, 199
Letting in the Rumour 8
'Llŷr' 121
'Roofing' 8
'Slate' 8
'Slate Mine' 8
'The Heaviside Layer' 123
'The King of Britain's Daughter' 9, 121–4, 185, 188n, 199, 205
'Wind Chimes' 8
Clarke, Ruth 71
Clifford, James 138, 144, 150, 191n, 192n, 199
Cluysenaar, Anne 7, 19, 21–3, 24, 25, 71, 136, 173n, 190n, 199, 201
'A Gap of Light' 21
'At Pantymaes Abandoned Quarry' 22
'Landfall' 21
'Llŷr' 123
Migrations 22
'On the beach, Ogmore by Sea' 22–3
'Quarry' 21
'Through Time' 22
Timeslips 21
Coleridge, S. T. 54, 178n, 207
'The Rime of the Ancient Mariner' 54
Coles, Gladys Mary 7, 101, 119, 123, 185n, 188n, 199
Colley, Linda 113, 119
Connolly, Claire 112, 113, 171, 186n, 199, 202
Connor, Stephen 162–4, 194n, 195n, 199
Conran, Tony 9, 10, 19, 122, 135, 170n, 172n, 190n, 199
Constantine, David 88

Cook, Captain 130
Corbett, Sarah 6, 7, 20, 32–3, 39
'Athena' 33
'Bitter Fruit' 33
'Black Crow Woman' 33
'Dark Moon' 33
'Little Bitch' 33
'My Three Dead Daughters' 33
'Night Flying' 33
'Ocyrhoe Becomes a Horse' 33
Other Beasts 32–3
'The Electric Dead' 33
The Red Wardrobe 33
The Witch Bag 33
Cordelia 121, 122, 188, 199
Cosgrove, Dennis 20, 172n, 200
Crawford, Robert 5, 51, 168n, 169n, 200
Cronin, Michael 42

Davies, Grahame 42
Davidson, Ian 146, 155, 156, 191, 192, 193, 200
de Certeau, Michel 28, 152–5, 192n, 193n
Delargy, J. H. 115, 187n
Derrida, Jacques 17, 45, 137, 141, 171, 191, 200, 204
Dickinson, Emily 9
Donahaye, Jasmine 5, 6, 7, 159, 169n, 179n, 200
Doorly, Third Office Gerald 161
Dowson, Jane 114, 171n, 173n, 190n, 191n, 200, 205, 209
Duce-Mills, Alexandra 159
Duncan, Andrew 142
Dyfrig, Saint 126

Earle, Jean 9
Elfyn, Menna xi, xv, 6, 11, 15, 20, 30–32, 40–6, 84, 159, 167, 171, 175, 176, 177, 201, 203
Cusan Dyn Dall / Blind Man's Kiss 32
'*Cusan Hances* / Handkerchief Kiss' 44
'*Cysgu ar ei thraed* / Asleep on her feet' 32
'*Dim ond Camedd* / Nothing But Curves' 32
'*Diwinyddiaeth Gewallt* / Theology of Hair' 32
Eucalyptus / Detholiad o Gerddi 31
'*Geiriau Lluosog am Gariad* / Ten Words For Love and Longing' 44
'*Nam Lleferydd* / Malediction' 41
Perffaith Nam/Perfect Blemish 31, 32, 41, 44–5
'Siesta' 31
Elgar, Saint 126–7
Eurydice 149
Evans, Christine 6, 13, 14, 69–91, 92, 100, 112, 114, 120, 124–8, 143, 180n, 181n, 182n, 183n, 185n, 188n, 201
'Adjusting the Focus' 79
'Another Season' 125
'Between Waking' 86
'Bonanza' 83, 84, 91
'Broc Môr' 73, 74
Burning the Candle 87, 88, 89, 90, 91, 183, 201
Call Us Peasants 84
'Callers' 81
Cometary Phases 78, 80, 81, 86, 87, 201
'Compline' 127
'Crossing from the Island' 73
'Driving Home' 77
'Enlli' 73
'Falling Back' 85
'In Women's Thanatological' 85
'*Insula Sanctorum*' 127
'Island of Dark Horses' 74, 75, 126
Island of Dark Horses 69, 70, 73, 74, 75, 76, 78, 82, 125–8
'Keeping in Touch' 80
'Lauds' 127
'Llŷn' 76, 78
Looking Inland 71, 72, 77, 80, 81, 86, 125
'Meanwhile, In Another Part of the Island' 85
'Meeting the Boat' 85
'Mrs Crusoe' 85

'Mynydd Rhiw' 77, 80
'None' 127
'Off Camera' 80
'On Retreat' 82
'Out of Season' 85
'Peninsular' 77, 80
'Prime' 127
'Pulpit Enlli' 82
'Second Language' 81
Selected Poems 74, 125
'Sevens: the Death of Elgar' 126–8
'Sext' 127
'Songline' 75–6
'Sounding' 73
'Storm' 73
'Summer in the Village' 83
'Terce' 74, 82, 127
'The Blacksmith's Son' 89
'The Scritch of the Match' 90
'The Way Light Falls' 89
'Through the weather window' 73
'Tree Wife' 85
'Unseen Island', 72, 73
'Watchers', 73
'Waves' 69, 70, 76
'Weaning' 86
'Whale Dream' 85
'Winter Visiting' 85
Evans, Donald 171n, 201
Evans, Estyn 115, 116, 187n, 202
The Personality of Ireland 112, 187n, 202
The Personality of Wales 112, 202
Evans, Margiad 9, 10, 170n, 186n, 202
Evans, Wil (Wil Tŷ Pella) 83, 181n, 182n
see also Bardsey boatman

Faraday, Michael 88, 89, 90
The Chemical History of A Candle 89
Finch, Peter 159, 212
Fisher, Catherine 6, 14, 24–5
Altered States 129, 130, 132
'Blodeuwedd' 130
'Estuary Poems' 129, 131–3
'Great-grandmother' 133–4
'Gwern-y-Cleppa' 128
Immrama 129, 130, 133, 202
'Llanddewi Fach' 130
'Teyrnon looks at Gwent Iscoed' 25
'The Unexplored Ocean' 130
The Unexplored Ocean 25, 128, 129, 130, 202
'III' 132
'V' 132
'XI' 132
Foucault, Michel 97, 104, 169n, 184n, 202, 204
Franklin, Lady 139–41
Friedman, Susan Stanford 5, 17, 18, 70, 117, 118, 119, 128, 133, 134, 136, 163, 165, 169n, 172n, 181n, 185n, 187n, 190n, 194n, 202
Freud, Sigmund 48, 144, 177n, 202
Furber, Jo 113, 114, 186n, 202

George, Rosemary Marangoly 48, 63, 177n, 202
Gide, André 5
Gilbert Roger 155, 193n, 203
Gilbert, Sandra 149
Gill, Jo 19, 96–8, 104, 114, 172n, 184n, 194n, 195n, 203
Gilmore, Leigh 6, 29, 96, 97, 104, 118, 119, 170n, 174n, 187n, 203
Goodby, John 142, 191, 203
Gormley, Anthony 138
Gramich, Katie 3, 19, 64, 78, 79, 83, 91, 112, 113, 136, 140, 168n, 172n, 180n, 182n, 186n, 187n, 189n, 191, 199, 203
Gray Christopher 154, 193n, 203
Gray, Kathryn 33, 34, 135–6, 159, 175n, 190n, 203, 206
Greene, Roland 100, 184n, 203
Gregson, Ian 46, 177n, 203, 206
Grosz, Elizabeth 29, 35
Gwyn, Richard 5fn, 6

Hallam, Tudur 42–3, 46
Hardy, Thomas 10

Harthill, Captain James 130
Harvey, Clodagh Brennan 115, 117, 187n, 204
Heaney, Seamus 131, 179n, 211
Heiland, Donna 48, 49, 177n, 204
Hemans, Felicia 64, 140
Hillis Miller, J. 15, 171n, 204
Hooker, Jeremy 2, 4, 24, 25, 48, 50, 64, 68, 146, 148, 168n, 169n, 170n, 173n, 177n, 178n, 180n, 192n, 204, 208 209
Hughes, Tristan 19, 172n, 204
Huk, Romana 168, 196, 204, 209
Humm, Maggie xvi, 29, 167n, 172n, 174n, 204
Humphreys, Emyr 116, 117, 187n, 204
Hussey, Leonard 161

Irigaray, Luce 11, 171n, 204

Jacob, Christian xviii, 167n, 205
Janovitz, Anne 53, 54, 65, 66, 178n, 179n, 180, 205
Jarvis, Matthew 4, 6, 59, 73, 169n, 170n, 174n, 178n, 179n, 180n, 181n, 205
Jarvis, Robin 152, 192n, 205
Jenkins, Lee M. 11, 150, 171n, 190n, 192, 205
Jenkins, Randall 11, 171n
Jenkins, Nigel 88, 183n
John, Angela 3, 168n, 186n, 202, 205
Jones, Bobi 205
Jones, David 88
Jones, Gareth Elwyn 204
Jones, Glyn 50, 116, 187n, 205
Jones, Glyn E. 180n, 205
Jones, Gwyn 205
Jones, T. Harri 62, 179n,
Jones, Noragh 205
Jones, R. Gerallt 205

Katz Cindy (and Neil Smith) 12, 171n, 212
Keats, John 35
Kelleher, Margaret 133–4
Kermode, Frank 99
Kerrigan, John 112, 113, 120, 122, 124,185n, 188n, 205
Kirby, Kathleen 14, 171n, 206
Kirkland, Richard 129, 189n, 206
Knight, Stephen 1, 2, 168n, 206
Kristeva, Julia 51, 55, 177, 178, 179, 206

Lefebvre, Henri xvii, 1, 14, 28, 168n, 206
Leighton, Angela xvi, xvii, 11, 40, 167n, 171n, 176n, 206
Lewis, Alun 10, 209
Lewis, Gwyneth xv–xviii, xix, 6, 7, 8, 11, 13, 20, 37, 38–40, 71, 92–111, 112, 114, 143, 165, 167n, 170, 172, 176, 183n, 185n, 186n, 206, 207, 210, 214
A Hospital Odyssey xvii, 39, 207
'A Poet's Confession' 106, 108,
'A Question' 109
'A Teenage Craze' 109
Chaotic Angels 38–9, 96, 102, 105–10, 184n, 206
'Finding the Bodies' 109
'Home Cooking' 107, 108
'How to Knit a Poem' 94–9, 105, 111,
'Keeping Mum' 96, 108
Keeping Mum 37, 96, 104–11
Parables & Faxes 20n, 101, 206
'Psychiatrist Twitcher' 110
'Six Poems on Nothing' 20n
Sunbathing in the Rain 93, 94, 95, 96, 102, 103, 104, 105, 167n, 184n, 206
'The Hedge' 96
'The Language Murderer' 37, 105, 106, 108, 110
'The Reference Library' 38–9
'Welsh Espionage' 38, 96, 99, 101, 102, 104, 108, 111
Y Llofrudd Iaith 37, 105
'Zero Gravity' 96
Lewis, Lisa 41, 176n, 207
Levertov, Denise 9, 10, 11, 170n, 206
Lir (see also Llŷr) 122, 124

Llewellyn-Williams, Hilary 6, 25–6, 173n, 199, 203, 207, 208
Animaculture 25–6
'Capel Mair' 26
'Maze Stone' 25
Lloyd, David 19, 131, 172n, 189n, 207
Llŷr 121, 122, 123, 124
see also Lir
Lopez, Helen 159
Lorde, Audre 29
Zami 29

Maitland, Sara 24, 148, 173n, 192n, 208
Massey, Doreen 1–2, 7, 8, 70, 75, 78, 79, 119, 157, 168n, 170n, 181n, 182n, 193n, 207
Masson, Ursula 3
Matholwch 122
McElroy, Ruth 105, 187n, 207
McFarland, Thomas 54, 178n, 207
Mechain, Gwerful 117
Merlin 130
Mew, Charlotte 10
Morton, H. V. 16, 17, 26, 112, 172n, 208
Morton, Angela 178n, 180n, 197
Muldoon, Paul 129, 189n,
'Immram', 'Immrama' 129, 189, 206
To Ireland, I: An Abecedary of Irish Literature 129
Mulford, Wendy 6, 14, 19–20, 23–4, 25, 84, 135, 136, 137, 142–50, 173n, 190n, 191n, 192n, 201, 204, 208
ABC of Writing 143, 144
'l' 145
'p' 144–5, 147
's' 144
'y' 143
'Alltud' 23–4, 25, 146–50
And suddenly, supposing 143, 144, 145
'Elennith' 149
The Land Between 144
'The Question' 146, 147
'The Return' 148
Virtuous Magic
'Yr Heniaith' 144

Nietzsche, Friedrich 51
Nightingale, Benedict 83, 183n, 213
Noah 130
Norquay, Glenda and Gerry Smyth 113, 186n, 208, 209

Ó Conaill, Seán 117
Olds, Sharon 33, 175n, 202
O'Leary, Paul 112, 113, 131, 133, 134, 189n, 208
Olson, Charles 10
Ong, Walter J. 115, 116, 117, 119, 187n, 208
O'Rahilly, Cecile 113, 186n, 208
Ostriker, Alicia 30, 174n, 209

Parry, William 139
Peach, Linden 7, 113, 114, 170n, 183n, 186n, 209
Perloff, Marjorie 119
Petch, Melanie 139,190, 191, 209
Petit, Pascale 6, 20, 32, 33–6, 39
'King Vulture' 34
'Lungfish' 34
'Motherfather' 34
'My Father's Body' 34
'My Father's Lungs' 35
The Huntress 34
The Zoo Father 34–5
'Trophy' 34
Pfeiffer, Emily Jane 113
Glân-Alarch: His Silence and His Song 113
Plath, Sylvia 85, 97
Pocock, J. G. A. 113, 210
Ptolemy 126
Pugh, Sheenagh 7, 9, 14, 135–42, 143, 183n, 190n, 210
'Amy Flew Away' 138
'Another Place' 138
'Buffalo Bill in Pontcanna' 138
'Climbing Hermaness' 138
Crowded by Shadows 138

Earth Studies and Other Places 138
'Fanfic' 139
'Fixed' 138
Id's Hospit 138
'Lady Franklin at Muckle Flugga' 139
'Lady Franklin Begins to be Concerned' 139
'Lady Franklin Hears a Ballad in the Street' 140
'Lady Franklin Refuses to Wear Mourning' 140
'Lady Franklin Resumes her Travels' 140
'Lady Franklin's Man' 139
Long Haul Travellers 138, 139, 141
'Murat Reis' 141
'Saxa Ford' 138
Sing for the Taxman 138
Stonelight 138
'The Arctic Chart' 138
The Beautiful Lie 139, 140
'The Door to the Sea' 138
'The Parry Islands' 139
'What if this Road' 138

Pugh, Simon 172n, 210
Punter, David 54, 67, 178n, 180n, 210

Ramazani, Jahan xvi, 12, 135, 141, 167n, 169n, 190n, 194n, 210
Rees-Jones, Deryn 6, 20, 36–8, 39, 172n, 175n, 176n, 188n, 194, 199, 202, 207, 210
'Afterthought' 37, 39
'Half Term' 36
'Oral Tradition' 36
Quiver 37–8
The Memory Tray 36
Signs Around a Dead Body 36
Rees, Alwyn and Brinley 56, 112, 115, 116, 179n, 187n, 189n, 210
Rees, Gareth 200
Rees, Teresa 168n, 196, 201
Relph, Edward 1, 79, 168n, 182n, 210
Rexroth, Kenneth 9
Rhydderch, Francesca xix, 5, 18, 31, 168n, 170n, 172n, 175n, 210
Rhys, Keidrych 10
Rice, Matthew (aka Murat Reis) 141
Rilke, Rainer Maria 27–8
Roberts, Dewi 120, 211
Roberts, Enid 124, 211
Roberts, Lynette 9, 10, 11
Roberts-Jones, Sally 7, 63, 170n, 180n, 197, 209
Robinson, Jeffrey C. 152, 191n, 192n, 211
Rose, Gillian 3, 14, 169n, 171n, 211
Rosenthal, M. L. 96, 99, 184n, 194n, 211
Rousseau, Jean-Jacques 152
Royle, Nicholas 48, 63–4
Rumens, Carol 159

Schlovsky, Victor 48
Scott, Captain 160, 165
Seidel, Michael 140, 190, 191
Sexton, Anne 97, 106, 108, 111, 184n, 203
Shackleton 160
Shapcott, Jo 7, 20, 26–7, 28, 96, 173, 174, 184, 209, 212
'Gladestry Quatrains' 26–8
'Llan' 27
'Over the Col' 27
'Radnorshire' 26
Tender Taxes 26–8
'Wye Marches' 27
Skoulding, Zoë 7, 14, 20, 28, 135, 136, 137, 150–8, 190, 191, 193, 200, 212
'Baths of Amnesia' 154
'Building Site' 153
'Bureau for the Suspension of Control' 154
'Disobedience: collaborative writing and the walk poem' (with Ian Davidson) 155–6
'Forests with A-Z of Cardiff' 155
'Llanddwyn Beach with directions for Copenhagen' 156–7

'Preselis with Brussels Street Map' 151
Remains of a Future City 28, 153, 192n, 212
The Mirror Trade 28
'The New Bridge' 28
'The Old Walls' 28
'Wandering Where I Am' 150–1, 192n, 212
Smith, Kenneth R. 24, 49, 52, 59, 169n, 170n, 173n, 180, 183, 212
Smith, Neil and Cindy Katz 12, 171n, 212
Smyth, Gerry (and Glenda Norquay) 113, 186n, 208, 209
Soja, Edward 28, 174, 212
Solnit, Rebecca 152, 153, 155, 192n, 193n, 212
Sommer, Doris 41–2, 176, 212
Stallybrass, Peter and Allon White 32, 175n, 212
Stammers, Ben 151
Stevenson, Anne 7, 9, 16, 17, 20, 21, 172n, 173n, 190n, 209, 213
A Report From the Border 173n, 213
Between the Iceberg and the Ship: Selected Essays 16, 172n, 173n, 213
'Binoculars in Ardudwy' 16, 17
'Poetry and Place' 16, 172n, 173n, 213
'Some Poems From Cwm Nantcol' 173n, 213
Stoeltje, Beverley 80
Swift, Jonathan 129

Taliesin 23, 119, 187, 204
Tennyson, Alfred Lord 66
Thomas, Edward 10
Thomas, M. Wynn 5, 44, 45, 168n, 170n, 177n, 190n, 196, 199, 213
Thomas, Ned xix, 6, 168, 170
Thomas, R. S. 44, 71, 79, 83, 84, 91, 125, 181n, 182n, 183n, 186n, 213, 214
Thrift, Nigel 15, 135, 136, 171n, 190n, 213

Van der Hoorn, Melanie 52
Vidler, Anthony 50, 178n, 213

Webb, Harri 91
White, Allon (and Peter Stallybrass) 32, 175n, 212
Williams, Chris (and Jane Aaron) 196
Williams, Daniel G. 20, 169n, 170n, 172n, 174n, 176n, 186n, 200, 202, 203, 205, 214
Williams, Frances 6, 170n, 214
Williams, Gwyn Alf 2, 56, 179n, 214
Williams, Merryn 214
Williams, Nerys 6, 159, 214
Williams, Raymond 29, 65, 174n, 214
Wills, Clair 18
Windsor, Penny 7
Wintle, Justin 71, 181, 214
Woodham-Smith, Cecil 189n, 214
Woodward, Christopher 53, 54, 178n, 214
Wyn Jones, Nesta 30
Wynne Rhydderch, Samantha 6, 29, 159–66, 194n, 195n, 214
Banjo 159, 161, 162, 164, 165, 194n, 214
'Blackout' 161
'Decoupage' 161
'Erratics' 159–65
'First Aid Class' 161
'In My Arms' 162
Not In These Shoes 161, 214
'Ponting' 161
Rockclimbing in Silk 161, 214
'The Minstrels at Minus Sixty' 161
'The Piano' 161
'The X-Ray Room' 161

General Index

abbeys 5, 147
Aberdaron 71, 76, 77
Abergavenny 64
Abergwaun 78
Abergwesyn 58–60 passim
Aberystwyth 78, 160, 161
aesthetic(s) xv, xvii, xviii, xix, 1, 3, 4, 6, 8, 9, 11, 12, 14, 18, 28, 30, 32, 37, 39–43, 45, 46, 48, 50, 64, 65, 66, 68, 79, 86, 88, 89, 90, 92, 104, 114, 117–19, 124, 128, 141, 150, 154, 157, 165
Afrikaans 46
Alexandria 126
alienation 16, 50, 82, 91, 143
Amazon, Amazonia 33–4
America, American 16
  North 30
  South 33
ancestors, ancestral 27, 129, 133, 145, 186n, 209
anchorite 88
Anglesey 125, 156, 186
Antarctic 160, 163
archipelago, archipelagic 113, 120, 186n, 188n, 206
architecture, architectural xv, 9, 13, 38, 52, 53, 88, 147, 161, 178n, 191n, 195n
Arctic 138, 139
Ardudwy 16, 17
Arthurian 20, 37
arwydd 116
Asian 28, 34
'A Symposium on Gender and Poetry' (*Poetry Wales*) 84, 175n, 183, 201
Athens 120,
Athlone 123
Atlantic (Atlantic Ocean) 10, 120, 122, 186n, 190n, 191n, 208, 209, 211
atom bomb 88
authentic, authenticity 5, 9, 77, 90, 91–111, 169n, 170n, 183n, 198
  see also forger, forgery
autobiography, autobiographical 63, 84, 93, 97, 122, 123, 170n, 174n, 182, 183, 184, 187, 203, 213

Bangor 10, 19, 151
banjo (banjo-playing) 161
bard, bardic 30, 46, 101, 116, 117, 119, 120
bardd 5, 46, 59, 176n, 177n, 203
bardd gwlad 59
Bardsey boatman 71, 83, 182n
Bardsey Island 10, 13, 69, 70–5, 80, 87, 88, 120, 124–8, 181n, 182n, 188n, 201, 205, 211
  see also Ynys Enlli
Bardsey Sound 71, 88
BBC 69 98 112
  TV 69, 180, 201, 202
  Radio 4 98
Beaumaris 20
Belgium, Belgian 21
'beyond' xviii, 2, 11, 15, 19, 20, 28, 49, 55, 68, 70, 129, 145, 165
bilingual, bilingualism xv, 5, 19, 27, 28, 36, 38, 40, 41, 42, 90, 92, 95, 151, 157, 176n, 212
body, bodies, embodied, embodiment 13, 18, 28, 29–46

border(s), borderland ix, 5, 12, 16–46, 47, 58, 63, 61, 70, 78, 79, 120, 122, 128, 135, 140, 159
boundary, boundaries 11, 12, 17, 24, 25, 26, 27, 28, 30, 35, 40, 44, 46, 52, 53, 70, 80, 92, 99, 136, 140, 155, 158, 169n, 175n, 178n, 179n, 183n, 190n
Bradford 151
braint 56
Brecknockshire 169n
Brecon, Breconshire 49, 58, 179n, 180n
Bristol, Bristol Channel xv, 128
Britain, British (Isles) 3, 5, 9, 10, 20, 34, 54, 74, 75, 95, 121, 122–4, 127, 131, 135, 140,
Briton, Britonic 113, 122, 199
  see also Brythonic
Brittany (Llydaw) 78, 79, 125
bro 5, 57
Bronfelen 53
Brussels 150–1
Brythonic 95, 124
Budapest 28
building, buildings 26, 47, 48, 50, 52, 53, 54, 55, 65, 74, 75, 125, 153, 160, 175n

Caeglas 55
Caernarfon 20
Cambrian Mountains 105
Cambridge 142, 143
canu gwerin 116
Cardiff xv, 4, 19, 112, 120, 123, 155
  Bay xv
Camarch (also upper Camarch) Valley 60, 61, 65
canhwyllau llygaid 90
Carmarthenshire 10
cartography *see* maps, mapping
castle, castles 20, 52, 54
Catholic 24–5, 129, 131
Cefn Gilfach 61
cefn gwlad 57
Celtic, ism 26, 112–14, 116, 119, 121, 122, 123, 129, 187n, 189n, 192n, 200
cenedl 56
cerdd xv, 43, 63
Ceredigion 4, 179n
chapel 40, 61, 82
Chernobyl 88
child, childhood, children 19 29, 31, 32–6, 37, 38, 41, 43, 50, 51, 57, 60, 62, 63, 72, 79, 102, 120, 121, 122, 126, 132, 143–5, 147, 149, 185n
China, Chinese 28, 37
Christian, Christianity 23, 25, 26, 127, 129, 148
Church, churches, 26, 52, 54, 59, 125
Cinnamon Press xviii
Cistercians 147
Clynnog Fawr 125
coal 24, 27
  see also mine, mining
coast, coastal, coastline 13, 18, 19, 25, 69, 70, 74, 76, 77, 78, 79, 80, 120, 121, 122, 124, 125, 128, 141, 163
Coedtrefan 60, 62, 63
community, communities, communal 2, 4, 6, 7, 15, 16, 18, 40, 42, 43, 50, 55, 56, 57, 59, 60, 61, 62, 63, 64, 71, 75, 77, 79–83, 84, 91, 105, 112, 125, 131, 135, 160
Conwy 20, 179n
Copenhagen 156, 157
Cornwall (Cernyw), Cornish 75, 78, 79, 125
croeso 132
Crosby Beach (Merseyside) 138
Crynant, Glamorgan 57
Cwm Nantcol 20
cultural dislocation, displacement, estrangement 10, 13, 16, 27, 57, 58, 82, 83, 91, 133, 143
  cultural heritage/legacy 81, 95, 128, 133
  geo-cultural xvi, 26, 131, 157, 165
  intercultural 5, 6, 18, 27, 132
  multiculturalism 37, 54

socio-cultural xvii, xviii, 3, 4, 8, 13, 15, 30, 44, 55, 56, 60, 62, 70, 75, 80, 115, 117, 118, 156
transcultural xviii, 19, 28, 32, 46
curator, curatorial 52
cyfarwydd, *cyfarwyddyd* 115, 116
cyheuraeth 61, 180
Cymraeg 5, 146, 158
Cymru 7
cynefin 4, 71
cynfeirdd 101, 119
cytiau Gwyddelod 126

dechreunos 62, 63, 180n, 205
dérive 154, 156
depression 93, 96, 104, 167, 184, 206
desire, desiring, desirous xvi, 15, 29, 31, 32, 44–6, 94, 99, 106, 118, 139, 149, 161
Devon 75, 126
dialogue(s), dialoguing, dialogic(ally) xv, 5, 6, 12, 13, 14, 15, 28, 43, 46, 88, 89, 90, 109, 119, 146, 150, 157
documentary 103
domestic, domesticity, 7, 8, 13, 51, 52, 55, 62, 63, 64, 107, 139, 147, 202
Dyfed 121

East Anglia 143
Edwardian 16, 139, 164
Egypt 57
Elizabethan 47
England 18, 25, 69, 79, 200, 205
English 3, 5, 6, 12, 19, 20, 27, 31, 36, 37, 40–2, 44–6, 57–9, 71, 81, 83, 95, 101–3, 105, 109, 113, 115, 121, 126, 131, 135, 141, 157–8
environs 13, 21, 26, 27, 42, 49, 51, 57, 59, 62, 77, 79
environment, environmental 4, 21, 22, 29, 62, 73, 80, 85, 142, 154, 156, 163, 169n, 178n, 179n, 180n, 181n, 205
Erwood (Powys) 147
Essex 75

estrangement 37, 39, 50, 51, 55, 58, 67, 82, 83, 144, 177n
see also alienation
estuary, estuarine 21, 22, 128, 129, 131, 132, 133
see also Fisher, 'Estuary Poems'
ethnic, ethnicity 5, 6 41, 74, 136, 137, 190, 211
ethnography, ethnographical xvi, xviii, 3, 12, 15, 18, 30, 40, 92, 137, 141, 159, 165
Europe, European, Europeanism 28, 108, 139, 151, 154, 158, 177n, 200, 208
Ewenny 147
exile 23, 50, 81, 129, 135, 136, 138, 142, 144, 146, 148, 150, 171n, 190n, 191n, 192n, 197, 208, 211

fabric, fabrication 13, 15, 48, 94–9, 105, 108, 110, 111
family, familial, families 13, 16, 27, 29, 30, 32, 33, 36, 38, 52, 56–7, 58, 62, 71, 72, 75, 81, 82, 87, 91, 112, 113, 117, 129, 113, 143, 144, 160, 181n,
famine (Irish) 129, 131, 133, 189n, 196, 200, 205, 208
farm, farmer, farming 13, 17, 57, 59, 60, 61, 62, 71, 72, 73, 82, 115, 121, 144, 181n
farmhouse 121
father(s) 34, 35, 36, 38, 57, 71, 72, 81, 88, 102, 121–3, 124, 132, 166, 181n, 182n, 185n
feminism, feminist xvi, 3, 18, 30, 31, 64, 85, 139, 142, 144, 148, 163
Fforest (Pembrokeshire) 121, 122
field, fields 4, 10, 17, 20, 26, 34, 49, 50, 59, 73, 82, 113, 131, 182, 201, 212
foreign, foreigner 16, 36, 51, 55, 67, 131
forest 33, 34, 35, 37, 47, 59, 62, 130, 155, 156, 157
see also rainforest
Forest of Dean 26

Forestry Commission 60
forger, forgery, forging 25, 92, 94, 96, 111
form(s) (*poetic/generic*) xvi, xvii, 5, 6, 11, 12, 13, 14, 15, 18, 23, 30, 31, 40, 47, 48, 51, 52, 53, 55, 64, 65, 66, 79, 86, 87, 100, 101, 103, 113, 114, 116, 117, 118, 119, 159, 160, 162
formal, formally (*of poetry*) xvi, 4, 8, 9, 10, 11, 12, 14, 23, 24, 25, 38, 44, 47, 48, 86, 90, 92, 99, 100, 103, 113, 118, 119, 124, 136, 141, 147, 149
Formalism 48
fragment, fragmentary, fragmented, fragmentation 7, 21, 22, 47, 52, 54, 61, 65, 68, 75, 79, 86, 93, 100, 108, 110, 119, 126, 128, 136, 145, 157, 160, 178n, 207, 213
France, French 27
frontier(s) 13, 16, 19, 69–91, 170n, 180n, 182n, 199, 213

Gavenny valley 147
genealogy 120, 133
genre, generic xvii, 4, 12, 13, 15, 18, 30, 44, 48, 65, 66, 67, 89, 91, 92, 93, 94, 99, 101, 103, 105, 111, 113, 114, 118, 119, 128, 129, 134, 152
gentry 52
geography (ies), geographer, geographical 1, 13, 15, 19, 24, 27, 28, 29, 32, 50, 51, 70, 80, 112, 113, 124, 135, 136, 137, 138, 139, 142, 143, 144, 147, 155, 157, 163, 164
  cultural geography 1, 28, 50, 112, 163
geology, geological 16, 20–4, 46, 70, 76, 121, 125, 148, 189, 165
geopolitics, geopolitical xviii, xix, 3, 4, 6, 12, 20, 28, 46, 90, 93, 114, 137, 141, 142, 144, 157, 165
German 10, 27
Gibraltar 125
Gladestry *see* Shapcott, Jo
Glamorgan, Glamorganshire 57, 58, 131
Gomer xviii
Gothic 48, 177n, 178n, 200, 204, 210
Green Man, the 25, 51
Grwyne, River 64 65 66
  Grwyne Fechan, 65
  Grwyne Fawr, 65
Gwent 24–5, 128–34
gwerin 5, 116
Gwynedd 16, 77, 81, 173n, 179n

Haarlem 141
Halley's Comet 87
Harlech 20, 78
Hay on Wye (Books/Literary Festival) 69, 122
hiraeth 43 45
history xvi, 1, 2, 7, 8, 16, 20, 21, 22, 34, 53, 54, 56, 60, 61, 63, 65, 74, 75, 78, 82, 97, 104, 110, 112, 113, 114, 115, 117, 118, 119, 124, 126, 127, 128, 131, 132, 133, 134, 145, 147, 164, 165
  cultural history 34, 60, 74, 78, 114, 115, 116, 124, 128, 131
  local history 52, 53, 58, 59, 117
  poetic/literary history 30, 101, 119, 135, 142
home, homes, homely, homeliness 6, 8, 13, 21, 27, 28, 30, 32, 35, 36, 40, 46, 48–68 passim, 69, 71, 72, 75, 77, 79, 83, 91, 107, 108, 121, 125, 126, 127, 128, 132, 136, 137, 138, 142, 143, 144, 146, 150, 153, 160, 169n, 172n, 173n, 177n, 180n, 182n, 193n
homeland 32, 144, 150
horizon(s) xv, xviii, xix, 3, 4, 6, 8, 11, 12, 15, 32, 45, 46, 49, 78, 93, 114, 125, 128, 165
house, houses 8, 16, 34, 47, 48, 49, 50, 51, 52, 53, 58, 59, 60, 61, 62, 63, 64, 65, 82, 87, 93, 107, 115, 117, 121, 135, 143, 145, 182n
housewife, housework 85, 93

identity 2, 3–6, 16, 29, 37, 48, 52, 53, 56, 63, 70, 83, 88, 99, 103, 111, 118, 128, 133, 134, 140, 148, 149, 154, 158
cultural identity 2, 7, 18, 49, 65, 70, 75, 79, 101, 102, 103, 108, 109, 113, 120, 133, 148, 165
poetic identity 93, 94, 150
Welsh identity 6, 79, 96
see also Welsh
Illyria 150
incomer 58, 59, 79, 83, 91, 136,
India, Indian 28, 34
intertextual *see* textuality
Ireland, Irish 3, 5, 14, 30, 34, 36, 37, 72, 78, 112–34, 171n, 173n, 176n, 177n, 185n, 186n, 187n, 188n, 189n, 190n, 191n, 198, 200, 202, 203, 204, 205, 206, 207, 208, 209, 210, 212
see also famine
Irish Sea 72, 113, 120, 121, 122, 126, 134
Italy 163

kin, kindred, kinship (see also *cenedl*) 14, 55–6, 57, 58, 78, 112, 113, 197, 198
Kington (Powys) 26
knitter, knitting 94, 98, 99, 105, 111, 164, 180n, 205

Lake District 105
landscape 4, 5, 8, 13, 16, 17, 18, 19, 20–9, 34, 51, 56, 57, 70, 77, 79, 80, 83, 92, 120, 121, 130, 134, 147, 149, 151, 153, 154, 156, 178n, 194n, 199, 200, 205, 206, 210, 213
Latin America 10
legend, legendary 25, 37, 61, 114, 115, 124, 126, 127, 130, 132, 140, 141, 194n,
Leinster (Ireland) 124
lighthouse 72, 74, 75, 181n
Liverpool, Liverpudlian 36–7
Llandaff 126, 127
Llandysul 40
Llangoed 66
Llangollen 16, 19
llatai 44
Llanwrtyd Wells 48–9
Llŷn Peninsula (Pen Llŷn) 13, 69, 70, 71, 72, 76–8 *passim*, 79, 80, 82, 83, 120, 123–6, 182n, 188n, 203, 213
local, locale, locality, localism 5, 6, 7, 20, 43, 50, 59, 60, 61, 62, 75, 79, 80, 84, 112, 117, 122, 124, 126, 130, 152, 154, 158, 164, 180n, 182n, 185n, 188n, 205
location, dislocation, relocation 3, 5, 10, 11, 12, 29, 36, 49, 125, 132, 133, 136, 137, 150, 152, 157, 160, 162, 165, 167n, 170n, 171n, 172n, 174n, 176n, 177n, 178n, 180n, 181n, 197, 198, 202, 208
London 10, 57, 71, 143, 144, 162
Ludlow 16
lyric *see* poetic form

Mabinogion, the 20
manmade 13, 51, 52, 156
maps, mapping, map-making, map-reading, xviii, xix, 14, 19, 24, 26, 27, 50, 51, 60, 74, 77, 120, 126, 139, 150, 151, 152, 154, 155, 156, 157, 164, 167n, 169n, 171n, 172n, 181n, 185n, 187n, 188n, 194n, 195n, 197, 202, 205, 206, 214
March, Marches, Marcher lords 18–20, 27,
Margam 25
'Mariana in the Moated Grange' 66
see also Tennyson
marriage 10, 56, 61, 71, 79
Mediterranean 125
Menai Straits 28
migrant, immigrant, emigrant, migration 5, 6, 10, 13, 14, 22, 23, 75, 87, 113, 125, 131–4, 138, 158, 163, 173n, 179n, 189n, 199, 200, 203, 207, 208

Millennium, millennial, post-millennial xv, xviii, xix, 1, 5, 7, 8, 11, 28, 151, 165
mine, mines (mine buildings), mining 8, 27, 42, 52, 57
  see also coal
mineral 87, 107
modernism, modernist 142, 171n, 191n, 192n, 197, 211
Monmouthshire 131, 143
monument, monuments, monumental 52, 55, 179n, 211
mother (including great/grandmother), motherhood 3, 10, 12, 19, 33, 34–5, 38, 56, 67, 71, 72, 81, 84, 85, 87, 93, 102, 106, 107, 121, 122, 133, 134, 143, 144, 149, 168, 178 186, 189, 197, 205, 212
  mother country 48
  mother-tongue 106, 107, 207
mountain(s) 10, 16, 20, 22, 24, 65, 66, 71, 77, 105, 107, 145, 179n
Muckle Flugga 139–40
Muse, the 139
music, musical, music-making 67, 68, 122, 132, 149, 161, 176n, 177n, 201
Mynydd Carningli (Preseli Hills) 150
myth, mythic(al), mythology, mythopoeic 17, 18, 20, 23, 24, 33, 34, 114, 121, 123, 126, 128, 130, 134, 149
mythologised 17, 19

narcissism 98
narrative 7, 20, 84, 93, 101, 109, 114, 115, 116, 117, 124, 128, 134, 148, 160
  see also narrative poetry
National Eisteddfod 101
nation(s), national(ity), nationhood xv, xvii, xviii, 2, 3, 5, 6, 7, 17, 24, 28, 29, 31, 48, 49, 54, 56, 57, 83, 91, 107, 113, 114, 120, 134, 136, 137, 142, 158, 159
  national identity 2, 78, 158
  international 6, 20, 115, 158
  nationalist/ism xvi, 113
  nation state 125
  transnational 3, 6, 20
native 10, 19, 20, 24, 27, 29, 30, 36, 38, 44, 50, 58, 59 91, 95, 101, 103, 115, 131, 150, 165, 194n,
neighbour, neighbours, neighbourhood 4, 14, 46, 55, 5, 93, 105, 114
Neolithic 16, 121
Newport 128, 129, 131
Norman 20, 192n

Offa's Dyke 26
Ogmore-by-Sea 22
Old English 73
oral literature 114–17, 119, 187n, 188n, 208
  see also oral poetry, poetic form
Ordnance Survey 120
outsider 19, 34, 40, 59, 79, 82, 83, 135, 136
Oxford 57, 73, 94

Pacific, South 130
Pantycelyn 61
parallel texts *see* poetic form
Paris 28, 34
Parthian Books xviii
Pembrokeshire 121, 122
Persia 28
Phoenician 126
pilgrimage 24, 88, 148
Pillgwenlly 129
place, places 1–7, 9, 10, 12, 14, 15, 19, 20, 22, 24, 27, 29, 36, 40, 43, 48–53, 57–9, 61–3, 65, 69, 70, 72, 73, 74, 75, 77–81, 83, 91, 95, 103, 104, 116, 124, 127–31, 135–40, 142–54, 156, 158, 160, 162–6
  place-name(s) 23, 27, 78
Pleistocene 24, 148
poetic convention 28, 44
poetic form(s)
  confessional 12, 13, 33, 34, 92, 96–8, 106, 108, 175n, 184n, 203, 209

couplets 8, 38, 47, 109, 138, 164
courtly love song 48
dialogic 46
dramatic monologue 160, 162–4, 194n, 212
elegy 30, 60, 122, 124, 133, 141, 147, 193n, 200
epic xvii, 37, 39, 88, 113, 118, 185n, 188n, 194, 198, 205
epistolary 9
facing-page (parallel) texts 13, 32, 42–6
found poetry 12, 13, 66, 67, 68
lyric 3, 9, 10, 12, 22, 30, 37, 38, 47, 65, 84, 88, 96, 97, 98, 99, 100, 101, 103, 106, 107, 109, 114, 118, 119, 120, 121, 124, 125, 129, 134, 160, 161, 165,166
macaronic poetry 12
murder-mystery 37
narrative poetry 9, 12, 61, 99, 101, 103, 106, 108, 109, 111, 114, 118, 119, 120, 123, 124, 129, 134, 160
'non-mainstream' / experimental 10, 142, 157, 159
ode 30, 141
pastoral poetry 12, 27, 30, 154, 156
quest poem 12
riddle poem 24
ruin poem 53, 54, 68
sequence 12, 21, 22, 25, 26, 31, 32, 37, 38, 64, 65, 71, 74, 86, 87, 89, 92–112, 114, 118, 119, 121, 122, 123, 124, 126, 127, 129, 130, 133, 139, 140, 141, 146, 147, 149, 160, 161, 163, 165
sonnet 47, 48, 123, 131, 132,
travel/travelling poem 12, 141
verse-novel 37
walk poem 152, 155, 193n, 200
Poetry Wales 28, 84, 137
politics, political xvi, xvii, 1, 2, 3, 4, 5, 6, 11, 12, 13, 14, 15, 18, 19, 20, 29, 30, 32, 38, 40, 41, 45, 46, 63, 66, 67, 68, 84, 85, 94, 101, 102, 113, 114, 116, 117, 118, 125, 134, 137, 138, 139, 140, 142, 143, 144, 145, 148, 150, 151, 152, 154, 155, 157, 159, 162, 163, 165
cultural-political xvii, xviii, 2, 3, 9, 11, 12, 14, 18, 19, 28, 29, 30, 31, 38, 42, 46, 48, 92, 112, 113, 140, 152, 156
see also cultural-political
Pont Britannia (Anglesey) 156
Port Talbot 26
postcolonial/ism 4, 48, 49, 170n, 171n, 177n, 189n, 194n, 196, 198, 202, 207, 210
Powys 13, 26, 58, 147
Preseli Hills 150, 151, 152, 157
pryddestau 101
psychiatrist 108, 109
Pwllheli 71

quarries 10, 21, 22, 52, 107

radio 98, 121, 123
rainforest 33, 35
remembrance, remembrancing 52, 54, 61
repetition 53, 54, 67, 116, 119, 121
Rhaeadr 61
river(s) 22, 24, 26, 34, 35, 61, 64, 132, 146, 194, 198
roads 25, 26, 52, 59, 60, 77, 80, 138, 152
Roald Dahl Plas xv,
Roman, Romans, Rome 20, 95, 127, 160, 161
Romantic, Romanticism, romanticised 8, 54, 139, 161, 178, 186, 192, 205, 207, 211, 212, 214
ruins, ruined, ruinous 13, 26, 47, 49, 50, 52, 53, 54, 55, 59, 60, 65, 66, 67, 68, 147, 178n, 180n, 200, 205, 207, 209, 214
rural, rurality 13, 19, 21, 26, 27, 28, 33, 49, 50, 52, 56, 81, 105, 112, 115, 155, 156, 157, 158, 171n, 182, 190, 205, 213

Saxon 75, 95
Scotland, Scots, Scottish 3, 5, 30, 51, 113
sculpture 8, 25–26, 35, 138
sea (sea-bed, sea-faring, sea-god, sea-route, seascape, seaside, seaway) xv, 26, 39, 69, 71–8 *passim*, 82, 113, 120, 121–4, 125–7, 129, 138, 139, 141, 147, 149, 160
  see also Irish Sea
seanchas 117
Second Flowering 135, 170n, 174n, 190n, 199n, 205
Seren Publishing xviii
Seven Sisters (Neath) 57
Severn (River) 24
sex, sexism, sexuality 10, 31, 33, 36, 45, 84, 102, 161, 168n, 171n, 184n, 195n, 198, 202, 205, 206, 207, 212
Shetland 138, 140
shore, shoreline (foreshore, offshore, seashore) 22, 69, 70, 72, 73, 76, 121, 127, 128, 129, 138, 186n, 206
site, sites 14, 17, 18, 29, 31, 38, 40, 50, 53, 63, 64, 70, 124, 136, 140, 141, 143, 147, 153, 154, 155, 158, 162, 171n
site-specific 151, 157
Situationists, situationism 28
Skirrid (Skirrid Fach, Skirrid Fawr) 147
solar system 87
South Pacific 130
Space, spaces xv, xvi, xviii, 1, 3, 4, 11–15, 20, 26, 28, 29–42, 49, 51, 53, 61–3, 65, 69–71, 79, 80, 86, 87, 100, 101, 114, 116, 119, 124, 128, 135–54, 158, 160, 163, 166
Stalinist Gulag 88
stories, story-telling 2, 14, 37, 53, 62, 65, 66, 67, 68, 84, 93, 98, 99, 101, 103, 106, 108, 112, 114–21, 122, 123, 124, 128, 129, 130, 132, 134, 139, 141, 144, 154, 165
Suffolk 23, 143
Surrey 57
Swansea 40, 194
Swiss, Switzerland 27, 28

Talley 147
territory, territorial (extra-territorial, non-territorial, re-territorialisation) xviii, 5, 8, 18, 19, 24, 29, 30, 34, 42, 49, 58, 70, 71, 76, 86, 101, 113, 128, 131, 134, 140, 141, 156, 159, 165, 168n, 200
textuality 12, 13, 14, 119, 124
  textual space (spatio-textual) xvi, xix, 1, 7, 12, 15, 18, 71, 86, 87, 88, 146, 150, 153
  intertextual(ity) 12, 108
  metatextual(ity) 89
therapy, therapeutic, therapist 96, 108–10
Tilley lamp 88
topos, topoi xvii, xviii, 30, 49, 50, 53, 54, 61, 63, 65, 67, 147, 161
topology xix, 5, 13, 20, 28, 114, 150, 155, 165
topography(ies) 10, 13, 15, 17, 18, 23, 32, 42, 59, 70, 129, 149, 153, 173n
Tower Hill 75
translation, translator(s) xv, 11, 12, 13, 31, 41–5, 73, 109, 126, 128, 136, 139, 141, 142, 154, 159, 164, 176n, 177n, 183n, 188n, 199, 200, 201, 207, 212
transnational *see* nation, national
travel, travelling, travelogue xix, 10, 12, 16, 25, 30, 77, 96, 125, 136, 138–43, 158, 160, 176n, 181n, 191n, 192n, 199, 200, 205, 210
Tywi (valley) 59

uncanny 47–50, 52, 55, 63–5, 67, 68, 108, 177n, 178n, 179n, 180n, 202, 210, 211, 213
unhomely 47–68, 178, 213
urban 19, 28, 153–6, 158

Usk 21, 64, 128, 131
Uwchmynydd 71, 76, 79, 182n, 201

Valais 27
valley(s) 4, 40, 50, 59, 60, 61, 63–7 *passim*, 145, 147
Venezuela 33
Venice 28
Ventriloquy, ventriloquised, ventriloquism, ventriloquising 122, 130, 160, 162–5, 194n, 199
Victorian 139, 191n, 196
Village 57, 58, 59, 60, 76, 83, 105

Wales
  contemporary 19, 40, 87, 114, 117, 163
  identifying 6, 9, 13, 23, 113
  linguistic communities of 32, 42, 122
  mid 13, 27, 28, 34, 47–68, 112, 177, 179
  north 10, 32, 83, 95, 134, 159
  north-west 13, 69
  patriarchal 7, 9, 30
  political devolution of 1
  post-millennial xv, xix, 1, 5, 28
  south 34, 95, 134, 138, 194
  twenty-first century xvi, 6, 28, 136–7, 158, 165
  Ireland 112, 113, 114, 120, 124, 131, 133, 134, 186
  Millennium Centre xv
  women in, of, on xvii, xviii, 3, 64, 114, 119, 124, 136–7
  Welsh-speaking 40, 81
  west 10, 78, 105, 134,151,157, 163
  see also landscape, border(s)
walking 59, 60, 61, 69, 73, 76, 77, 121,122, 130, 149–53, 155–6, 165, 180n, 181n, 182n, 183n, 189n, 192n, 193n, 198, 200, 201, 203, 211, 212, 213
Welsh 1, 2, 5, 6, 12, 19, 20, 23, 24, 25, 36, 37, 34, 36, 40, 42, 49
  'elective' 2, 6
  literature 30
  Mam 108
Welsh-language poets, poetry, texts xv, 11, 12, 30, 31, 41, 45, 95, 101, 105, 159
West country 57
whodunnit 37, 105, 106
World War Two 57, 122, 172n, 204
Wye, River 27, 66, 147

y bardd gwlad 5
Ynys Enlli 71, 73, 74, 76, 77, 79, 80, 82, 127, 181n, 182n, 188n, 198
  see also Bardsey Island
Yorkshire 13, 69, 71, 105
ystyr 115
  see also story, story-telling